SOCIETY AND POLITICS

Society and Politics
in Hong Kong

Lau Siu-kai

The Chinese University Press
Hong Kong

International Standard Book Number: 962-201-336-8

The Chinese University Press
The Chinese University of Hong Kong
SHATIN, N. T., HONG KONG

Typesetting by The Chinese University Press
Printing by Ngai Kwong Printing Co., Ltd.

To Sophie and Poon-yung
with deep affection

Contents

Preface

For many years I have been baffled by the problem of political stability in Hong Kong and the heap-of-sand character of her Chinese majority. It is only in the last six years that I was seriously engaged in research and publication on the political and social aspects of this economically successful British colony. This book represents a modest effort at a systematic and theoretical analysis of Chinese society and politics in Hong Kong. In the process, I also attempt to synthesize, as far as possible, the findings of myself and those of other students of the area.

As social scientific research in Hong Kong is still in its formative years, the secondary studies on which I can draw on are meagre. Moreover, many of them have been conducted by expatriates whose knowledge of Chinese is minimal and who tend to approach their subject-matter with preconceived notions derived from their own cultural upbringing. As the readers can readily see for themselves in the book, data gaps preclude exhaustive elaboration and theoretical generalization about many crucial points. In a deplorable sense, each social scientific study in Hong Kong has to start almost from scratch, and the ordeal each researcher has to undergo is considerable. Fortunately, this has its own advantage, for it bestows upon the researcher, bold enough to open up virgin territories, the liberty to let his creativity and imagination take charge, without being encumbered at every point by well-established and jealously-defended dogmas and perspectives. Nevertheless, this marginal advantage is more than offset by the disadvantages which the researcher has to endure from the paucity of sharpened theoretical tools and corroborative empirical evidence.

My purpose here is also to alert the readers to my subjective bias which has unintentionally crept into the arguments whenever interpretations and explanations have to be made against a background of data vacuum. Being a native of Hong Kong, and having sufficient identification with her to call it home, I find it extremely difficult, if not impossible, to extricate myself from the people and things which surround me, and the likes and dislikes I have for them. Thus, readers are requested to bear with me, and to be wary while pondering my contentions.

It can readily be seen that research on this scale cannot be accomplished by the author alone. I would like to extend my gratitude to the Harvard-Yenching Institute, which not only funded the 1977 survey research, that provides the book with much of the data, but also granted me a Harvard-

Yenching visiting scholarship in 1980-81 so that I could stay at Harvard University for a year writing. For the past six years, the Social Research Centre of The Chinese University of Hong Kong provided the serious, yet friendly, academic environment in which intellectual pursuits were an enjoyable undertaking. And, as readers can witness for themselves, the research reports published by the Social Research Centre (known previously as the Survey Research Centre) constitute a major source of information for this book.

Interest in social science research on the part of the Hong Kong government is growing, and this is an encouraging sign. I have no doubt that in the social-political setting of Hong Kong, social science research can not only contribute knowledge but also mediate between government and citizens. While this book is primarily theoretical, it is also hoped that it can have some policy implications. At this juncture, I would like to express my appreciation to three government officials who have given me encouragement and support. They are: Sir Jack Cater, Chief Secretary, Mr. David Akers-Jones, Secretary for the New Territories, and Mr. John Walden, the former Director of Home Affairs.

Over the years I have benefitted from discussions, formal and informal, with the following colleagues in the Chinese University: Drs. Ambrose King, Kuan Hsin-chi, Rance P. L. Lee, Ho Kam-fai, Mr. Andrew W. F. Wong, Ms. Barbara Ward, and many others. Credit for many of the ideas in the book should be shared with them.

Lastly, I would like to express my gratitude to my wife, Sophie. Marrying a bookish and absent-minded academic is an ordeal many women would find hard to endure. Nevertheless, through her patience, affection and sense of humour, Sophie has managed to turn this ordeal into a satisfying undertaking, and to enliven her not-always-grateful husband. My year-long absence from home, during my stay at Harvard, imposed tremendous hardship on her and my two-year-old son, Poon-yung. To express my appreciation and respect for her, I would like to dedicate this book to Sophie and Poon-yung, with deep affection and devoted love.

LSK
Cambridge, Mass.
March 1981

1. Economic Development and Political Stability

In the last three and a half decades, the tiny but densely populated British colony of Hong Kong has displayed a developmental pattern which has no counterpart in the world.[1] Rapid economic growth, urbanization, a colonial regime professing laissez-faire and social non-interventionism, and political stability are the salient features of the colony's recent history. This feat of intermeshing all these sociological phenomena which, in many other cases, are mutually contradictory has drawn envy and amazement from some quarters, jealousy and resentment from others. In this book, the problem posed is the existence of political stability under highly destabilizing conditions. And an attempt is made to develop a systematic explanation of this twentieth-century "miracle."

"Political stability," to be sure, is a nebulous concept (Hurwitz 1973; Ake 1974). Its meaning ranges from a positive sense of the presence of a high level of political and moral consensus, the existence of a legitimate constitutional order with which everyone identifies, and the establishment of an integrated political system which allows for popular political participation and the resolution of conflicts in a peaceful manner, to a neutral sense of the absence of political conflicts and violence, a chaotic succession of regimes or to structural changes in the political system or the rules of the political game. "Political stability" in Hong Kong, very obviously, does not fall on the positive end of the scale. In the neutral sense, Hong Kong has experienced a relatively high level of political stability. In terms of institutional longevity, Hong Kong's record is remarkable. In Hong Kong,

> the constitution is basically and formally the same as when Britain first annexed the territory in 1843, with all power concentrated in the hands of the Governor and the bureaucracy. All the unofficial members of the Executive and Legislative Councils are still nominated, not elected, and officials still control a majority of the votes in the Legislative Council. None of the unofficials is associated with government departments or the colonial secretariat in a quasi-ministerial role. With regard to personnel, the emphasis on seniority in colonial service promotions ensures that heads of departments reach their positions at a mature age and then mostly serve until retirement. No senior official has ever been prematurely retired as a result of public pressure. (Miners 1975:26)

---

[1] With a land area of only 1,061 square kilometres, Hong Kong at the end of 1979 had an estimated population of 5,017,000. About 98 per cent of the population can be described as Chinese on the basis of language and place of origin.

Conflicts and violence, on the other hand, did occur in 1956, 1966 and 1967. Except for the last one, they were primarily social conflicts not directed specifically against the government. In the case of the 1967 riot, it was in essence a spin-off from the Proletarian Cultural Revolution in China, not spontaneously generated out of hostility to the government. For most of the leftists and their sympathizers who participated in the political campaign, there was no real intention to topple the colonial government. Moreover, all three instances of conflict were, relatively speaking, small or moderate in scale. And, what is more significant, their political reverberations were minimal.

In many developing countries, according to cross-national studies, economic growth is accompanied by political instability (Olson 1963; Feierabend *et al.* 1969). One of the connections between the two phenomena is the high level of economic inequity among various socioeconomic groups (Adelman and Morris 1973), which is conducive to group conflicts and a surge of political demands overloading the capacity of the political system. Particularly ominous is that, along with economic growth, social mobilization proceeds at a hectic pace to expand the politically relevant sectors of the population, produce mounting pressures for the transformation of political practices and institutions, raise political aspirations to unrealistic levels and promote ethnic conflicts (Deutsch 1961; Connor 1972; Young 1976). Economic growth is oftentimes cited as the cause of anomie and role conflict which, as socio-cultural phenomena, do not fail to wreak political havoc (Pye 1962; Apter 1965). Consequently, the destabilizing effects of economic growth are alleged to be reinforced by those originating from sociocultural transformation.

Urbanization, usually a partner of economic growth and sociocultural change, takes its own toll of political stability. The momentous rate of rural-urban migration in many developing countries has created urban populations too large to be integrated socially, economically, or politically into the cities. Though the evidence is far from conclusive (Cornelius 1969, 1975; Nelson 1970, 1979), it is still true that the traumatic experiences of the migrants in the cities have generated their feelings of frustration and insecurity, and driven them to resort to political means for the resolution of their difficulties or problems.

In some of these countries, the simultaneous presence of all these destabilizing factors has led to the breakdown of political institutions. And, for many countries, after the dismantlement of traditional authorities and institutions, few viable political institutions remain (Huntington 1965, 1968; Huntington and Nelson 1976). Granted that harmonizing economic growth and political stability is a herculean task facing both the underdeveloped countries and those which are more modernized (Brazil, Argentina and Mexico), many have taken the "difficult path" of pursuing economic growth at the expense of political participation. As a result, in the last two decades or so, the Third World has witnessed the rapid emergence of a medley of "exclusionary" regimes: military dictatorship, neo-fascist regime, bureaucratic-authoritarian polity, charismatic leadership, authoritarian government, one-partyism, multi-partyism with one-party dominance, patrimonialism, modernizing monarchy, so on and so forth (Zolberg 1966; Huntington 1968; Collier 1979; O'Donnell 1979).

Like many other developing countries, Hong Kong has undergone breathtaking changes. Starting from scratch immediately following the Second World War, Hong Kong is today a highly industrialized society, as well as a major commercial and financial centre in the world. In real terms, the Gross Domestic Product of Hong Kong increased at an average annual rate of about eight per cent over the thirty years from 1948 to 1977. Starting with a per capita money income of US$182 in 1948, Hong Kong by 1977 had reached US$2,611 in current prices, representing a fivefold increase in real terms. As an economy geared to production for export, Hong Kong's performance again is magnificent. In the early 1950s, the share of locally produced exports in total exports was between five per cent and fifteen per cent. Today, it is about eighty per cent. Evidently, this marvellous economic success is the result of the drastic transformation of the economic structure of the colony.

The rate of urbanization in Hong Kong, like her economic achievements, is equally phenomenal. Even though in composition Hong Kong is a city of immigrants, the flow of immigrants into Hong Kong has never been steady or smooth. Before the Second World War, most of the Chinese people coming to Hong Kong from China came in uneven waves, largely reflecting the existing political situations in China. As mere sojourners, they did not heavily tax the capacities of the society and the government. Since the Second World War, and particularly in the wake of the communist takeover of China, there have been a number of influxes into Hong Kong of Chinese refugees who came as settlers. The largest number entered Hong Kong in the late 1940s and early 1950s. In 1945, the population of Hong Kong was slightly over 500,000. The number swelled to 1,800,000 in 1947, and to 2,424,700 in 1953. Since then, both natural population growth and the continual arrival of refugees resulted in a population of 3,209,500 in 1961, 3,936,630 in 1971 and 4,986,560 in 1981. In terms of the rate of urbanization and the erratic pattern of population increase, Hong Kong's experience is highly extraordinary.

What is peculiar in Hong Kong, and such peculiarity would demand explanation, is that, despite rapid economic growth and urbanization, Hong Kong is singularly immune from sociocultural breakdown or political instability. The cultural system in Hong Kong is heterogeneous, with the division between Western and Chinese cultures. Even among the Chinese themselves, variations in dialects, customs and styles of living, as well as lingering hostilities among locality groupings, would be readily available cleavage lines to divide society into antagonistic fragments. In terms of political orientations, ideological identifications run the gamut from the extreme right (in support of the Nationalist regime in Taiwan) to the extreme left (in support of the Communist regime in Mainland China). Even though Hong Kong has been exempt from some other kinds of divisions such as religious conflicts, territorial rivalries, centre-periphery competition and the struggle for power between modernizing elites and traditional authorities, the two kinds of cleavages mentioned above—cultural heterogeneity and political identification—would be sufficiently destabilizing, at least potentially. Furthermore, the staggering inequality in the distribution of income in Hong Kong would have the potential of generating class conflict and industrial hostilities, which she can ill afford to have. Nevertheless, none of these potential conflicts have materialized. In fact, aside from the riot in 1956, which saw leftists fighting with rightists over an incident which however minor had great symbolic political meaning (*Report on the Riots in Kowloon and Tsuen Wan, 1956*), residents with different political inclinations are able to live peaceably, as are sociocultural and economic groups.

Finally, amidst such potentially destabilizing factors, that political stability in Hong Kong can still be maintained under a colonial government adhering to the now outmoded doctrines of economic laissez-faire and social non-interventionism needs exploration. The problem can be posed in this way: given the limited economic and political capacity and adaptability characteristic of a colonial regime, how can it maintain political stability (and also its own political survival) in face of all these potentially disintegrative factors which can rapidly politicize society and mobilize people into political action? While many other countries which display higher levels of "state activism" are not able to guarantee political stability, why is the colonial government of Hong Kong capable of doing so?

To disentangle the puzzle posed by the peculiar developmental pattern of Hong Kong, it is futile to try to find analogous cases and draw explanations through comparisons. Undoubtedly, successful cases of economic growth and political stability can be found, such as South Korea, Taiwan, Singapore, Brazil, Mexico and the Ivory Coast. But they all differ from Hong Kong in at least one aspect: they are all sovereign states which perform a full battery of state functions, while Hong Kong is not. A significant consequence ensuing from this difference is that the government in Hong Kong is more constrained in its capability to deal with the society under its rule. As the constitutional form of governance is practically speaking "fixed," adjustment in the relationship between the government and society hence requires delicate political skills. The fact that an "anachronistic" polity can coexist harmoniously with a modernizing society would therefore necessitate an analysis of both the polity and the society and their relationship with each other. In the case of Hong Kong, given the limited adaptability of the government, the structural characteristics of the Chinese society and the sociopolitical proclivities of the Chinese populace would provide us the key to an understanding of political stability in Hong Kong.

HONG KONG AS A COLONIAL SOCIETY

Perhaps the most tempting way to explain political stability in Hong Kong is to resort to the theories of colonial societies. Some classify Hong Kong as a colonial society from the outset and then compare it with the colonial societies of the past and draw their conclusions. Not only is this approach common among many Chinese inhabitants in Hong Kong, but it is also attractive to those who intend to discredit the Hong Kong government and to castigate the society of Hong Kong as an archaism (Association for Radical East Asian Studies 1972; A Group at the Hong Kong Research Project 1974).

In brief, most theorists of colonial societies (Furnivall 1948, for example) portray them as immoral societies marked by sociocultural segmentation or pluralism. As societies devoid of social or moral constraints, economic forces loom large and economic relationships, market relationships in particular, are the common denominator structuring interpersonal relationships. Political order in the colonial societies, under such socially disorganized conditions, will have to be coercively imposed from above by the colonial authorities.

The "colonial situation," as seen by G. Balandier, a distinguished French anthropologist, describes societies "in a state of crisis, . . . [which] are involved to some extent in a kind of social pathology" (1966:37). In colonial societies, "the liberation of economic forces from the moral restraint imposed by social obligations is detrimental to social and individual welfare" (Furnivall 1948: 303). Moreover, "individual demand for private gain prevailed over the social demand for common welfare, and prevailed the more readily because society was no longer homogeneous" (*Ibid.*: 309).

Colonial societies according to conventional wisdom contain a hodgepodge of ethnic groups. However, as social groups, they rarely interact with one another. As individuals, nevertheless, their relationships are mediated through economic transactions.

> In Burma, as in Java, probably the first thing that strikes the visitor is the medley of peoples—European, Chinese, Indian, and Native. It is in the strictest sense a medley, for they mix but do not combine. Each group holds by its own religion,

its own culture and language, its own ideas and ways. As individuals they meet, but only in the market-place, in buying and selling. There is a plural society, with different sections of the community living side by side, but separately, within the same political unit. Even in the economic sphere there is a division of labour along racial lines, Natives, Chinese, Indians and Europeans all have different functions, and within each major group subsections have particular occupations. There is, as it were, a caste system, but without the religious basis that incorporate caste in social life in India. (*Ibid*.: 304–5)

In addition to the horizontal division of labour among ethnic groups, theorists also arrange them in a graded hierarchical political system, at the top of which are the white colonists.

The [colonial situation] may be defined by singling out and retaining the most general and most obvious of these conditions: (1) the domination imposed by a foreign minority, racially (or ethnically) and culturally different, acting in the name of a racial (or ethnic) and cultural superiority dogmatically affirmed, and imposing itself on an indigenous population constituting a numerical majority but inferior to the dominant group from a material point of view; (2) this domination linking radically different civilizations into some form of relationship; (3) a mechanized, industrialized society with a powerful economy, a fast tempo of life, and a Christian background imposing itself on a non-industrialized, "backward" society, in which the pace of living is much slower and religious institutions are most definitely "non-Christian"; (4) the fundamentally antagonistic character of the relationship between these two societies resulting from the subservient role to which the colonial people are subjected as "instruments" of the colonial power; (5) the need, in maintaining this domination, not only to resort to "force," but also to a system of pseudo-justifications and stereotyped behaviours. (Balandier 1966:54–55)

Similarly, Schermerhorn used the term "hierocratic" to describe a political order based on coercion:

This implies a structure of domination in which one cultural section with its own set of segmentary institutions imposes its rule upon one or more other cultural sections, each with its own set of segmentary and historically unrelated institutions which remain at least partially intact during the period of reign. In the colonial case (particularly the instances of limited and substantial settlement) maximal enclosure occurs on both sides of the boundary lines separating superordinate and subordinate sections. . . . The integration of such a society is clearly not consensual but coercive with the political institution the central organ in the hands of the dominant cultural section, actually the only institution that in any sense unites all people. (1970:148–49)

Furthermore, in order to maintain this unequal distribution of power, something else, aside from coercion, has to be instituted:

(a) keeping contacts at a bare minimum (segregation); (b) offering the European as the model for emulation, while effectively blocking any means to that end (assimilation is held out as the basis for equality—because it is known full well

that assimilation is either impossible of attainment or is restricted to a very
limited few); (c) maintaining ideologies justifying the position of the dominant
group; (d) employing political tactics designed to preserve the imbalance in favor
of the colonial power (and its European homeland); (e) more or less deliberately
transferring to certain groups the attitude and feelings provoked by political and
economic domination. (Balandier 1966:47)

These ideal-typical conceptualizations of colonial societies advocated by
the social scientists quoted above, when applied to Hong Kong, produce
either partial truths or outright distortions. This incompatibility between
theory and reality can be attributed to the particular historical setting,
environmental conditions and socioeconomic characteristics of the people
which exist in the colony. They are drastically different from those found in
the colonies of the past. Since a detailed description and analysis of the polity
and the Chinese society of Hong Kong will be conducted in the following
chapters, it is sufficient here to outline in broad strokes the uniqueness of
Hong Kong as a colony in comparison with the prevailing ideal-type
characterizations.

(1) Hong Kong as a colony was acquired by the British in 1843 primarily
for serving as a basis of free trade in the Far East, and only marginally for the
sake of territorial gain or the inculcation of Western culture to the "barbarian"
natives.

(2) Instead of imposing an alien government or the natives in the colony,
the pattern of alien rule in Hong Kong is just the reverse. The colonized
Chinese people came to Hong Kong to subject themselves voluntarily under
the rule of an alien colonial administration.

(3) From the very beginning, the development of Hong Kong was based on
a kind of partnership between the British and the Chinese with a common
goal of economic gain. Even though this is an unequal partnership in the
political sense, coercion has never been the sole means to consolidate it. In
the past, the Chinese always had the option to return to China. Today, the
delicate relationship between Hong Kong, Britain and China, as well as anti-
colonial international sentiments, would make any blatant and arbitrary
exercise of coercion in Hong Kong virtually unthinkable.

(4) As Hong Kong suffers from a scarcity of natural resources, the acquisition of Hong Kong can never be justified in terms of securing the supply of
key raw materials for the mother country. The prosperity in Hong Kong
depends on the development of human resources, particularly entrepreneurial
initiative and labour productivity. An oppressive political and social environment would only smash all hopes for economic advancement. The rationale
of government in Hong Kong, thus, can only be to provide a stable political
framework in which economic initiative can have full play so that, with the

increase in the well-being of the people, the government can also be benefitted. Any exercise of political muscle must be conducted cautiously and skilfully.

(5) In a rough sense, division of labour along ethnic lines is, to a certain extent, true in Hong Kong, as the Britons in Hong Kong are mostly of middle-income status and above, while a predominant majority of the Chinese are in the lower-income and lower-middle income categories. However, this observation must be qualified. In colonies of the past, racial or ethnic status is the major, if not the only, criterion of social stratification, and it thus determines an individual's socioeconomic status and life chances. Such arrangements are tantamount to the installation of a caste system where upward and downward social mobility are well-nigh impossible, as all social positions are ascribed. In Hong Kong, it can safely be claimed that the racial or ethnic factor is still of some importance, but it has already receded to secondary status. As an achievement-oriented society, Hong Kong's populace are stratified mainly along the economic dimension with each ethnic section pursuing a wide spectrum of occupations, though the range of that of the British and other Europeans is much narrower and falls within the upper ends of the occupational prestige hierarchy.

(6) Though there is, to a certain extent, social, cultural and institutional segregation between the British and the Chinese in Hong Kong, the barrier between the two groups is far more permeable than allowed for by the theories of colonial societies. In earlier times, discriminative measures against the Chinese on racial and cultural grounds were to be found, but over time they were gradually withdrawn. Today, racial discrimination and stereotyping have not totally vanished, but they tend to assume a more covert and subtle form, and their political significance is negligible. Residential segregation between the two races is still obvious, and can be explained largely in terms of the differential economic power of the two ethnic groups, and voluntary choice. Moreover, industrialization in Hong Kong has not failed to create new groups and affiliations which involve both the British and the Chinese, and this zone of social and cultural interaction between the two groups is fairly broad, though confined perhaps, on the part of the Chinese, to the upper-middle class and above. Cultural and linguistic differences are further reduced through the process of Westernization among the Chinese who increasingly pick up Western life-styles and the dissemination of Western education. More accommodative attitudes towards the Chinese culture can be detected from the British too, and this is instrumental in alleviating ethnic strain. In a survey of adult Chinese in 1977, for example, it is interesting to learn that while 22.2% of the respondents had Western friends, 36% of them would like to have friends who were Westerners (Lau 1977:178-80).

After this item-by-item comparison between Hong Kong and the ideal-typical characterizations of colonial societies, how would we conceptualize Hong Kong as a colonial society? Basically, Hong Kong is a society where political power is concentrated in the hands of a particular racial/ethnic group, where different ethnic groups share certain assumptions about the importance of economic goals, where accommodative attitudes hold in both groups, where cultural diversity is held within tolerable limits and prevented from spilling over into the political arena, where coercion is not the most important means to maintain social and political order, and where nationalist feelings do not loom large. What this conception implies are that ethnic conflict or nationalist fervour is not a destabilizing factor in the case of Hong Kong, and that we should look elsewhere for an explanation of political stability in Hong Kong. More specifically, given the rapid economic growth in Hong Kong, how can political stability be maintained in an "anachronistic" colonial regime, whose capacity for meeting political demands and expanding channels for political participation is limited, and which coexists with a Chinese society faced with an increasing volume of problems arising from industrialization and urbanization, with these problems having enormous political relevance? Evidently, the resolution of this problem would call for a thorough investigation of the polity and the Chinese society of Hong Kong, particularly the latter, as well as their relationships.

Several approaches are currently in vogue to explain political stability in Hong Kong, and they deal in one way or another with either the government or the Chinese society or both. These approaches are shared by many people in Hong Kong, and are basically folk theories rather than formal, internally consistent or rigorous formulations. Admittedly each of these approaches has its own merits, but in general they suffer from oversimplicity and weaknesses in explanatory power. Individually, each of them has pinpointed one or two elements in the polity or the Chinese society of Hong Kong as the fundamental cause of political stability in the colony. Even combined, however, they fail to piece together a coherent explanation. To scrutinize these approaches to see what they have included and left out, is a necessary prelude to the construction of a more adequate and powerful theory of political stability in Hong Kong.

THE CHINA FACTOR

Historically, the various parts of Hong Kong were ceded to the British by the moribund Manchu government over several time periods, through a number of unequal treaties. The island of Hong Kong was ceded in 1843, the Kowloon Peninsula in 1860. The New Territories, which constitute the rural hinterland of Hong Kong, were acquired through a lease for ninety-nine years in 1898.

Legally, the New Territories, which now contain most of Hong Kong's industrial establishments and her vital sources of water, is due for return to China in 1997, and the consummation of such an act would spell the doom of Hong Kong. Even though no one can predict as of now the chances of a communist takeover of the New Territories or the whole of Hong Kong at that date, at a later date, or even sooner, the haunting spector of the return of the New Territories to Communist China, from where many of the Hong Kong inhabitants have fled, has definitely not failed to make its marks on the society and people of Hong Kong.

Under the perennial condition of "borrowed place, borrowed time" (Hughes 1976), the China factor is pertinent to the political stability of Hong Kong, as the argument goes, in two ways.

First, it is believed that China is willing, though reluctantly, to tolerate the existence of Hong Kong as a British colony, despite her strident anti-colonial posture, because of the economic and other values of Hong Kong to the achievement of her national goals. Hong Kong is a major source of China's earnings of foreign exchange. In fact, since the mid-1960s, some forty per cent of China's foreign exchange earnings has come from Hong Kong alone (Rabushka 1979:25). These earnings are accumulated from a variety of sources: exports to Hong Kong, economic operations (banks, warehouses, factories, shipping firms, insurance companies, real estates, cinemas and others), remittances from Hong Kong and overseas sent to Chinese citizens on the Mainland and using Hong Kong as a redistribution centre for Chinese-made goods. Aside from these tangible economic benefits, Hong Kong also contributes to the Chinese economy through rendering intangible economic benefits, since China can make use of Hong Kong's economic and financial institutions and her stature as an international commercial centre for trade contracts, financial negotiations, and access to Western technology and knowhow. It is possible that China's total earnings from foreign exchange in Hong Kong may have reached US$1,700 million in 1975, perhaps even more (Miners 1977:19). Non-economic importance of Hong Kong to China, particularly her utility as a contact point with the West, is considerable, though it is declining with the gradual entry of China into the international scene.

In view of the enormous importance of Hong Kong to China, to take over Hong Kong would be tantamount to killing the goose that lays golden eggs, as the common saying in Hong Kong has it. Even at a time when revolutionary extremism galvanized the whole China during the Cultural Revolution, no official attempt to take over Hong Kong was ever made. As a matter of fact, through the control of the leftist trade unions in Hong Kong, China has so far reined in any militant labour actions that might have jeopardized the economic and political situation of Hong Kong. And she is also prepared to denounce those activities of the leftists which are seen as disruptive of the political order, and these include those of her sympathizers (as in the 1967 riot) and the "unorthodox" Marxist and Trotskyist zealots. Without exaggerating, China's tolerant attitude towards Hong Kong constitutes a crucial factor for her continual existence as a British colony.

While China's policy to preserve the colonial status of Hong Kong is a major explanatory factor of the inability of Hong Kong to install another type of political system (e.g., political independence under local Chinese rule, a fully democratic political system with possibly a Chinese governor), it cannot account for political stability in Hong Kong under *a colonial constitution*. Put another way, even though it is generally acknowledged that the colonial political system in Hong Kong cannot be changed, it does not necessarily mean that political stability, which also has endogenous origins, must be the logical outcome. To explain it, we have to move away from the China factor.

Second, it is argued that most of the refugees who fled to Hong Kong since the late 1940s left China because they harboured intense and uncompromising hostility towards communism and towards the communist Chinese government. Consequently, they abhor any political conflict, particularly those suspected of being instigated by Communist China, which might have the intended or latent effects so embarrassing to both the British and the Chinese governments that a takeover of Hong Kong by China would become unavoidable, in spite of the extreme reluctance of China to do so. The British in Hong Kong are not alone in deliberately promoting the impression that given the potential cleavages in the colony, the ignition of a small conflict might unleash political forces of unknown magnitude to inflict severe damages upon Hong Kong among the Chinese populace, as they are accompanied by a majority of the mass media in the colony. Many politiking activities, including those which in many other places would be considered as legitimate actions directed at the government, have been popularly branded as moves to "rock the boat" and summarily condemned. Though this pervasive fear of conflict among the Hong Kong Chinese is receding, it undoubtedly is still a restraining force on political activities in Hong Kong.

Without questioning for a moment that the China factor in the second sense is relevant to political stability in Hong Kong, it can still be argued that it fails to provide an adequate explanation. First of all, the hostility of the Hong Kong Chinese towards the communist Chinese government seems to have been overstated. According to a survey of the refugees in Hong Kong conducted by the United Nations, it was found that among the pre-World War II refugees, 17.4% came to Hong Kong for political reasons, while 79.6% came for economic reasons. The situation is reversed for the post-World War

II refugees, with 64.1% of them coming to Hong Kong for political reasons
and 34.3% coming for economic reasons (Hambro 1955:154). Taking into
account the comparatively larger number of post-World War II refugees, it
might be said that in the immediate periods since the end of the Second World
War, more than half of the Hong Kong residents might not be sympathetic to
the Communist regime in China, but a substantial minority of them were
either neutral or even pro-communist. Second, even those who fled China for
"political reasons" might not necessarily be die-hard anti-communists. In a
rare study of the political attitudes of post-World War II refugees in Hong
Kong, Covin identified three political subcultures in the sixty refugees which
constituted his sample. The largest subculture was an apathetic-subject one.
Members of this group expressed neither strong negative nor positive feelings
about the Peking regime. While only mildly critical of the communists, their
major reasons for leaving China were staying with their families, hunger and
general poverty. Very little which was specifically political could be connected
with their refugee status. The second largest political subculture was alienated-
subject. The members of this group expressed strong negative feelings towards
the communists. They considered themselves to be politically oppressed.
Many of them gave explicitly political reasons for fleeing China, and all of
them saw themselves as having escaped from a country which was politically
suppressive. The smallest group was allegiant-subject. Men in this category
showed positive feelings towards the communists. They had supported
communist policies, and they felt that communism was good for China. Most
of them came to Hong Kong in order to be with their families or because of
economic hardships they had suffered. Those who came for the latter reasons
did not blame the communists for the economic plight. Overall, as only the
members of the alienated-subject category were strongly against the Communist regime in Peking, the conclusion is that anti-communists were only a
minority of the sample. There is another interesting finding in this refugee
study, and it is that the former "exploiters," who had been picked as the
target to struggle against by the Chinese communists, were not more prone to
be hostile to the Peking regime (Covin 1970). While representativeness of the
sample refugees selected by Covin can be questioned, we still cannot escape
the conclusion that the Hong Kong Chinese are not as antagonistic to the
Communist regime as has been believed to be the case.

Third, the economic and political achievements of China, particularly the
international status which she has managed to attain, have not failed over the
years to instill a sense of national pride among the Hong Kong Chinese,
especially among the younger generations. Five hundred and fifty adult Chinese
in Hong Kong were asked in 1977 to choose between an egalitarian society
where opportunities to advance socially or economically were limited but yet

polarization between the wealthy and the poor was minimal, and a society where disparities between the rich and poor were glaring but then the people had the chance to advance socially and economically. The proportions of respondents picking the first and the second options were 48.4% and 38.7% respectively (Lau 1977:200-201). While the conclusion is that the Hong Kong Chinese would in general prefer Hong Kong to China, the impression created by the finding is certainly not feverish anti-communism on the part of the people.

Lastly, to say that the Chinese are not as hostile to communism as has been said to be of course does not mean that the Hong Kong Chinese are willing to come under communist rule. To be sure, 81.6% of the adult Chinese respondents in a sample were found in 1977 to endorse the status quo of Hong Kong (Lau 1977:199). What all this means is that the fear of Communist China could not provide as powerful a means of restraining the political activities of the Chinese as alleged to be. The riots of 1956, 1966 and 1967 are vivid evidence of the capability of the Hong Kong Chinese to engage in conflictual behaviour. Among these three riots, the first and the last one are notably significant as they were politically and ideologically charged, the first one involving rightists taking on leftists in a historical moment when the political future of China was still rather uncertain, and the last one intentionally instigated by the local communists to challenge the extant political order and to draw into their camp a not insignificant number of people who were politically neutral before the event took place through nationalist and patriotic appeals. Over the years, the Chinese in Hong Kong have learned that conflicts, if kept within certain limits, would not provoke intense reactions from China, and the willingness of the poor Chinese to confront the government in a mild way recently is a telling indicator of a changing mood.

Obviously, the appeal to the China factor without a careful analysis of the Chinese society and the polity in Hong Kong is not sufficient to establish a solid explanation of political stability in Hong Kong.

POLITICAL APATHY OF THE CHINESE

The Chinese people are oftentimes characterized as politically apathetic, and their political passivity is frequently adduced to explain political stability in Hong Kong. Most of the times, however, the term "political apathy" is used in an undiscriminating manner. As a result, it at once explains too much and too little. Rarely has an attempt been made to distinguish between political apathy based on satisfaction with the performance of the government and apathy springing from deprivation of channels for political participation. Apathy has been commonly treated as an inherent trait in the Chinese national character, and seldom is it considered to be a psychological and behavioural manifestation contingent upon structural conditions. Furthermore, it is rare for the users of the term to dimensionize the concept, or to recognize that it is possible for the affective, evaluative, cognitive and behavioural dimensions of "political apathy" to vary independently without changing in the same direction to form a consistent syndrome.

Judging from the political behaviour of the Chinese in history, in China and in Hong Kong, it is reasonable to conclude that while there is a cultural tendency to be politically passive, this passivity will recede into the background whenever structural conditions change to make political activism either possible, appropriate or necessary. We might not agree with Pye (1968) and Solomon (1971) that intense, even feverish, political activities and sentiments will be unleashed to create utter chaos whenever the authority system in China breaks down and fails to keep a tight rein on human aggressive tendencies. Still, it cannot be denied that the history of China is interspersed with thousands of peasant riots and rebellions which, under extreme conditions, toppled governments. In Hong Kong, political conflicts and violence are not nonexistent, though they are extremely rare. Aside from those we have mentioned before, Hong Kong in the early twentieth century had witnessed quite a number of cases of political activism among her Chinese populace. The activities of Sun Yat-sen and his Hong Kong clique, the excitement produced by the 1911 Revolution, the strikes of the 1920s and the persistent attempts of the Chinese Communist Party to organize the Chinese residents in the colony demonstrate that Hong Kong can be prone to conflict and violence. And, more importantly, not all these events were the result of political manipulations by forces outside of Hong Kong. The 1925 strike by the seamen, although precipitated by events in Shanghai and Canton, had as one of its goals the extension of political and social rights in the colony, and a large proportion of the Chinese population were involved for a longer period during that strike than is true in most full-scale revolutions (Catron 1971:30-31). Even though political activism among the Chinese has declined since the Second World War, it can only be explained by the changed structural conditions mainly inside and outside the colony, with the former seemingly more important. If political apathy is a cultural trait of the Chinese, it should remain more or less constant in its behavioural manifestations. Yet while the former is held to be constant, the latter has changed with time. Even in today's Hong Kong, the Chinese are not as apathetic as they are said to be. As will be discussed in more detail in Chapter 4, the Chinese are fairly active in the cognitive dimension of political culture. What this means is that whenever they feel the necessity to participate politically, they will not be totally ignorant as to how to proceed.

THE SUPPORT OF THE CHINESE ELITE

Another approach to explain political stability in Hong Kong verges upon a "conspiracy theory" of political stability. And it runs as follows: Hong Kong can remain politically stable because the Chinese elite shares identical interests, which are predominantly economic in nature, with the British elite (government officials and business groups). And they are willing to give full support to the government to maintain political order.

It is almost commonplace to say that elite support is essential to the survival of any political regime. Nevertheless, to what extent is elite support effective in maintaining political order would depend very much on the type of elite concerned and their relationship with the masses. Presumably, elites with independent political, social or military power bases are the most effective as a politically stabilizing force to a government aiming at political stability. In the case of Hong Kong, such elites with independent power bases are nonexistent. The Chinese elite in Hong Kong comprise entrepreneurs, industrialists, social notables and other prominent individuals. They are successful individuals, but generally speaking are not recognized leaders of solidary social or political groups. Their support for the government represents basically individual support. Organizational solidarity among the Chinese elite members is far from substantial.

In a passive sense, elite support does contribute to political stability in Hong Kong. By siding with the government, competitive mobilization of the masses by the elite for political purposes is precluded. This will deprive the masses much of the needed leadership and organizational resources. Elite support will also in a positive sense furnish the government with an aura of prestige and legitimacy, thus bolstering the government's status in the eyes of the public. Elite support will also exert a moderating impact upon the Chinese society and cool down political heat. Moreover, the Chinese elite can also be made to serve as middlemen or liaison persons for the government to bargain with the masses whenever direct confrontation between the government and the people is to be avoided. One such case in point is the 1925 seamen's strike (Catron 1971:31).

Elite support, on the other hand, is no guarantee of political stability in Hong Kong. The lack of powerful linkages between the Chinese elite and the masses means that whenever political troubles break out, the Chinese elite cannot be relied upon to contain or dissipate them, and this observation is particularly pertinent in cases of anomic riots or movements led by anti-government leaders. The resolution of the conflicts in 1956, 1966 and 1967, for example, was accomplished largely by the deployment of coercive means controlled by the government, and the government can do the job because of the limited scope of the riots and the non-involvement of the general public. During the 1967 riot, the most serious of the three, a substantial number of the upper elite were panicky, and they chose to leave Hong Kong. As for the lower-level elite, their performance in containing violence was far from impressive. The Kaifong (neighbourhood association) leaders, for example, were criticized by the leading newspapers for their ineffectiveness in assisting the government to maintain law and order; one of which complained caustically:

> There is another fact that the people concerned will find painful—the "civic leaders" who claim to represent the people, and whose appeals for the restoration of law and order came so belatedly, were ignored by the very citizens whose spokesmen they claim to be. If this is a sample of their hold on the masses, the so-called democratic movement in Hong Kong is best dead and buried.

The tone of another editorial was equally acrimonious:

> It seems incredible but, nevertheless, very true, not a single leader of the Kaifongs or clansmen associations and other similar organizations came out to help the authorities restore law and order in Kowloon.
> The Kaifong leaders have remained strangely silent when they and others could have exerted considerable influence to bring about an earlier end to the lawlessness due to their being in much more direct contact with the ordinary people. (Both passages quoted from Wong 1972a:198.)

If we cannot explain Hong Kong's political stability by looking only at the Chinese elite, it is imperative that we pay attention to the political orientations and behaviour of the common people, their relationship to the elite and to the government.

OTHER EXPLANATIONS

Besides the three major approaches discussed above, other explanations of political stability in Hong Kong are available. However, since these explanations are scattered explanatory sketches falling short of full-scale explanations, they will only be briefly touched upon:

(1) Hong Kong's phenomenal rate of economic growth and the resultant rise in living standards for a majority of her residents predispose them towards acceptance of the existing conditions.

(2) The efficiency of the government, as witnessed in its housing policy, administration of trade and commerce, educational facilities, etc., forecloses many issues of civil discontent.

(3) Since few Chinese expect British rule to continue beyond 1997, if indeed it lasts as long as that, those who are discontented with life in Hong Kong and apprehensive for the future would prefer to emigrate, if they have

the requisite qualifications, rather than strive to ameliorate conditions in a "borrowed place" with limited "borrowed time," for any efforts they may make are unlikely to lead to any permanent changes.

(4) There are no political parties in Hong Kong to channelize discontent into political action or violence.

(5) Not much frustration has been felt at the denial of the basic democratic right to vote and participate in government.

(6) The Chinese in Hong Kong tend to treat the colony as a temporary resting place rather than as a permanent home. This lack of a sense of commitment to Hong Kong would prevent them from taking any drastic political action.

(7) The Chinese people are known for their resiliency and ability to endure hardships. Put in a desperate situation, they would prefer to stay away from the government and from political activities.

(8) The government of Hong Kong has been able to make itself legitimate by modelling its institutions and attitudes on the paternalistic and authoritarian regimes which the Chinese have been accustomed to for millenia.

These variegated explanatory sketches, ranging in different levels of generality and abstraction, contain some truths which deserve serious consideration, though some of them are patently false (such as the alleged desire of the Chinese to emigrate, which in fact is confined to an extreme minority of the people, see Lau 1977:150). What is needed, however, is to integrate them into a more comprehensive theoretical framework so that their interrelationships and their relationships with other elements relevant to political stability in Hong Kong can be arranged in order.

HONG KONG AS A MINIMALLY-INTEGRATED SOCIAL-POLITICAL SYSTEM

The approach to political stability advocated in this book is a comprehensive and systematic framework focusing upon the polity and the Chinese society of Hong Kong, and their relationships with each other. By analyzing the core features of the social-political system of Hong Kong, this approach will locate the fundamental causes of political stability in the colony. As such the approach can be used as an interpretative schema to make sense of the social and political phenomena in Hong Kong in the last three and a half decades. Basically, the approach to political stability advanced here is a structural approach. Even though the normative orientations of the government and the Chinese society will also be described, their concrete manifestations are assumed to be conditioned by the structural setting involved. Therefore, without denying that cultural traits have their own historical continuity, they are not treated as immutable, for structural changes will call for selective emphases on cultural tendencies, modifications in their specific contents, and the emergence of new cultural orientations.

The presupposition of this approach, and there are ample reasons to consider this presupposition to be sound, is that given a colonial-bureaucratic system whose capability to expand political participation and political functions is limited, political stability in a society undergoing dramatic economic and social change has to be explained by relying more on uncovering the nature of that society. The structural and normative features of that society which enable the "anachronistic" colonial political system to remain viable have to be attended to.

In essence, our approach conceptualizes Hong Kong as a minimally-integrated social-political system, and, in such a social-political system, political stability can be maintained even if an "anachronistic," non-participant polity is superimposed on top of a rapidly modernizing Chinese society. The basic process at work in this type of social-political system is "depoliticization," and both the polity and the Chinese society deliberately and spontaneously operate to bring it about. In Hong Kong, in addition to the intentional efforts at depoliticization by both the government and the Chinese society, objective factors beyond policy control also impinge upon the system to facilitate the process. Consequently, the viability of the minimally-integrated social-political system in Hong Kong is a result of both deliberate human strivings and the fortuitous coincidence of a host of objective factors which represent the particular historical and geographical setting wherein Hong Kong finds herself.

In a succint schematic form, the core features of a minimally-integrated social-political system are:

(1) The coexistence of a bureaucratic polity and a Chinese society, with limited linkages and exchanges between them.

(2) The bureaucratic polity is dominant in the political sector of the colony. In fact, it defines the basic configuration of the political arena in Hong Kong. It is an autonomous political actor and is largely exempt from interference by social and economic forces in the system. In fact, it arduously maintains its political autonomy by limiting its functions, by preventing the emergence of other autonomous political actors and by depoliticizing the Chinese society. In a sense, it is a "secluded" bureaucratic polity.

(3) The Chinese society of Hong Kong comprises basically a conglomeration of familial groups, which constitute the most significant social groups with which a majority of the Chinese people identify. These familial groups function largely as networks for the exchange of resources among their members, and hence are non-political in nature. By meeting many of the

needs of the Hong Kong Chinese, they represent a politically conservative and stabilizing force in society. Interactions between familial groups are rare. While there is no paucity of voluntary associations in Hong Kong, a predominant majority of them are social and cultural in nature, and are not viable political actors. Many of them are particularistic or ascriptive in membership, and thus are familial groups writ large. Anyway, participation in groups beyond the familial groups is low among the Hong Kong Chinese. What results in Hong Kong therefore is a Chinese society with low political mobilizability, since there are no mechanisms to tie these small familial groups together to form large, cohesive groups for political action.

(4) Both the bureaucratic polity and Chinese society are "boundary-conscious." Each is wary of "intrusion" by the other. On the part of the bureaucracy, politicization of the civil service by the entry of political forces from society is a nightmare. On the part of the Chinese society, being left alone by the bureaucracy is the most desirable state of affairs. Consequently, the *modus vivendi* between the bureaucracy and society in Hong Kong has these features: a minimum consensus on the division of labour between the two and a fairly high degree of mutual insulation. Politics in Hong Kong, if any, takes place largely at the boundary between the bureaucratic polity and the Chinese society, and involves generally officials charged with dealing with the Chinese society and members of the Chinese elite who are in the main pro-government. As this elite does not have popular power bases, their "political" role is mainly one of liaison or information transmission. Moreover, politics at the boundary is not highly institutionalized in a formal/legal sense. In fact, covert and informal politics is of enormous importance in the boundary zone.

(5) A minimally-integrated social-political system can be maintained only under two conditions. First, society is resourceful enough to deal with its salient problems and it is normatively inclined to be apolitical. Second, the bureaucracy does not pursue "state activism" nor intrude unnecessarily into society to restructure it, and it is successful both in depoliticizing society and in resolving the residual and outstanding societal problems left unsolved by society. Needless to say, compartmentalization of the two cannot, in reality, be complete or watertight.

(6) As the maintenance of political stability in Hong Kong hinges upon the mutual adjustment between the polity and society, it has to be a continuous process, and there is always a degree of uncertainty and maladjustment in the final outcome. In the last three and a half decades, there have been changes both in the polity and in society, and adjustments in their relationship have been made, though they are not substantial. Compared to the modernization process, these changes in the boundary relationships are gradual and small in

scale, and the basic relationship between the two has remained constant.

(7) Even if the minimally-integrated social-political system works well, it is unavoidable that conflicts will arise from some sources. The most obvious of these are conflicts instigated by forces outside the colony, and conflicts launched by small groups of disgruntled and socially unattached individuals. Furthermore, the possibility cannot be ruled out that social discontent can lead to anomic, relatively unorganized forms of political action involving a small number of frustrated persons. Nonetheless, the nature of Hong Kong as a minimally-integrated social-political system would lead us to expect that these conflicts will be confined in scale because, under normal conditions, it is extremely difficult to mobilize the Chinese people in Hong Kong to embark upon a sustained, high-cost political movement.

To conceptualize Hong Kong as a minimally-integrated social-political system enables us to steer away from the pitfalls which beset the other approaches to political stability in Hong Kong we have alluded to and criticized. Unlike the colonial society model, our approach does not set great store on the factors of coercion and racial discrimination. While we agree with the colonial society theorists that the polity is indispensable to the maintenance of political order in Hong Kong, we are however more inclined to attribute a much greater role to the Chinese society in the maintenance of political stability. As a result, the interplay between the bureaucracy and the Chinese society is of major concern to us. In comparison to the China-factor approach, which sets out to explain political stability in Hong Kong by adducing exogenous factors, our approach focuses on the operation of political and sociocultural forces which are internal to Hong Kong. There is also a difference in the explanandum in our approach and the China-factor approach. Whereas the China-factor approach is largely engrossed in the problem of the continuity of the constitutional status of Hong Kong as a British colony, our approach is more concerned with the problem of political stability *within* a British colony. More precisely put, given the facts that Hong Kong is a British colony and that a majority of the Hong Kong Chinese agree to keep this constitutional status intact, we would still be interested to know the reasons for, besides the absence of anti-colonial movements, the rarity among the Hong Kong Chinese of political actions which have less radical goals. There is no denying that the China-factor approach can contribute to some sort of understanding of the phenomena which interest us. Nevertheless, in itself the China-approach is far from an adequate approach.

While recognizing the political apathy of the Hong Kong Chinese, our approach, in contrast to the one based on political apathy, does not stop here. We try to lay bare the structures of political apathy, and trace their relationships with each other. In such a fashion, political attitudes are treated explicitly as a result of contextual factors, and not as inherent in Chinese political culture. Pushing the argument a step further, our approach is basically a structural approach to political stability in Hong Kong. Political apathy, as a situationally contingent construct, has to be rejected as a sufficient explanation. The elite-support approach has much to recommend itself, but it suffers from an implicit misunderstanding of elite-mass relationship in Hong Kong. In our opinion, the elite-support approach would furnish a much better explanation of political stability if it can be proved that there are strong linkages between the elite and the masses, so that when the elite chooses to support the Hong Kong government, the masses will follow suit. But such elite-mass linkages do not fit the situation in Hong Kong. Therefore, by unilaterally concentrating on the will of the Chinese elite, the will of the masses will be overlooked. In comparison with the elite-support approach, our approach underscores the essentiality of an understanding of the organizational patterns of the masses.

As the data presented in the following chapters will demonstrate, the application of this approach to political stability in Hong Kong will organize salient social and political phenomena of Hong Kong into a theoretically and empirically meaningful whole. Still, several caveats have to be borne in mind in evaluating this approach. First, we are adopting a basically theoretical approach to the study of society and politics in Hong Kong. As a result, the Chinese society, the bureaucratic polity and their relationships are conceptualized in an ideal-typical way so as to bring out the crucial features in the phenomena under study. To pursue this end, many historical and empirical details have to be omitted so as not to burden the descriptive process or to add unnecessary qualifications and ambiguities to the fundamental issues we are focusing upon. Our descriptions may occasionally seem overly clear-cut or to be oblivious to some counterevidence, but that is unavoidable. Anyway, we are fairly certain that no significant counterevidence which can turn the whole model around has yet been encountered.

Second, our approach is supposed to apply *only* to the period after the Second World War. It is possible that it can also serve some explanatory purposes when applied to the pre-World War II period, but there is no intention here to stretch the applicability of the approach too far. The major reason for confining the scope of explanation of the approach is a recognition of some salient differences between Hong Kong in the past and modern Hong Kong. For one thing, the demographic structure is different, the extreme skewness of the sex and age distribution of pre-World War II Hong Kong contrasts sharply with the more balanced demographic structure in modern Hong Kong. Another thing is that the economic structure in pre-World War II Hong Kong, which was based on entrepôt trade, differs from the industry- and export-based economy of modern Hong Kong. The Japanese occupation of Hong Kong during the Second World War had also left its imprint on the normative and institutional patterns of the polity and society of the colony (Lethbridge 1969), and that also adds some unique features to modern Hong Kong which were absent in the past.

The descriptions and analysis in the following chapters rely on the following sources of data: a survey conducted by the author in 1977;[2] original documents published by the government and other public bodies;

---

[2]Data and findings from a questionnaire survey conducted in 1977 will provide an important source of information in the chapters which deal with the normative and organizational features of the Hong Kong Chinese. Therefore, unless the source of particular pieces of data or findings is specifically spelled out, it will automatically refer to the 1977 survey.

The sample of respondents in the survey was derived from the sample of respondents used in the Biosocial Survey conducted by the Social Research Centre of The Chinese University of Hong Kong (in cooperation with the Australian National University) in 1974. The sampling frame of the Biosocial Survey was a stratified sample with equal probability in the selection of sampling units. The sample thus derived was a proportionate stratified random sample with 4,001 sampling units in the form of living quarters. In addition, a supplementary list of 1,600 addresses was also randomly drawn to replace those unsuccessful interviews in order to obtain the required number of 4,001 completed cases. At the completion of the survey, a total of 3,893 households had been successfully interviewed, and they represented cases from both the original sample and the supplementary sample.

These 3,893 completed interview cases constituted the sampling frame of our survey with one modification: cases from some of the census districts had been deleted because these census districts lay outside the urban centres of Hong Kong and Kowloon, and the inclusion of them would have substantially increased interview costs. A systematic sample of 735 addresses was taken from this modified sampling frame. Students from The Chinese University of Hong Kong were employed as interviewers, some of whom had accumulated some experience from previous surveys conducted by the Social Research Centre. A total of 550 interviews were successfully completed, thus obtaining a response rate of 74.8 per cent, which was not at all unsatisfactory given the difficulty of interviewing in Hong Kong.

Among the 550 respondents, most were males (59.5%), married (77.5%), largely located in the lower educational levels and in the low or moderately low income categories. The socioeconomic profile of our respondents can be said to be biased towards the lower ends of the social hierarchy in Hong Kong. Nevertheless, as the Chinese people who are low in socioeconomic status constitute the majority of the Hong Kong population, they are pivotal to the political stability of Hong Kong. We can safely assume that the upper and middle classes in Hong Kong are staunch supporters of the status quo. The same assumption, on the other hand, cannot be made with impunity with regard to those in the lower rungs of the social hierarchy. In fact, it is the reticence and resilience of the lower classes which intrigue us the most. The intensive attention to the lower-class Chinese which our sample of respondents affords us should be greeted with delight rather than deplored.

tions with individuals inside and outside the
dary works on Hong Kong which are relevant
blished materials). In a sense, this book is at
id *synthetic* in nature, synthetic in the sense
attered research on Hong Kong conducted in
 theoretical framework so that its relevance to
 of Hong Kong can be discerned.

2. The Bureaucratic Polity

The swelling of bureaucratic power is a universal phenomenon. It has a lot to do with the rise of the welfare states in modern Western countries, and the need for the state to assume the critical role of promoting national and economic development in both the socialist and the non-socialist developing countries. Despite its structural dominance, bureaucratic power is checked in varying degrees in most places by other political institutions which, rightly or not, represent the people—political parties, elected legislatures, politicians, charismatic leaders, the judiciary, ruling monarchs, and so on. Elite groups, such as traditional notables, modern pressure groups, or even counter-elites, also keep bureaucratic power within bounds in one way or another. In countries where the bureaucracy appears to be unchallenged by other autonomous political institutions, the military (a bureaucracy in its own right) is most of the times the underwriter of bureaucratic domination.

Formally at least, the political system of Hong Kong approximates an ideal-type version of a type of polity which is conceptualized as the "bureaucratic polity." "The concept of bureaucratic polity is distinguishable from other forms of government by the degree to which national decision-making is insulated from social and political forces outside the highest elite echelons of the capital city" (Jackson 1978:4). Indonesia and some of the relatively modernized Latin American countries such as Brazil and Argentina are usually cited as proto-typical cases of such kind of polity. What makes the bureaucratic polity of Hong Kong distinctive is that, while the bureaucracy reigns supreme there, it does not rely on military support for survival. Even though theoretically, as a colonial administration, Hong Kong's bureaucracy is subjected to control from the mother country, in practice its exemption from interference from the "top" is almost complete. In essence, it is a "secluded" bureaucracy—secluded from political and social forces which might threaten to undermine its autonomy.

As a developing country, Hong Kong's bureaucracy is remarkable in its continuity, stability, efficiency in delivering services, respectable status in society, relative freedom from corruption and political legitimacy. In a society characterized by sociocultural and ideological heterogeneity, the bureaucracy is a potent political institution maintaining order in society. The "seclusion" of the bureaucracy is a quite significant factor in the low level of politicization in Hong Kong. In other countries, the inability of the bureaucracy to withstand the intrusion of political and social forces has brought about the not unfamiliar result of "bureaucratic feudalism" (Baker 1978), where the administration is riven by factional infighting; or politicization of the bureaucracy (LaPalombara 1967:15), where the bureaucracy becomes the battleground of political struggle by societal forces and loses its separate existence. The bureaucracy may also take on the prevailing values and structures of society, be stripped of its distinctive features as a rational organization, and be crippled in performing its functions by rapacious nepotism and corruption (Price 1975). The loss of bureaucratic autonomy in turn fuels political mobilization and participation in society and creates a situation of overload of political demands, which inevitably generates political instability and institutional breakdown. The "seclusion" of the bureaucracy of Hong Kong is both a significant cause and the logical outcome of political stability in the colony. A careful analysis of the nature and causes of the "secluded" bureaucracy in Hong Kong will definitely provide us one of the most important keys to the explanation of political stability in Hong Kong. In this chapter we shall focus on the characteristics of the bureaucracy and, through their relationships, trace its "seclusion." In the following chapters, the deliberate efforts of the bureaucracy at maintaining seclusion as well as the environmental factors which function to facilitate it will be explored.

STRUCTURAL POSITION OF THE BUREAUCRACY
IN SOCIETY

Generally, the administrative bureaucracy in Hong Kong, consisting of officials directly or indirectly appointed by the British Crown, is the only significant political institution in the colony. Without overstating, the boundary of the bureaucracy almost coincides with the boundary of the polity in Hong Kong. Thus, the bureaucratic polity and the bureaucracy in practice are more or less the same thing. In jealously guarding the boundary of the bureaucratic polity, the bureaucracy is highly exclusionary. It lays down the rules of the political game in Hong Kong, and it almost always is the winner. Other political actors, as individuals or as groups, are inducted into the polity primarily upon the initiative of the bureaucracy, and hence they are dependent on it for maintaining their political privileges.

For administrative purposes the bureaucracy is assisted by two advisory councils: the Legislative Council and the Executive Council (Miners 1977:63-76, 99-131). The composition of these two Councils attests unmistakably to the political dominance of the bureaucracy, as they are filled with bureaucratic officials and unofficials appointed by the Governor of Hong Kong. The political will of the officials usually prevails with no difficulty in both Councils. Even though unofficials of the Chinese stock have increased over the years, both in absolute number and in proportion (to total membership) in the two Councils, their dependency on the government for appointment, their narrow socioeconomic background (being mostly big businessmen), their lack of effective organization, and their pro-establishment stance generally render them powerless to be a decent "opposition" or balance to bureaucratic hegemony.

As an institution, the bureaucracy enjoys longevity and continuity. This structural continuity contrasts sharply with the Chinese society (onto which it is superimposed to administer), which has been undergoing rapid changes in form and substance. As soon as the British took over Hong Kong, the bureaucracy was created both to symbolize British rule and to provide the necessary political order so as to allow free trade and physical construction to take place. Despite some attempts at reorganization of the civil service, the basic structure of the bureaucracy has remained largely the same. This tenacity in maintaining its structural features amidst drastic changes in its environment is a truly remarkable sociological phenomenon.

The bureaucracy is the only repository of legitimate political authority in Hong Kong. As such it is not merely an instrument for the implementation of policies made elsewhere. The Governor of Hong Kong, as the representative of the British Crown, is not simply a "neutral" chief administrator in the civil service. The rituals and symbols affixed to his office would be an unmistakable guide to his actual role as the "head of state" in Hong Kong, and he commands enormous prestige and power in the colony. As the "head of state," his relationship to the people in Hong Kong is not simply one of bureaucrat-client, which is marked by aloofness and impersonality, but one of patriarch-subject. He is the symbol of the colony and is held to be the representative of common interests.

> The submission to him of petitions (of which he may receive hundreds in a year) is eloquent testimony of the fact that he is regarded as something more than an official, hopefully as the repository of the true will (to use Rousseauistic terms) within the colony. Yet the very delicacy of this task is such that he must, in dealing with those very petitions which seek to determine the general good, never appear to favour particular groups or sectional interests. (Harris 1978:33)

Formally, the legitimacy of the power of the bureaucracy is derived from "above," from the Crown of Britain under whose sovereignty Hong Kong is the colony. Nevertheless, if legitimacy is defined as the felt obligation of the ruled to obey the order of the ruler, it can definitely be said that this legitimacy is also rooted in the Chinese society, setting aside the issue of whether this legitimacy is voluntarily and enthusiastically granted by the Chinese or not. Two of the major reasons why a colonial administration can enjoy legitimacy willingly granted by the colonized are the traditional Chinese respect for governmental authority, and the relative satisfaction of the Chinese with the benefits accruing from continued British rule. Blessed with this legitimacy, the government is not only the conferee of social prestige, it functions also as a conferer of status to those who are favoured by it. And this status-conferral capacity is a major cause of its general success in co-opting the Chinese elite in Hong Kong.

Ironically, for all its dominance in the polity, in terms of resources controlled and activities undertaken, the bureaucracy and correspondingly the polity are only a small sector in the colony. Even though the bureaucracy monopolizes almost all functions in the polity—from policy making to policy execution, and from law making to law enforcement—it actually is not an activistic, omnipotent, all-pervading force in society. In thus confining its scope of activities, it can better insulate itself from social and political forces which might be forced to emerge to impact on the bureaucracy, and make more bureaucratic involvement in social affairs unavoidable.

In view of the sociocultural diversity in Hong Kong, the capacity of the bureaucracy to maintain its relatively high degree of autonomy is magnificent. This autonomy can be described in various ways. First, the bureaucracy is ideologically neutral, and bureaucrats are independent from political groups both left and right. Second, no social or economic groups are able to "capture" the bureaucracy to serve their own partisan interests. Of course the bureaucracy has not infrequently been accused of serving the interests of commercial and industrial groups, and there is certainly some truth to the charge. However, given the economic context of Hong Kong, a government, whether it is against business interests or not, would most probably follow the same line of policy as that currently followed by the Hong Kong government. Otherwise, the economic prosperity of Hong Kong would be jeopardized. In the history of Hong Kong, however, it is not uncommon to find the government pursuing policies against the wishes of the business groups in the name of "common good." In dealing with a variety of social and economic groups, the bureaucrats are always able to maintain a united front. Though this united front was somehow "forced" upon civil servants by regulation since 1866 (Endacott 1964a:158), it is voluntarily subscribed to by most civil servants. Third, no other political actor or institution is capable of challenging the dominance of the bureaucracy in the polity. Many of the ostensibly independent political actors are in fact creations of the government and serve largely a supportive role. Fourth, there are no effective institutionalized channels whereby bureaucratic power can be checked by society. If it is checked at all, it is mainly the outcome of the voluntary effort at self-restraint made by the bureaucracy itself, though it in fact may have taken public opinion into account. Fifth, in spite of its formal subordination to the British government, the Hong Kong government is in actuality granted wide-ranging discretionary decision-making power. Since 1958, financial and budgetary autonomy has been given to it by the mother country. Except for policies which might have drastic implications for the constitution of the polity, the bureaucracy is insulated from interference from above. This, as a matter of fact, is extremely important in securing the autonomy of the bureaucracy, as it will enable it to be immunized from the volatile politics in Britain, which, if not curbed, could easily galvanize the Hong Kong government and turn it into a dependent institution subjected to political whims.

Compared to the society and economy of Hong Kong, the bureaucracy represents a totally different type of organizational entity based on different organizational principles and rationales. If the Chinese society is organized according to particularistic and emotional ties, and if the economy is integrated by the market system and based on the profit motive, then the bureaucracy is a formal organization integrated by rational rules and geared to the pursuit of collective societal goals. In many developing countries, the bureaucracy tends to be a microcosm of either society or market, and loses its distinctive organizational characteristics. Consequently, its ability to keep politics in bounds or to resolve conflict is paralyzed. Unlike these countries, the autonomy of the bureaucracy in Hong Kong is due in no small measure to its ability to maintain itself as a different cultural and organizational entity.

It has been well recognized in comparative studies that an autonomous bureaucratic administration is critical to political stability in societies marked by cultural and ideological diversity and by a paucity of other legitimate political authorities. In such a situation, the bureaucracy provides the most coherent set of rules the enforcement of which serves to bind the various social and political groups together. And, given the continuity, the stability and the respectability of the bureaucratic administration, its political function in stabilization is neither dispensable nor replaceable. And Hong Kong is an illustrative case of a bureaucratic polity playing this vital political role.

BUREAUCRATIC ROLE DEFINITIONS

An understanding of the role definitions of the bureaucracy is extremely important in uncovering its relationships to the Chinese society and its behaviour. As bureaucratic role definitions are made by individual officials, particularly the Governor, who may differ in their conceptions, it is not an easy job to describe a consistent set of role definitions for the bureaucracy as a whole. In the process of trying, unfortunately, we are also handicapped by the lack of empirical research on this highly important subject. Consequently, all we can do here is to present a general, though somewhat simplistic, picture of bureaucratic role definitions, utilizing scattered pieces of information largely in the form of statements and actions by government officials which can throw light on their role orientations. As a result of this exercise, a number of salient themes can be identified.

Government by Consent

In an age when the ideals of participatory democracy and national independence go virtually unchallenged, the government is to some extent hard-pressed to legitimize its rule in Hong Kong. The declaration of the principle of government based on the consent of the governed goes somewhat along the way to ease the ideological dilemma for both the British and the Chinese, and to make the status quo more acceptable to both. In its various forms— government by consent, government by consultation, government by discussion, government by consensus or government by compromise—this principle has been proclaimed and reiterated in numerous occasions by government officials and by academics (Endacott 1964b:229-41).

As the government sees it, "consent" has both a substantive and a procedural meaning. Substantively, it means that the Chinese voluntarily consent to continued British rule because they consider it to be in accordance with their best interests. These interests are to improve their economic well-being under a politically stable regime which also ensures a certain degree of individual freedom. In this sense, the expression of consent is tantamount to the bestowal of a mandate to rule to the British. With this mandate, the British government ruling over Hong Kong has to be considered a fully legitimate government. With this consent, Hong Kong is colonial in form but not in substance. To the Chinese officials serving in the government, the conception of government by consent helps to alleviate any mixed emotional feelings which might arise in connection with serving an alien government.

As "consent" is not a thing always constant in supply, the "consent" the government enjoys can also diminish. Moreover, even after it has been bestowed to the government, it can also be withdrawn. Therefore, to ensure that an "adequate" supply of consent is forthcoming, procedures which enable the government to maintain it or even increase it are necessary. The key to its maintenance, according to the government, is to formulate policies and take actions which are in accordance with the wishes of the ruled and are capable of meeting their needs, or at least do not seriously violate their wishes. Since it is impossible, under a colonial constitution, to assess the "popular will" directly through the popular vote, it is necessary to install a consultative or advisory system so that information about the opinions of the people can be collected. Moreover, as it is impossible to consult every individual or group affected by a specific policy, the government has to solicit ideas and advice from a select group of personalities whose positions in society and whose demonstrated expertise in particular fields have unmistakably shown that they can reflect the wishes of the others not consulted. Furthermore, as a government owing ultimate allegiance to Britain, and as an autonomous organization in its own right, the government is oftentimes inevitably put into a situation wherein the interests of Britain, its own interests and the interests of the ruled are in conflict, and compromises have to be struck in order to bring about harmony. In some cases, though they are rather rare, failure to compromise might result in leaving one or two sides dissatisfied (the decision to abolish the death penalty despite opposition by the Chinese is a case in point).

To govern by consent in Hong Kong is not tantamount to total control of governmental policy-making by the Hong Kong Chinese. Far from it. What it in practice means is that the government is prepared to cater to public wishes when its resources allow it, when by doing so its own principles are not compromised, and when the policies involved does not have adverse repercussions on the basic contours of the system. In reality, also, the system of consultation has incorporated only a tiny, select group of individuals into the decision-making process in the government, and their actual influence there, however, is rather limited. Despite these deviations from the proclaimed ideal, it can in general be said that the Hong Kong government is a fairly responsive and responsible government. As such, the use of the principle of government by consent should not be seen as a hypocritically declared ideal to camouflage despotic rule. Its avowal by the government reflects a realistic recognition by it that in a society such as Hong Kong, a certain amount of public consensus as to societal goals is necessary to secure continual British rule. Such a voluntary concessionary posture by the bureaucracy is an essential ingredient in creating a harmonious relationship between the government and the Chinese society, since there is no institutionalized means or sanctions whereby the public can compel the officials to act in designated ways or to remove them from office when they refuse to do so.

Bureaucratic Paternalism

Basically, the government of Hong Kong is a paternalistic administration, though this paternalism is ameliorated to a certain extent by the need to obtain consent from society. The people are largely seen as subjects who are indifferent to collective decision-making as long as its results are not detrimental, and they are willing to leave it to those in authority, seen as their superiors, to decide their fate for them. The following passage in a booklet written by government officials reflects the government's view of the relationship between itself and the people:

> The traditional Chinese view of the ideal relationship between government and people . . . is analogous to that which should exist between parents and children, or between a shepard and his flock. The actions of both parties should be in strict accordance with a moral code, under which the rulers of a society, who should be men of learning, virtue and ability, must ensure that the community enjoys peace, order and security, leaving individuals free to pursue their affairs without undue governmental interference. In return, the people must impose their full trust and confidence in their rulers, and have cause to oppose them only if the regime fails to provide the conditions of peace, order and security to which the community is entitled. Save for such opposition, this traditional concept does not contemplate the direct participation of the population in the organization or process of government. (The Working Party on Local Administration 1966:11)

Moreover, the Hong Kong Chinese are often seen by the British and Chinese officials alike as being too preoccupied with their private affairs that, even given the opportunity, they will be hesitant to participate in collective decision-making. In addition, the shortage of leadership talent among the Chinese and their overconcern with "face" (which might be lost in unsuccessful political endeavours) also deter them from being politically active (*Ibid.*: 81-82).

These paternalistic and authoritarian attitudes among the officials have roots both in the British and the Chinese political cultures. The dominance of the imperial bureaucracy in China for more than two thousand years has not failed to produce a mentality among Chinese officials who demand respect and docility from their subjects. Under the supremacy of bureaucratic officials,

> citizens never demanded their rights, they sought instead the sympathy, and indeed the pity, of those more powerful than themselves. . . . Above all else citizens were taught that they should never be aggressive or demanding in their relations with public authorities; and officials were expected to be considerate and understanding of those who were docile and properly dependent. (Pye 1968:19)

On the part of officials,

> . . . the fundamental belief remains that the masses of the people can be readily satisfied and, more important, kept docile and compliant merely by the appearance of a potentially sympathetic and not unreasonably hostile system of official authority. (*Ibid.*: 22)

Though Pye's description is somewhat overstated when applied to Hong Kong, it manages still to contain a grain of truth in the attitudes towards their authority on the part of government officials.

In Britain, the aristocratic tradition in her political culture is clearly revealed in the arrogant and supercilious posture of the authorities and the "deferential" attitude of the common people (Bagehot 1955; Nordlinger 1967). In the British colonies, it has been found that these attitudes have become even more rampant.

Bureaucratic paternalism in Hong Kong gains reinforcement by the crossbreeding of both the Chinese and the British administrative cultures. This attitude serves to enable the bureaucracy to assert its autonomy vis-à-vis society; and it unavoidably keeps the efforts at obtaining popular consent within certain limits, short of the point whereat the bureaucracy will find itself losing "face" and respect in the eyes of the subjects.

Guardian of Common Interests

The government does not consider itself as just one among a number of groups in society, each pursuing its own partisan or sectional interests in competition with others. Instead, it sees itself as the guardian of the "common good," and is over and above partisan conflicts and interests. What this in practice means is that the government does not identify itself with any particular group in society. It is an autonomous actor whose activities are essential to secure a stable environment wherein all groups can live together peacefully. In Hong Kong, it is assumed that only by the installation of a set of impartial laws and bureaucratic regulations can intergroup relations be harmonized and intergroup conflicts kept within bounds. Underlying all this is a view of society flooded with potentially antagonistic forces, a conception of human nature as basically self-seeking and needing control, and a faith in the essentiality of the political institution to control it.

In reality, as to be expected, impartiality in the treatment of different groups and individuals is impossible to attain. Nevertheless, it is certainly not true that the government is the obedient servant of business interests, particularly those of the British themselves, as argued by Hughes:

> Power in Hong Kong, it has been said, resides in the Jockey Club, Jardine and Matheson, the Hong Kong and Shanghai Bank, and the Governor—in that order. There is more than a grain of truth in the observation. A vulnerable but durable colony, with a sturdy, old-fashioned, free trade philosophy, and uncompromising dedication to the principles of Adam Smith, requires an Establishment whose order of precedence expediently unites Big Business with Government. (1976:23)

While as a journalist Hughes' description is intentionally exaggerated to create a forceful impact on the mind of his readers, it cannot be denied that business groups and elites get more favourable attention from the government than that received by the less advantaged. However, the government is far from being so dependent on the business groups that its autonomy has to be forfeited. Throughout the history of Hong Kong, it is not uncommon to find the government defying business groups even though there is no risk at all of opposition from other sectors of society if the demands of the business groups are met.

In the period before the Second World War, for example, the bureaucracy had several times turned down demands by the British merchants that they be

given almost sole representation in the government which, if granted, would
mean the establishment of a system wherein the Chinese populace were ruled
by a minority of British mercantile interests (Endacott 1964b:43, 73, 75-76,
109, 119, 123, 137 and 140-41). Even though it can be said that the government was determined to stand firm because in conceding to the British
merchants its own tax base would be so constrained as to thrust it into
financial difficulties, the determination of the government to ward off
attempts to impose dominance by one group over another, powerless, group
was also operative. In connection to this point, the reasons given by a high-
level British official in 1845 is illuminating; and I believe the points raised
then are still pertinent today:

> Sir James Stephen, at the Colonial Office, defended the Governor and criticized
> the memorial sent by the merchants. . . . He said the objections to municipal
> government [requested by the merchants] in Hong Kong were: (i) "The English
> minority can hardly be entrusted with the powers which it would give them over
> Chinese and other alien and ignorant ratepayers"; (ii) Its existence would probably
> be incompatible with that "decisiveness and energy of proceeding which are
> almost necessary for the very existence of a European government surrounded by
> millions of Asiatics." Thus very early in Hong Kong's history the doctrine that the
> fate of the native inhabitants must not be entrusted to a comparatively few British
> residents was recognized; but there was for long to be an incompatibility between
> this paternalist attitude and the growth of self-governing institutions. (Endacott
> 1964b:75-76)

Again, the same arguments were put forth in rejecting another petition of
the British residents for political autonomy:

> Lord Ripon's reply to the 1894 petitioners was conclusive, and its subsequent
> support by Joseph Chamberlain in 1896 proved that the two main British political
> parties agreed that the conferring of greater political autonomy on the British
> residents was incompatible with the moral obligation to protect the interests of
> the Chinese inhabitants. The principles of Crown Colony government were there-
> fore even more firmly entrenched in Hong Kong as a result of the 1894 petition.
>
> The main argument was that the interests of the Chinese were likely to be
> better safeguarded by the Colonial Office than by a small local European
> oligarchy, however democratically elected amongst themselves. At the same time,
> it was held that the Chinese majority were not ready to assume political control,
> particularly in view of the Colony's economic importance and magnitude of the
> imperial interests involved. In a shifting society in which Chinese and European
> alike came to Hong Kong from choice, generally in pursuance of self-interest, the
> existing government answered essential needs, and provided the necessary minimum
> framework of control within which the different Hong Kong communities could
> work and live together. (*Ibid.*: 135)

When change did occur, it was to give greater representation in the bureaucracy to the Chinese.

Rule by Law

In the eyes of the bureaucracy, the Hong Kong society is potentially turbulent because its members are forever predisposed to flout public interests in their frenetic pursuit of private ends. The institution and enforcement of a set of public rules are thus rightly regarded by it as of critical importance in the maintenance of public order. In other words, law, backed by the coercive apparatus of the government, is considered to be the prime integrative mechanism in a fragmented society which lacks a sense of moral community. A set of specific, clearly spelled-out, stable laws, which define the public order and public interests, thus serve as the ground rules for activities in society, afford predictability in interpersonal encounters, and provide the framework for highly interdependent behaviour in an industrializing society.

While the bureaucracy monopolizes the law-making and law-enforcement functions, law adjudication is the reserved duty of a relatively independent judiciary. Under these arrangements, the legal order, which is supposed to stand above the conflicting groups, is indispensable in limiting the powers of all the groups; and it pretends to the posture of impartiality, impersonality, or providential harmony while sanctioning its claim to their allegiance.

With the law-making prerogative under the control of the bureaucracy, the laws in Hong Kong unavoidably reflect the bureaucratic will. Arbitrariness in the making and application of the laws, however, is more true in theory than in practice. The bureaucracy is constrained in its legal power by the need to take into consideration the prevailing legal norms in England, the customary practices of the Chinese people, the vested interests of the bureaucracy itself, and the political imperatives of the times. Compromises often have to be struck, and expediency is not infrequently the guiding principle in the selection of legal means. The limited government which the bureaucracy professes also constricts the volume of law flowing out from the bureaucratically dominated legislature, and this accords well with the bureaucratic goal of general depoliticization.

Even though the bureaucratic law constitutes the administrative tool reflecting the bureaucratic will, it is not necessarily held to be illegitimate by the Chinese people. While a cynical attitude towards the colonial law is oftentimes expressed by the populace, in general it is true that they are ready to abide by it, if for no other reason than the fear of punishment. Bureaucratic laws in Hong Kong, without any doubt, are insufficient to justify the political and social order, and they are rightly recognized as inherently authoritative, objective or necessary. But it does not mean that they are totally devoid of moral implications. As the bureaucracy is itself willing to conform to the rules it makes, and as these rules appear to embody some inherently desirable or necessary order, they by and large are treated by both the government and the governed as standards that even the former cannot or should not disturb. By a very gradual process, the legal order in Hong Kong is able to gain some legitimacy in its favour.

The substance of the law in Hong Kong is regulative in nature, as it is geared very much to the purposes of stability and administration. But it accords quite well with the needs of a Chinese people weary of turmoil and disturbance and steeped in a legal culture dominated by the unilateral transmission of rules from the top. This explains its ability to demand conformity. As the Chinese people are prone to be suspicious of others' motives and apprehensive about the precariousness of the political order, they are receptive to the imposition of regulations on each others' behaviour so that social and political peace can be preserved. In view of such a general acceptance, it is easy to see that while at times conflicts between the legal norms and the Chinese customary practices do flare up, they more often than not fail to bring about serious disruptions in the legal process.

Depoliticizing Society

Like other bureaucratic polities, the Hong Kong government looks at politics and political activities outside the bounds of the bureaucracy with abhorrence and consternation. Politics is seen to threaten the hegemony of the bureaucratic regime. What is equally objectionable is that it will inject irrational criteria into the public decision-making processes which would divert resources away from rationally-designed collective goals set by professional administrators. The term "politics" has an extremely obnoxious connotation in Hong Kong, and is associated by society with malicious plots, violence, dirty tricks, instability and self-seeking behaviour. The government is not innocent of spreading these connotations both to discourage politics of all kinds and to discredit any would-be "trouble-makers" or do-gooders.

Since the early histories of Hong Kong, the policy to eradicate politics in the colony has been laid down by the government. This policy was, and is still now, justified in terms of common interests. In connection with this the following statement by Sir Alexander Grantham (the Governor of Hong Kong from 1947 to 1958) to the Legislative Council on March 8, 1950 is representative of the view of the government:

> We cannot permit Hong Kong to be the battleground for contending political parties or ideologies. We are just simple traders who want to get on well our daily round and common task. This may not be very noble, but at any rate it does not disturb others. (*Hong Kong Hansard*, 1950:41)

Hong Kong has been and still is a haven for those Chinese who are hostile to or disillusioned with the ruling Chinese governments. First the anti-Manchu

newspaper clippings; conversations with individuals inside and outside the government; and all the secondary works on Hong Kong which are relevant (including published and unpublished materials). In a sense, this book is at once theoretical, descriptive and *synthetic* in nature, synthetic in the sense that it tries to assemble the scattered research on Hong Kong conducted in the past and subsume it under a theoretical framework so that its relevance to a comprehensive understanding of Hong Kong can be discerned.

revolutionaries, then the anti-Kuomintang Communists, and then the anti-Communist Nationalists sought refuge in Hong Kong and used her as the base to launch subversive manoeuvres against the neighbouring Chinese authority. The apprehension of the Hong Kong government that these activities would antagonize the Chinese governments and hence expose the colony to unpredictable forms of retaliation from them is certainly justified. However, this anti-political stance has in many times carried to the other extreme that political activities of all kinds, even including those representing legitimate claims against the government, are looked at with suspicion and disapproval.

This oversensitive posture to politics can be accounted for easily. First, this is a correlate of the anti-political professionalism characteristic of practically speaking all bureaucratic cultures, British colonial administrative culture in particular. Secondly, this is in connection with the intention by the government to stamp out all nascent sources of independent political power. And, finally, this is used as an excuse to divert attention away from real issues, discredit the "trouble-makers" and to rationalize inaction. In particular, the government is extremely apprehensive about its ability to regulate the behaviour of the people at the grass-roots level, where both their lack of "viable" organizations and their "overorganization" would be causes of serious concern. In the first case, the anxiety of the government can be detected in the following remark by Sir Grantham when speaking in the Legislative Council on March 2, 1950:

> We are, for the first time, bringing large numbers of people within the orbit of established government. . . . A squatter area is virtually impossible to administer; it cannot be policed by normal methods; none of the legislation governing buildings can be applied, for the buildings are themselves illegal; there is no hope of enforcing the sanitary or health regulations, for the area has no drains, no roads, no sewers, no mains water. Now in this great settlement experiment, these people are being given the chance to learn some of the privileges and some of the obligations of citizenship. (*Hong Kong Hansard*, 1955:40)

In the latter case, the reason given by Mr. John Walden, the Director of Home Affairs, for disapproving the amalgamation of Mutual Aid Committees in high-rise residential buildings, where most of the Chinese residents are accommodated, is revealing of the anti-political attitude of the government:

> As for the MACs, Mr. Walden said they were never intended to be used for political purposes.
> "The idea was to get people together to solve common problems within their own buildings. They were not intended as evidence of grassroot democracy in a political sense." Mr. Walden explained.
> "We don't encourage MACs to group together because by so doing they might be involved in the game of politics and tend to be diverted from the original objective and instead try to gain political power and prestige," he said. (*South China Morning Post*, April 19, 1978)

Most trade unions in Hong Kong are politically sympathetic either to the Communist regime in Peking or to the Nationalist regime in Taipei. The deliberate efforts of the government to prevent them from engaging in political activities through both stringent regulations and measures which would foster trade-union fragmentation, furnish another instance of the determination of the government to depoliticize the colony (England and Rear 1975).

In the eyes of the government, even if a depoliticized society is not an ideal society as advocated by political philosophers, it definitely is the type of society which both it and the Hong Kong Chinese would like to live in.

Bureaucratic Centralism

Closely related to the theme of depoliticization is the theme of bureaucratic centralism, namely, the concentration of political power in the hands of the government. The logical connection is clear: for if politics is to be eradicated, it is imperative that political power be taken away from potential trouble-makers and controlled by the government which has always had the public interests in mind.

Since the establishment of the bureaucratic administration in 1843, no one group in the colony has succeeded in compelling the government to relinguish a portion of its public decision-making power. In the political landscape of Hong Kong, there is no division of power, no checks and balances, no independent local government, no viable political parties, no independent parliament and no judiciary capable of curbing executive power. Many of these "absences" are stipulated by the constitutional arrangements of Hong Kong; the others, the non-existence of political parties for example, are the derivatives of a system which does not provide for an arena where political power can be obtained through institutionalized political competition.

In Hong Kong, it is understandable that the government disapproves of any attempt to install political institutions of any kind which are capable of challenging bureaucratic power at the centre. It is startling to see, however, that the government is in no mood to tolerate even local administrations which are on the whole dependent on the centre, but are granted a certain amount of decision-making power at the local level as well as independent purse-strings.

For example, the various attempts at local administrative reforms which have been proposed since the Second World War have been abortive. The first attempt was the so-called "Young Plan" proposed by Sir Mark Young, the Governor of Hong Kong, in 1949. It called for the transferring of certain functions of internal administration to a new Municipal Council which would be constituted on a fully representative basis. The new Council was to have an elected majority with the franchise open to all who were permanent residents and were literate in either Chinese or English; it was to be financially autonomous, funded out of the revenue from rates and licenses, employ its own staff and would eventually take over all urban services, education, social welfare, town planning and other functions (Endacott 1964b:179-95; Miners 1977:190-91). The proposal met with strident opposition both within the government and by some top Chinese elite. It was ultimately abandoned when the Communist takeover of China and the influx of refugees gave priority to other urgent issues on the administrative agenda. Another round of talks on administrative reform came in 1966, when a working party on local administration (the Dickinson Party) was appointed by the Governor to study the possibility of instituting local administrative devices so as to improve administrative efficiency in the colony. About the same time, the Urban Council set up an *ad hoc* committee to formulate proposals on local administrative reform which would result in enlarging its own power and jurisdiction at the expense of the central government (The Urban Council 1966, 1969). While both the Dickinson Report (Working Party on Local Administration 1966) and the Urban Council proposed largely similar programmes of reforms, there were nonetheless some differences:

> The difference between the two schemes can be summarized as follows: the Urban Council proposed a three-tier structure for the government of Hong Kong, with a debilitated central government at the top, a powerful new municipal council in the middle and new district authorities at the bottom; the Dickinson Report more parsimoniously proposed a two-tier structure, with the central government at the top left much as before and a number of new local authorities at the bottom which were to be called into existence by the dismemberment of the Urban Council and the Heung Yee Kuk. (Miners 1977:193)

While it is natural that the more radical proposal of the Urban Council was doomed from the very beginning, that the more moderate proposal of the Dickinson Report had also fallen on deaf ears is telling evidence of the reluctance of the government to decentralize.

When we recall that both the 1949 and the 1966 attempts at reform were initiated by the government, there is no reason to question the sincerity of its motive. Nevertheless, the fact that events immediately following the initial proposals, the influx of refugees in the first instance and the outbreak of the communist-led riot in 1967, could so easily dishearten the government and push it swiftly back into the protective shell of inaction bespeaks only too well of the basic ethos of bureaucratic centralism of the bureaucracy. In this connection it is amusing to note that after the riot was over in 1968, in an effort to "console" the Urban Council, it was given financial autonomy and some additional responsibilities in 1971 (*White Paper: The Urban Council*,

1971). But in return the standing orders of the Urban Council were changed so that thereafter it was not allowed to discuss, debate or talk about public issues beyond its jurisdiction (*Hong Kong Standard*, April 5, 1972).

Similarly, attempts of other kinds which threaten to budge the concentration of political power from the government meet with the same fate—being brushed aside. The most notable of these attempts were the call for the election of unofficial members in the Legislative Council by popular vote (*South China Morning Post*, November 30, 1977) and the call for the appointment of an ombudsman who could challenge bureaucratic power by public opinion in the years between 1967 and 1969 (Cheng, Lin and Kuan 1979: 257-58).

Two passages from the speeches of high-level government officials reflect the strong link between political reform and political instability in Hong Kong in their mind. The first one came from Mr. Dennis C. Bray, the then District Commissioner for the New Territories, in 1971:

> Hong Kong's political and geographical location rules out any radical change in the form of government, says New Territories District Commissioner Mr. Dennis C. Bray.
>
> "... there is no hope for either substantial shifting of power to bodies such as the Urban Council or for any forum of independence such as an elected parliament.
>
> "Fundamental changes in the nature of the central government seem to me to be ruled out because they would destroy the stability of Hong Kong," he said.
>
> "Hong Kong's stability rests on a tripod of consents which are each necessary for continuation of anything like the present way of life.
>
> "These three consents are the consent of Hongkong people, the consent of China and the consent of Britain." (*Hong Kong Standard*, November 13, 1971)

The other piece was from Mr. David Lai, the City District Commissioner for Kowloon,

> [Mr. Lai] declared that there was nothing in the quality of the Colony's people or the strength of the economy standing in the way of change in the political set-up.
>
> "But if we headed that way, we should certainly be running a serious risk of upsetting Hong Kong's political stability—the key to our prosperity and the steady improvement to the general living of the people." (*South China Morning Post*, July 25, 1971)

Economic Laissez-faire

In many developing countries, the scarcity of capital and entrepreneurial skills, and the pursuit of the national goal of economic development have impelled the state to take on a highly active and interventionist economic role. In sharp contrast, the economic role of the Hong Kong government is extremely limited (Owen 1971; Cheng 1977; Beazer 1978; Rabushka 1979). The government limits its economic functions to those of provision of an economic infrastructure and the creation of a favourable economic climate for private enterprise. It owns no industries or economic undertakings. In the case of economic infrastructure, however, some of its important components are in fact owned by private concerns, the most notable examples are energy supply and telephone services. The government does provide roads and fresh water, and operates the port and airport, as well as promotes exports through the establishment of some para-official agencies such as the Trade Development Council and the Hong Kong Productivity Centre. Aside from a few exceptions, the most important of which is its monopolization of the sale of Crown land, the private sector in Hong Kong is given the free rein by the government. There is in general an absence of tariffs and other restrictions on imports and exports, which is paralleled by the non-existence of controls on the movement of capital, and complemented by low rates of direct taxation. Through the maintenance of balanced or even surplus fiscal budgets, the government is exempted from the onus of having to borrow from the money market or to create and service a large national debt, both of which would have serious effects on the financial sector of Hong Kong. In the absence of price and wage rigidity, the 100-per cent backing system is supposed to be self-regulating and thus prevents administrative problems and the necessity of clumsy intervention. In addition, the backing is a major source of confidence in the currency of Hong Kong, thus serving to attract capital inflow and investment (Cheng 1977:34-35). The market forces of supply and demand, or in the words of Sir Philip Haddon-Cave, the Financial Secretary, the "automatic corrective mechanism," are allowed to reign supreme in the economy of the colony. Defunct industries will not be bailed out by the government, and it endorses no redistributive policy in favour of the labour sector. Even the government itself considers its economic fate to be largely determined by market forces, both domestic and international, and they are seen to be beyond its control.

This policy of economic laissez-faire has its origin both in the economic philosophy of free trade in the nineteenth century and in the structure of the Hong Kong economy which defies bureaucratic manipulation.

When the colony was first acquired,

> what was sought was a commercial and not a territorial empire, and the island was taken over reluctantly, primarily for the purpose of establishing the necessary organs of law and order and administration, free from Chinese intervention or control. . . . The Colony was not thought of in terms of territorial gain, but as the minimum space required for what were thought to be the necessary British institutions. Its function was to be the headquarters of British trade, administration and general influence in the Far East. (Endacott 1964b:vii-viii)

The export-oriented character of the economy, the need to attract foreign investment, and the dependence of Hong Kong on the supply of raw materials and machinery from abroad would render any efforts by the government to manipulate supply, demand and the price structure ultimately futile. Any distortion in the price structure by the government will have long-term adverse effects on the economy, and they might even be disastrous.

In this connection, a note of qualification is in order. While it is warranted to say that in general the government's role in the economy is limited, it does not necessarily mean that it cannot be more economically active than what it is now. It has been argued by Owen (1971:170-75), for example, that the structure of the Hong Kong economy does permit a more active bureaucratic role and that the government has in fact, through its budgetary policy, exerted some positive effects on the running of the economy, notwithstanding repeated denials by it.

> But intentions may be one thing, the effects quite another. The budgetary pattern described is Keynesian in nature and must have played a role in steering the economy along a steady path. Indeed, we have explained reasons for supposing that the Government has much greater leverage over the economy than official denials of Keynesian policies would lead us to expect. We would therefore expect that the variations in the budget that have occurred in the past decade have played a significant role in promoting full-employment and avoiding inflation. Paradoxically, success in achieving these economic goals may have been due to Keynesian actions of a government which denies all Keynesian intentions. (Owen 1971:175)

We, looking from a political angle, would consider the government's deliberate refraining from utilizing its full, though limited, economic potential in society to be another indicator of its "seclusionist" character. A self-imposed limitation of its role in society contributes both to enhance its autonomy as a political institution and to depoliticize society by making economic matters outside of the jurisdiction of the government. As a result of the laissez-faire policy, the compartmentalization of the polity and the economy is accomplished.

Social Non-interventionism

Parallel to laissez-faire in the economic realm is non-interventionism in the social realm. In contrast to the Communist regime in China which is determined to weed out deep-seated Chinese values, norms and organizations, and to replace them with new ones befitting the ideals of socialism and the "new socialist man," the Hong Kong government deliberately refrains from tampering with the cultural predispositions and social norms of the Hong Kong Chinese. As a result of social non-interventionism, the Hong Kong Chinese are able to enjoy a measure of social, and of course also economic, freedom unsurpassed in the history of China.

The principle of social non-interventionism is followed because of a number of very obvious reasons. In all the former British colonies, the colonial officials' perception of cultural reality and their zeal to preserve the traditional values and institutions of the colonized subjects underlay the social policy of the colonial government. Moreover, when the British decided to acquire Hong Kong in the nineteenth century, they cherished no intention to build a society which could be rationalized on idealistic grounds. In order to build up a viable community in the colony, it was felt imperative that well-placed Chinese nationals would have to be lured to migrate to Hong Kong. Any social measures which violated the deeply ingrained Chinese view of society would hence only do more harm than good. On the other hand, it is undoubtedly true that the imposition of British laws upon the Chinese society has in the past generated conflicts between the legal norms and Chinese social norms. However, due to the generally cautious and compromising attitudes of the British authorities, which are facilitated by the relatively high degree of legislative autonomy of the Hong Kong government, these conflicts have been kept within bounds. In fact, many of the laws in force in Hong Kong tend to reflect Chinese norms and sentiments in varying degrees.

Another very important reason for the pursuit of a policy of social non-interventionism is the lack of administrative capacity of a colonial bureaucracy to undertake such a herculean task. When we examine the efforts at social reconstruction by Communist China, where both administrative penetration and mass mobilization are extensive, the results of societal transformation there are far from encouraging. In Hong Kong, we find a relatively small bureaucratic apparatus superimposed on a vast Chinese society. Short of a drastic expansion of the bureaucracy extending its tentacles throughout the breadth and depth of the Chinese society, any attempt at social transformation would have to be futile. Furthermore, and this is an important point to note, before any effort at social intervention can take place, the outlook of the bureaucrats themselves has to be modified ideologically. Obviously, both capacities of both the bureaucracy and the bureaucrats are not adequate to ensure even a modestly successful attempt at social intervention.

What the government has opted to do so far is to administratively adjust to the organization of Chinese society in Hong Kong, both to avoid unnecessary conflicts between the government and the Chinese society, and to supplement administrative control with social control (which emerges spontaneously from within the organizational fabric of the Chinese society) so as to achieve political stability in Hong Kong. In this sense, hence, British colonial policy is totally different from that of the French in whose colonies the social structures of the colonized are arbitrarily infringed upon for the sake of administrative standardization, and the process irreversibly destroy their long-

revered authority structures. The results, in the French case, are social
instability and the need to apply more coercion in order to maintain colonial
rule. In contrast, the efforts of the British to keep Chinese customs and organizations intact, and in some cases even strengthen them, have contributed,
inadvertently or not, to lessen the administrative burden of the government.
Hence under British rule, it is not surprising to find that Hong Kong is a society
very Chinese in character, and this fact was noticed by the British officials
themselves:

> ... under the protection of the British Government, Hong Kong has become a
> Chinese rather than a British community . . . and Chinese settlement . . . has been
> one main element in its prosperity. (Lord Ripon to Sir William Robinson, August
> 23, 1894. Quoted from Endacott 1964a:215.)

> It is extraordinary—not to say discreditable—that after fifty-five years of British
> rule, the vast majority of Chinese in Hong Kong should remain so little anglicized.
> (Sir William Robinson, Speech to the Legislative Council, November 25, 1895.
> Quoted from *ibid.*: 243.)

Changes in the Chinese soicety do happen, for sure. But they are primarily
the outcome of the unrelenting process of Westernization, which Hong Kong,
as an international port, can never be able avoid.

Provision of Social Services

In the capitalist society of Hong Kong, where the rampant market forces
reign supreme, it is not surprising to find glaring inequity in the distribution
of income and the inability of many people at the bottom to meet their basic
needs. Though the Chinese society itself, through the organization of charity
works of various kinds, has been able to alleviate many of the pains inflicted
on it by the merciless process of economic growth, it is true to say that,
without the stepping-in of the government to take over some of the responsibilities of social service provision, political and social stability in the colony
would be very much threatened. To say this of course does not mean that all
the need for social services have been satisfied by the government. Far from
it. Nevertheless, when we compare the social services delivered by the government with those by other Asian governments, the performance of the former
is highly impressive, though it falls far short of the "from-cradle-to-grave"
ideal as realized by some Western countries. Still, it is rare to find a colonial
government in history giving out so much for the governed.

First of all, we shall let the statistics tell the story. Between 1951/52 and
1965/66, government expenditure in Hong Kong, both in the aggregate or on a
per capita basis, and in money or real terms, rose faster than GDP and showed
fewer fluctuations. There was a pause in the growth of government expenditure
between 1965/66 and 1970/71. After the 1967 riot, the government had taken

on a more active role as service provider. Since 1970/71, the upward trend in government expenditure growth was again resumed (Ho 1979:25).

When the expenditure of the government is classified, the notable fact that emerges is the rapid growth in social expenditure in comparison with other types of expenditure. Expenditure on education, medical and health services, housing and social welfare represent the vast bulk, more than ninety-eight per cent of social expenditure. In fact, social services have been the most important expenditure category since the mid-1950s, and at present it constitutes over forty per cent of public spending. Within this plethora of social services, the most significant to note are the free compulsory education up to the Form 3 level, the close-to-half of the Hong Kong population living in public housing, the institution of a public assistance scheme on a cash-payment basis, and the availability of medical care to the poor who are only charged nominal fees. All these services are provided either directly by the government itself or, more importantly (except for housing), through government-subsidized agencies.

In view of the enormous need for social services in Hong Kong, it is no exaggeration to say that the social services provided by the government are still far from adequate. As we shall see in the next several chapters, were it not for the private help which society is able to garner for itself, the possibility of social unrest would be increased. On the other hand, given the dependence of government revenue on the fluctuating economic conditions and the low-tax policy of the government, there are serious constraints on the capacity of the government to deliver more services to the people, even if it were determined to do so. From 1949 to 1976, the expenditure of the government as a percentage of GDP (at current prices) ranged from 7.3% in 1950/51 to 18.7% in 1974/75, although during the period the trend was upward. The smallness of the public sector goes a long way to explain the meagre amount of resources which the government can mete out to meet social needs. Furthermore, it can be seen that close to half of the government expenditure goes to the emoluments of civil servants. The costs of salaries and pensions as a percentage of total government expenditure in selected years are presented in Table 2.1.

Granted that there are double entries of the same item of expenditure both as salaries/pensions and as social expenditure, it can still be said that the government of Hong Kong is to a substantial extent an organization geared primarily to organizational maintenance.

Next we come to the attitude of the government towards its role as a service deliverer. On the whole, up till the early 1970s, the government was extremely reluctant to expand its role as a deliverer of basic social services. One of the reasons is that the provision of services to the disadvantaged runs

TABLE 2.1

Costs of salaries and pensions as a percentage of total expenditures

Year	Percentage of total expenditure
1960/61	50.30
1966/67	48.59
1971/72	47.24
1976/77	40.87

Source: Calculated from the figures published in *Reports on the Public Service* (Hong Kong: Colonial Secretariat, selected years).

counter to the doctrine of laissez-faire and in itself represents the intrusion of the clumsy hand of the bureaucracy into the operation of the market. As a matter of fact, strong opposition to this role of the government by business interests has been documented in the past. Another reason is the inclination of the government to "seclude" itself from society so that social issues will not be converted into political issues demanding political attention. Taking up the service-provision role would force the government willy-nilly into social affairs, and as a result generate unwanted and unnecessary consequences. In the 1950s, the government not infrequently used as an excuse the transiency of the Chinese population to abstain from playing a more active role in service provision. As an example, it is interesting to note in the 1955/56 report of the Social Welfare Officer (the predecessor of the current Social Welfare Department) the following statement: "it is certain that more than half of the residents, of whatever nationality, consider their real home to be elsewhere" (1955/56:1). It is only since the mid-1960s that the service role of the government became more explicit, as evidenced in the following remark by the Director of Social Welfare in his 1965-66 *Report*:

> The partnership of official and voluntary social welfare effort in Hong Kong has matured steadily in recent years and notably in the year under review. The days of crisis when an uncritical welcome was extended to any organization willing to fill a gap in the welfare field are fading into memory: during 1965-66, heavy emphasis was placed by the Department [of Social Welfare] and the Council [of Social Services] on the need for consultation before action, and coordination in place of competition. (1965-66:4-5)

Since the quelling of the riot incited by local communists in 1967, the more active service role of the government has become more institutionalized. The speech by the Governor, Sir Crawford Murray MacLehose, to the Legislative Council on October 18, 1972, represented a landmark event. In his speech was outlined the future plans of the government in a variety of service fields (*Hong Kong Hansard,* 1972/73:1-23). Nevertheless, even up to the present day, a strain of ambiguity can still be discerned in the government's stand towards its role as a service deliverer; and this ambiguity is reflected in some internal discord among top officials themselves as to what extent this role should be executed:

> In the Fall of 1973 I interviewed a cross-section of Hong Kong's public officials. My analysis of these interviews and other materials disclosed political divisions within the government bureaucracy; which pitted the Finance Branch and its supporters in one corner, against the "policy" branches, the departments, and their spending allies in the other. It was my feeling then that the Governor better understood British social and economic thinking than the realities of an externally dependent resourceless economy; the recession of 1974, however, has evidently taught him greater appreciation for the market economy. (Rabushka 1979:95-96)

> When I returned to Hong Kong in December 1976, I found that internal administrative disputes had given way to a unified dislike and resistance against intrusions of Her Majesty's Labor Government into the territory's internal affairs. There were considerable fears in Hong Kong that Britain wished to impose a welfare state, with a concomitant increase in rates of taxation on business profits and salaries. Hong Kong officials, of all persuasions, are rightly irritated when the representatives of a demonstrably unsuccessful economy try to impose their profligate and interventionist policies on a fiscally responsible, autonomous territory. Restoration of Tory rule, under which Hong Kong would more likely to go its own way, might reopen internal bureaucratic lines, but perhaps all have learned their lesson from the 1976 perturbations in United Kingdom-Hong Kong relations. (*Ibid.*: 96)

In addition to the persistent, residual ambiguity about its service-delivery role, the government, in the execution of this role, displays also its paternalisic and centralist tendencies. In describing the welfare role of the British colonial government in Burma, Pye had this to say:

> The British emphasis upon welfare was not, however, matched by a warm or humane approach to government. British rule was extraordinarily impersonal, partly because it represented the novel concept of a rule of laws and not men, but above all because it took place in a political vacuum, for it was unresponsive to an open and acknowledged political process. (1962:100)

It can be argued that Pye's description also applies to Hong Kong, though to a lesser extent. There is no denying that the government, in deciding on the amount and package of services to be delivered, has made it a practice to consult a small number of social leaders and professionals. Still, the opinions of the common people, who are the beneficiaries of these services, have not occupied an adequate role in the decision-making forum. Basically, services are "handed down from above" by the bureaucracy, and complaints from the public about their inadequacy or mispackaging are greeted with hostility by the officials, as the following story by Mr. John Walden, the Director of Home Affairs, candidly shows:

I can well remember how in 1966 a very worried senior Secretariat officer voiced his vexation at what seemed to him to be gross public ingratitude for what the Government had done for the people of Hong Kong in the '60s. "What more do these people want?" he said, "we look after all their needs and even their foreign affairs".

He was one of those dedicated civil servants who was unable to believe that a communications gap or a groundswell of discontent could exist until he actually read about it, after the event, in the report of the Commission of Enquiry into the 1966 disturbances. Like many conscientious civil servants today, he was so sincerely convinced that what he was doing was right for the people that it would never have occurred to him to ask them whether they agreed. The ears of top government men were not very close to the ground in these days. (1980:2-3)

To conclude on the role orientations of the government, we may say that it is characterized by a fundamental inclination to jealously protect its autonomy from social and political forces arising from society and to maintain its monopoly over collective decision-making. It tries to minimize the entanglements between the polity and the Chinese society, through economic laissez-faire and social non-interventionism, so as to depoliticize society. Even when it is compelled by circumstances to play a more active role in seeking public consent and in delivering social services, such activities have not however created a high degree of integration of polity and society sufficient to close the gap existent in an essentially minimally-integrated social-political system.

BUREAUCRATIC STRUCTURE AND BEHAVIOUR

The role orientations of the government are to a large extent reflected in its structure and behaviour, which exert an independent force of its own to maintain its autonomous and "seclusive" posture as the dominant political institution in society. The major features which distinguish the modern British civil service are open entry based on academic competition, permanency of tenure irrespective of party political change, a division of grades or classes according to whether the function is responsible or merely routine, a regular, graduated scale of pay, and a system of promotion based on a combination of seniority and selection by merit (Tinker 1966:24). These formal features of the British civil service, however, did not originate in Britain. Instead, this pattern was largely derived from the evolution of a superior civil service in India. Not until after 1870 did the Home Civil Service begin to assume the present pattern (*Ibid.*: 25). The message this historical fact purveys is that a bureaucratic administration geared to the rendering of services in an efficient and politically neutral fashion was innovatively instituted in a colony in view of the exigencies of colonial governance. In the heterogeneous colonial setting, an autonomous civil service is the key to political stability. In India, for example,

> The higher civil services served as an integrative factor of considerable importance in a very extensive and highly populated country. Administrative unity of the country, maintenance of law and order, reasonable standards of integrity, systemization of the tax system, and also formalization of the relationship between the administration and the people in place of arbitrary dealings as in the past were the main achievements of the civil services. (Khanna 1970:223)

In Hong Kong, substantively speaking, the application of the general model of British civil service has produced several features which contribute in large measure to the maintenance of the political autonomy of the bureaucracy. They are, first, power concentration in the hands of generalists and expatriates in both the functional and territorial senses; second, a stratum of higher-level bureaucrats with professional-technical as well as privatistic orientations and, third, the high priority given to system (organization) maintenance as compared to development administration. While the bureaucracy is relatively efficient in the routine administrative duties and in maintaining law and order, it is deficient both in promoting development and in adapting to changing circumstances. In other words, political autonomy and "seclusion" are achieved while innovativeness and flexibility are impaired.

Bureaucratic Growth

Just like the society onto which it is superimposed, the bureaucracy has undergone rapid expansion both in size and in complexity, though its resource-acquisition capacity remains small when measured in terms of government expenditure as a percentage of the GDP. As a matter of fact, bureaucratic growth represents both the need to administer an increasingly complex and populated society, and the result of economic growth which makes available to it more resources in the forms of taxes and revenues from other channels. In 1947, there were thirty departments in the government, and by 1980 the number had expanded to forty-seven. The expansion of the size of the bureaucracy can also be gathered from Table 2.2.

From the table, it can be seen that the expansion of the bureaucracy is declining, which can be explained both by the increasing bases for the calculation of the percentages, and by the economy of scale resulting from larger sizes which reduces the need for ever-growing rates of expansion. Still, the bureaucracy itself represents the largest employer in Hong Kong.

When we break down the bureaucracy by the occupational classes of its employees on April 1, 1978, it is found that 2% of them were in housing, 2% in postal services, 2% in secretarial duties, 3% in fire services, 3% in prisons, 4% in education, 5% in nursing, 8% in construction, 10% in clerical and related grades, 15% in the Royal Hong Kong Police Force, while the balance were in "others" or were minor staff (*A Report on the Civil Service*, 1977-78:

TABLE 2.2
Authorized establishment and annual growth rate in selected years

Year	Authorized establishment	Increase (%)
1954/55	23,867	–
1955/56	26,113	9.4
1956/57	30,125	15.4
1957/58	36,071	19.7
1958/59	40,429	12.1
1959/60	45,546	12.7
1960/61	50,431	10.7
1961/62	53,267	5.6
1962/63	56,910	6.8
1963/64	60,297	6.0
1964/65	63,793	5.8
1965/66	68,467	7.3
1966/67	70,853	3.5
1967/68	73,182	3.3
1968/69	79,741	9.0
1969/70	82,529	3.5
1970/71	86,203	4.5
1971/72	94,417	9.5
1972/73	98,459	4.3
1973/74	104,896	6.5
1974/75	112,818*	7.6
1975/76	114,306	1.3
1976/77	114,692	0.3
1977/78	117,495	2.4

Source: Selected annual issues of *A Report on the Civil Service* (Hong Kong:
Colonial Secretariat).
*Starting from 1974/75, excluding supernumerary posts held against permanent
posts.

38). As such, the bureaucracy should be considered as primarily a municipal
government in charge of maintaining law and order and the provision of urban
and social services. The fact that the Royal Hong Kong Police Force alone
accounted for 17.5% of the civil service strength as of April 1, 1978 (*Ibid*.:
39), when the total establishment is broken down by departments, is surprising in comparison to many other municipal governments, which usually
have lower figures. It can be explained by the nature of the Hong Kong
government as both municipal and "national" governments combined which
has to rely upon itself in ordinary circumstances to apply coercive power
when the situation demand it.

    To operate such a large and structurally differentiated administrative machinery, modern administrative theories would recommend a more decentralized approach and a greater emphasis on specialists if administrative efficiency and effectiveness are to be attained. The case of the bureaucracy in Hong Kong, however, suffers from overcentralization of decision-making power.

Power Concentration: Generalists and Expatriates

In conformity with the British practice, the top decision-makers in the Hong Kong government are made up predominantly of generalists of the administrative class, the elite corps in the bureaucracy. Like their British counterparts, the generalists in Hong Kong are transferred from department to department fairly rapidly so that they can acquire a comprehensive understanding of the government *as a whole*. Ideally such a practice would enable the generalists to become more sensitive both to problems arising from interaction between government and society and the problems associated with inter-departmental coordination. In short, in view of the absence of politicians and elected representatives of the people in the colony, such constant reshuffling of top-level personnel is expected to be able to make "politicians" out of them. And in fact some of the ideals are realized. The top-level generalists, normally highly educated, many having university degrees, are recruited through a highly competitive examination, and they display a high degree of intellectualism and breadth of knowledge unmatched by those specialists who are immersed in particular kinds of callings. In fact, in a society such as Hong Kong, the generalists are very significant in maintaining order and stability:

> Particularly in the new states where the need for national integration is paramount, the proliferation of functional specialists in administration will add to the many centrifugal forces that already exist. When a society is rent by all sorts of social and political forces pulling in conflicting, disintegrative directions, the administrative generalist may be a vital cement, holding the system together. It may well be that programs of economic development require a certain amount of functional expertise in administration; indeed it is difficult to imagine how the many technical activities implied by economic modernization could evolve without them. But there must be accorded equal attention to the critical political role that the administrative generalist can perform. . . . (LaPalombara 1967:21)

While there is no denying the essential services which the generalists can deliver in Hong Kong, there are several factors which detract from their effectiveness and from the capacity of the Hong Kong government to be a more innovative and change-oriented bureaucracy. One of these can be discussed briefly, and that relates to the generally anti-specialist attitudes and intellectual snobbishness of the generalists, which make it difficult for specialist expertise to feed into the decision-making process at the centre. The monopolization of top-level positions by the generalists and their denial, barring a few exceptions lately, to the specialists or professionals tend to demoralize officials in professional grades and produce a defeatist attitude among them. This generalist-specialist gap is exacerbated, furthermore, by the frequent transferring of generalists among departments, which makes them unable to "settle down" on a particular field of expertise in their administrative career. The solidarity of the generalists vis-à-vis other bureaucrats, which is not without a modicum of self-defense and self-protection, is conducive to the development of a conservative and inflexible attitude in the upper echelons of the bureaucracy.

Perhaps the most important causes that serve to reduce the efficiency and effectiveness of decision-making and implementation in the government are the over-representation of expatriates in the top decision-making level and the over-concentration of power in the bureaucracy. Both of them will be elaborated in detail in the following paragraphs.

As Hong Kong is a colony of Britain, it is of course not suprising to find an over-representation of expatriates in top-level positions. However, as a corollary to rule by "consent," the British have made it a policy to recruit locals into the higher bureaucratic ranks as early as 1946. In a speech to the Legislative Council, the Governor of Hong Kong declared:

> The policy of the Government is to ensure that every opportunity shall be given to locally recruited persons not only to enter but to rise in the service of the public up to the highest posts and to fulfil the highest responsibilities of which they are capable or can be assisted to become capable. (*Annual Report on Hong Kong*, 1946:6)

Thereafter, the proportion of local (primarily Chinese) officers in the elite administrative class has in fact risen at a fairly steady rate, though because of the enlargement of the class as a whole, the absolute number of expatriate officers there has also increased, as can be seen in Table 2.3.

The progress made in the numerical sense, however, conceals a more important fact. Up to the present moment, the dominance of expatriates in the highest grades of the administrative class, the staff grades, is well-nigh complete. "Expatriates form 82 percent of the whole group. By excluding grade C officers the proportion is 87.9 percent. If one concentrates solely on the top five, the secretary rank and grade A officers, who often double as heads of departments, the proportion becomes 92.9 percent" (Davies 1977: 54-55).

Another measure of the same phenomonon can be provided by looking at the representation of graduates of the Hong Kong University in the top-level positions in the government. Taking into consideration that these graduates constitute the intellectual elite of Hong Kong, and that the University has continued to provide future officers to the government since its establishment

TABLE 2.3
Percentage of local officers to total in administrative grades

Year	Local officers	Overseas officers	Percentage of local officers to total
1950	1	42	2.3
1956	3	54	5.3
1960	7	36	16.3
1962	12	66	15.4
1964	13	67	16.3
1966	18	74	19.6
1968	23	75	23.5
1970	40	71	36.0
1972	50	67	42.7
1974	66	86	43.4
1976	78	101	43.6
1978	91	114	44.4

Source: Hong Kong, Colonial Secretariat, Establishment Branch, *Report on the Public Service*, various issues.

in 1911, the negligible representation of its graduates in top-level positions is astonishing, as Table 2.4 shows.

TABLE 2.4
HKU graduates serving in senior administrative grades
(Master Pay Scale point 46 or above) as of June 1, 1978

Grade (Administrative)	HKU graduates	Established and supernumerary posts
Secretaries	0	11
A.O. Staff Grade A	0	4
A.O. Staff Grade B	2	25
A.O. Staff Grade C	16	58
Senior Administrative Officers	8	23
Total:	26	121

Source: Hong Kong University, *Convocation Newsletter* (December 1979:2).

This sluggishness in the process of localization, especially at the top levels, naturally has drawn a lot of criticism and protests from local officers, and it is not uncommon to find the locals challenging the appointment of individual expatriates to senior bureaucratic posts. Among the reasons commonly adduced to explain the sluggishness are: (1) "The universities [the Hong Kong

University and The Chinese University of Hong Kong] here are not producing the type of people [the government] need[s] for quick sound decisions, people who know enough of world affairs. They are too inward-looking" (*South China Morning Post*, October 22, 1972). (2) "Localization has been somewhat bogged down by the rapid expansion of public services within the past two years and the consequent creation of a large number of additional posts. Recruitment of more staff from overseas is necessary to enable various departments to proceed on schedule within major projects, such as public works, housing and new towns" (*South China Morning Post*, March 4, 1979). And (3) the incomparable attraction of the private sector in terms of salaries and career prospects drains many enterprising locals away from public service (Podmore 1971).

While acknowledging that there is more than a grain of truth in these explanations, it is still possible to say that the unwillingness of the government to localize its top-level positions and the inadequate facilities for leadership training in the bureaucracy are major contributing factors. Whatever the causes may be, the disparity in power, status and remuneration between the locals and the expatriates has resulted in great dissatisfaction and frustration among the former. In a mailed questionnaire survey of 253 higher non-expatriate civil servants in Hong Kong in 1971, it was found that this dissatisfaction was couched in a more or less muted, but nevertheless palpable, form. The survey showed that 52.9% of the respondents agreed or strongly agreed that "expatriate officers in general do not understand local conditions to the extent that they can be good administrators in Hong Kong" (Wong 1972c:33). Moreover, 63% of the respondents thought that they could easily do the job of their immediate expatriate supervisors. Given this perception of their own abilities, it is not difficult to understand their frustration when 64.9% of them were convinced that, under the existing system, only the expatriates could really go to the top in the government (*Ibid*.: 33-34).

As of now, the local-expatriate schism is far from being so serious as to "polarize" the bureaucrats. However, it does have the effect of impairing the communication process inside the government. Ever since the early years of Hong Kong, most of the expatriate officers have been professionals rather than a mixed lot from varied backgrounds (Lethbridge 1978:40). Many of them were required to receive training in the Chinese language. With the increase in the number of expatriates recently, the proportion of them who can master the Chinese tongue has dwindled. To administer a Chinese society, however, the feedback of information from their Chinese subordinates is undoubtedly essential. The Chinese officers' dissatisfaction with their promotion prospects would prompt them, in one way or another and in varying degrees, to withhold information from their expatriate superiors, thus detracting from their administrative performance.[1]

The bureaucracy is also a top-heavy creature. Not only are important decisions made at the centre, probably by the Governor and a select group of senior officials, but many minor decisions are also channelled to the top for resolution. This overcentralization of power at the top is promoted and sustained by numerous regulations and enactments, which substantially deprive the lower and middle echelons of administrative autonomy. In addition, financial supervision constitutes the most formidable weapon in exercising control by the centre over the subordinates. A team of management consultants, upon the invitation of the Governor to look into possibilities for administrative reorganization so as to enhance the adaptive capability of the bureaucracy, did recommend in 1973 that more delegation of decision-making power to the lower levels be undertaken (McKinsey and Co., Inc. 1973). Some reorganization of the bureaucracy did subsequently take place, the most notable of which was the appointment of a number of secretaries who were held responsible for a number of policy areas, thus lessening the burden of the Governor and the Colonial (now the Chief) Secretary in policy-making. Judging from the results, however, the top-heavy character of the bureaucracy is still its organizational hallmark, while coordinated and farsighted policy-making is still not adequately institutionalized. In spite of the intention of the Governor to delegate authority, the centralizing inertia of the bureaucracy is still insurmountable, and the animosities of many top officials to the consultants' report was barely concealed (*South China Morning Post*, February 16, 1976).

Given the vast amount of paperwork moving through the administrative system, it is paradoxical that not much meaningful information is received by decision-makers at the top, especially on a regular basis. The explanation lies in the fact that form, not substance, characterizes much of the paperwork. Options for action based on meticulous and professionally-conducted analyses of the situation are seldom presented to the top for reference.

In fact, there is very little means available to the top bureaucrats to insure compliance at the bottom and to actually achieve direct control over day-to-day operations. The lack of sufficient initiative and discretionary power on the part of the middle-level administrators results oftentimes in failure to integrate effectively operational units so as to ensure the execution of decisions in accordance with stipulations. The inadequacy in the monitoring techniques inside the bureaucracy has been lucidly brought out by John Walden, the Director of Home Affairs:

[1] Since 1979 the process of localization has begun to pick up. If this trend carries into the future, which is very likely, some of the grievances related to the paucity of career mobility for local officials would be alleviated.

> Apart from such specialised surveillance and occasional proddings by Governors, departments and Secretariat Branches move steadily towards their appointed objectives without being very precisely accountable to anyone for their successes and failures, particularly their failures. There is no internal audit of administrative decisions, no systematic checks to ensure that the consultative system is being correctly used, no accepted procedure for conducting an independent internal enquiry into situations where it is clear that something has gone seriously wrong. Top civil servants working under extreme pressure and placing heavy responsibility and great trust in the men that underpin them, have neither the time nor the inclination to probe into the causes of yesterday's crises. (1980:7)

Moreover, the inability of the rank-and-file officers to make discretionary decisions in connection with their day-to-day operations results in a process whereby minor decisions are pushed upward for consideration. This overloads the centre, and cripples it from making quick and timely decisions. Delays in decision-making at the top not only undermine the adaptive capability of the government but also provide the lower echelons the excuse for inaction and absolve them from all responsibilities for poor performance.

THE BUREAUCRATS AND BUREAUCRATIC BEHAVIOUR

Recruitment of civil servants is done through a process which insures the political autonomy of the government. A system of civil service examinations, overseen by top officials and conducted in an objective manner, would allow only candidates with merit to enter into the bureaucracy. This, in addition to the absence of appointments through political patronage or the spoils system which tend to pervert public administration in many countries in Asia, Africa and Latin America, prevents any social group from monopolizing civil service posts. Even compared to the imperial civil service examinations in traditional China, which have been extolled for their impartiality, the administration in Hong Kong is far less contaminated by corruption. Needless to say, those with better socioeconomic backgrounds would be in a more advantageous position to make it in the tough examinations. However, as many of those in the upper and upper-middle classes are more attracted to opportunities in the private sector, either in business undertakings or in prestigeous professions, the socioeconomic profile of the civil servants consequently reflects a general middle-class coloration. In fact, for many in the lower-middle and lower classes, the bureaucracy provides an invaluable channel of upward social mobility. The relatively high pay offered to civil servants and the high level of job security, not to say the social status enjoyed by officials in a Chinese society, have resulted in a relatively low level of personnel turnover in the civil service.

This low turnover rate not only gives the bureaucracy its needed continuity and stability, it is also an essential ingredient in maintaining the political autonomy of the bureaucracy. In Japan, the U.S.A., and the Philippines, for instance, rapid movements of bureaucrats out of the public sector and into private business or politics have led to the subordination of the bureaucracy in many ways to outside influence, for bureaucrats have to establish the proper relationships with their prospective employers or patrons while still in office in order to make the future transition. In Hong Kong, hence, the fact that many civil servants do retire in bureaucratic service contributes immeasurably to the political autonomy of the bureaucracy.

In view of the high prestige enjoyed by the officialdom in Hong Kong, the security of bureaucratic employment and the assured promotion prospects through the seniority system, it is not surprising to find the civil servants a highly conservative and satisfied lot. In a rare study of higher non-expatriate civil servants in Hong Kong, Wong (1972c) found that her respondents rated the attractive features of their job, in descending order of attractiveness, as security, challenge, the responsibility demanded and pay. Seventy-nine and a half per cent of the 253 officers studied had high job satisfaction. Furthermore, they formed a group of highly self-conscious and assertive individuals. Their sense of self-esteem can be gleaned from the finding that 83% of them believed that their work was of essential value to the local community; and they tended also to rank their occupation as one of the most important occupations in the colony. It is therefore natural to find them basking in a sense of high achievement in life, with those in higher grades obviously more satisfied with their job and more appreciative of what they had achieved.

On the other hand, the same study also found that the civil servants were a highly privatized lot. What this means is that many civil servants tended to look after primarily their own interests, and they lacked an affective identification with or commitment to their own community. To them, the most important things in life were not wealth, power or status, but a happy life, interesting work and economic security. Only 49.4% of them said they would retire in government service (even though in fact many more than that would end up doing so). For those who said they would not or were uncertain, the main reasons given were pay and promotion prospects. They tended to separate their work from their family life as far as possible. Thus, they only sometimes brought their work home, and only occasionally saw their colleagues after work. They were concerned most with their own career and promotions within the bureaucracy. In addition, their opinions of the Hong Kong society were not favourable. Except for its standard of living, they had poor evaluations of its living environment, community spirit, law and order, education system and art and culture. As a result, most of them preferred to live in some other places (59.6%).

All in all, to most of the Chinese civil servants in the government, a relatively detached view of their job and their society is the norm. While such a posture will not deter a person from performing his job duties in an efficient and professional manner, it would certainly exert a serious dampening effect on their innovativeness and activism in involving in community affairs. In thus performing in an impersonal, business-like and socially-aloof fashion, the "seclusion" of the government from society is further enhanced.

When we gather together the role orientations of the bureaucracy, its structural characteristics, and the character of the officials, some salient behavioural tendencies of the bureaucracy and its officials show up. Many of these tendencies have been discerned and criticized by the public in Hong Kong. However, to complete our analysis of the "secluded" bureaucratic polity, they are summarized below in a schematic way.

Complacency

Complacency is a behavioural trait commonly attributed to the Hong Kong government by observers. Bureaucrats are generally speaking highly satisfied with what they have done and their own performance in Hong Kong. A prototypical case of complacency can be illustrated by the Governor of Hong Kong, Sir Alexander W.G.H. Grantham, whose speech to the Legislative Council in 1947 ran as follows:

> There does seem to be general apathy amongst the public as to what goes on here. I think that the reason for this is that by and large—and I use those words advisedly—the people of Hong Kong are well satisfied with the Government. . . . I do not want to be complacent about the matter, but if we look at what has been achieved in this Colony since it was founded, I think that the people have justification for being well satisfied in the manner in which we and our predecessors have served them. (*Hong Kong Hansard*, 1947:256–57)

There is reason to believe that the passing-by of thirty years has not seriously modified this complacent outlook of the government.

Defensiveness

Given this sense of complacency, it is small wonder that there is a conspicuous tendency of the bureaucracy to be self-righteous, thinking that it knows much better than anyone else where the public interests lie, and that it is always heading in the right direction. One indication is the common explanation given by the government for the complaints made by the ordinary people as a communication gap between the government and the people. Communication gap there may be, but the interesting thing to note, is the conviction of the government that once the people are informed of the government's decisions and actions, and the reasons behind them, their complaints will vanish. In such a manner, the possibility that there can be real clash of interests between the government and the governed is hence glossed over. This attitude of self-righteousness is in perfect harmony with the belief in the right to arrogance so eminently upheld by the traditional Chinese officials.

With a high sense of complacency and self-righteousness, it is easy to understand the feeling of being offended whenever criticisms are launched against the government. One of the editorials in the prestigious *South China Morning Post* has specifically addressed to this issue:

> No one enjoys criticism although the honest professional will generally welcome it if it is constructive. And he will take notice and do something about it if he feels that the criticism is valid and a wrong needs righting.
>
> Unfortunately, however, there are more than a few Government officials who do not fall into this category. You only have to read the correspondence columns of any newspaper to see the resentment stirred up by the slightest criticism of a particular department and the sensitivity of some of the people who head those departments.
>
> They are quick to seize on the smallest inaccuracy, blow it up out of all proportion to the general context of the criticism and make a savage and sarcastic attack on the critic. Presumably they then feel their job has been satisfactorily done. And the main point of the criticism is carefully ignored. (November 4, 1978)

This self-defensive posture on the part of the bureaucrats was also candidly admitted by Mr. John Walden, the Director of Home Affairs:

> Moreover, in a highly centralised City State, seemingly under continual siege, group loyalty fosters mutual tolerance by members of their misdemeanours whilst strengthening their resolve to stand shoulder to shoulder in defence of the establishment, right or wrong. In such a situation great effort is put into fending-off outside criticism through organised publicity but little into diagnosing and treating the causes of the trouble within the system. (1980:7)

Formalism and Legalism

In an overcentralized complex organization, it is commonplace to find bureaucrats developing a fetish for formal rules and codes, for most of them are hamstrung in their capacity to make decisions. Formalism and legalism are particularly rampant among middle and lower level officials, and in some cases have become pathological. Not empowered to make decisions of their own, and afraid of making mistakes which might jeopardize their promotion prospects, bureaucrats tend to seek refuge behind written rules and regulations. Administrative rules and regulations might even be ritualized and valued for their own sake, thus overlooking the spirit behind these rules and the vast differences in the special circumstances of the people to whom they are supposed to apply. For many Chinese officials, bureaucratic rules symbolize their power and status, and not uncommonly they manipulate them to create awe and fear among their clients and thus to assert their superiority. As a result of this addiction to rules, not only are decisions deferred or not being made, but the problems might even be papered over whenever formal and legal rules are of no help in particular instances, and the bureaucrats in charge do not want to appear foolish in the eyes of their superiors when their assistance or advice is requested. Moreover, legalism and formalism tend to build an invisible barrier between the government and the people, and, along the process, alienating the latter from the former.

While on the one hand this emphasis on formal and legal rules by the bureaucrats is a result of overcentralization in the bureaucracy, on the other hand it finds support from the traditional Chinese administrative culture. Chinese bureaucrats in the past were marked by a diffuse sense of insecurity in office, which made them afraid of decision-making of any kind, particularly when they found themselves in unfamiliar situations. Furthermore, hierarchalism and the tendency to defer to superiors prohibited independent thinking and action without permission from above. These traits can still be detected in the administrative behaviour of many Chinese officials in Hong Kong, and this timidity not infrequently even draws complaints from their expatriate superiors.

Inflexibility

Closely related to formalism and legalism is the inflexibility of the bureaucracy in formulating new goals and in designing alternative strategies to achieve them, which undermines its ability to adapt itself to social change in the colony.

> The Hong Kong bureaucratic system is a bureaucratic curate's egg—efficient in parts. Where it falls down so very often is in the area of discretionary power. As long as policies have to be implemented "according to the book" they can be relatively efficiently implemented. Where, however, it is necessary for officials to exercise a power of discretion, the system has on occasion broken down and opportunities for bribery have become enhanced. (Harris 1978:130)

It is now generally acknowledged that an innovative and adaptive organization will have the following characteristics: (1) fluid and personal communication links, (2) flexible definitions of authority, (3) absence of sharply-drawn lines between levels of authority, (4) authority based on skill, and (5) sufficient lower-level responsibilities for coordination of discrete tasks, each with a power base. Put in different terms, it would place a premium on face-to-face contact, non-authoritarian relationships, the absence of defined and continuing areas of authority and considerable individual initiative and responsibility (Zysman 1977:41). It can easily be seen that the Hong Kong government falls short of these organizational prerequisites and that its inflexibility can be easily understood.

It is also evident that one of the most important causes of bureaucratic inflexibility lies in its narrow role definition. Professor Leonard Minker, a professor of business organization at the University of Birmingham, who was invited by the government to conduct a series of seminars on management and organization for its directorate staff in 1978, was reported to have made the following comment on the bureaucracy:

> He said Government people here, in common with their counterparts in other countries, do not see themselves in a management role.
>
> He said they tend just to see themselves as administrators and are thus having the problem of what he termed "role shortsightedness".
>
> "Government people here are not specifically inclined to thinking in an economist's terms and to examining alternatives for their problems like an economist," he said.
>
> Formulations of objectives and policies within the Government has not always been entirely clear. Need for closer relationships between the formulation of objectives and the organization to achieve them.
>
> The rapid growth in the civil service has overtaken the supply of managerial skills and to cope with this situation the Government needs to improve the design of its organization.
>
> In Government business, he called for socio-economic considerations, organizational flexibility, the capacity for the Government to adapt to change, positive efforts to look for opportunities for improving its services and training facilities and opportunities for Government officers.
>
> He observed that one advantage of the present system of branch secretaries at the Government Secretariat is that it encourages more attention to policy formulation and generates more thinking about programmes and policies for public services.
>
> The system, he said, does not fully resolve the relationship of policy formulation and management. As between departments, there is some lack of clarity regarding the respective roles of the policy branches of the Secretariat.
>
> "I think the major problem the Government faces now is not the mechanistic relationship between secretaryships and departments as this will be resolved through the development of working relationships. The problem now is to cope with the rapid growth in the community and in Government organization."
> (*South China Morning Post*, December 6, 1978)

Aside from overcentralization, stringent financial control over the departments by the centre is usually cited as a major reason for the lack of flexibility and foresight in the bureaucracy. Evaluation of performance in the bureaucracy is largely by the resources spent and not by result. What this in fact means is that efficiency is the criterion of evaluation instead of effectiveness. Effectiveness can be defined as the extent to which a goal is achieved, while efficiency is basically a measure of the ratio between costs and benefits. In a situation where both low benefits and low costs are combined, it can still be considered as efficient, but certainly not effective. The over-emphasis on "resources consumed," together with a deficiency in the means to monitor programme performance, is certainly not a way to provide incentive to innovation and adaptability.

Another facet of inflexibility is the lack of centralized forward planning by the government. After 1973, following the reorganizations recommended by the McKinsey Report, the situation improved. A number of plans covering a variety of fields have been prepared. Still, some caveats have to be borne in mind in evaluating the planning process of the bureaucracy. First, these plans are concerned primarily with the provision of services by the government to the public, and, given the passivity of the latter, it is very difficult to judge the efficiency and effectiveness of the plans for want of reliable feedback. Second, in the formulation of these plans, involvement of the public is minimal, aside from a small number of social leaders and professionals. Technical criteria are generally used instead of political criteria. Plans are always much easier to make in a "political vacuum" because many of the complicating factors are either absent or can be easily passed over. Third, as has been noted by John Walden in a previous citation, there is a lack of internal monitoring devices to make sure that the planned targets are achieved in time. Fourth, in many cases, such as the provision of public housing, the planned targets have failed to be reached in time. Finally, the conservative and stringent fiscal policy is still in force.

Some of its characteristics which might exert an inhibitory effect on forward planning are: the practice and policy of balanced budgets; the maintenance of unnecessarily large fiscal reserves (which have historically ranged from one-half to one year's expenditure); the almost complete avoidance of any public debt; habitual underspending by government departments, conservative revenue estimating; a widespread economizing ethic throughout government; the absence of inflated requests in the budgetary process; and an average ten-year tenure of office for each Financial Secretary which creates a climate of stability (Rabushka 1976:4). Whenever the fiscal budget has to grow or shrink in line with the unpredictable Hong Kong economy, forward planning is extremely difficult to formulate or to implement.

Technicalism

We have mentioned in the first part of this chapter that there is an abhorrence of politics on the part of the government. This, in terms of bureaucratic behaviour, is reflected in the relative inability to play the role of the "politician" by the bureaucrats. It can easily be seen that the role requirements of a politician and those of an administrator are frequently incompatible. A politician's success or sheer survival is dependent on the support of his constituents, while that of the administrator is not. A politician is inclined to compromise, to bargain and even to change established rules if they are found to be paralyzing; the instinct of an administrator is to operate within the secure environment defined by a set of "rationally-designed" rules which are considered to be fixed, at least in the short term. The criterion used by politicians to set priorities is the balance of social and political forces in society (which to a certain extent might be supplemented by the philosophical principles of individual politicians); the criterion of the administrator is technical, informed by his professional expertise and is politically neutral. According to Pye, British colonial officials are particularly fond of "pure administration":

> First, the British officials became very quickly a distinctive class of man with extremely strong feelings for their profession, which they saw in terms of the rationalistic standards of public administration. The colonial society, in which they were never challenged by the conflicting demands and emotional pressures of an open political process, offered a unique opportunity for pure administration, for rational and efficient government. British officials were able to convince themselves that good government was essentially an administrative phenomenon in which routine service functions were the ultimate test, that in the good society, specialists and technicians could apply their skills without being harassed by the irrational acts of popular politicians. In short, they saw themselves as administrators who should properly be judged according to the skill with which they provided services for the community. (1962:100)

Given this emphasis on administrative expertise, it is understandable that whenever they are put into a dilemma where they are forced to play an explicit political role, they find it difficult to meet the challenge. Some find a way out of the dilemma by becoming self-deprecatory; avoiding public discussion of certain issues; making decisions in secrecy and presenting the public with a *fait accompli*; and admitting in public the contraints they are under in arriving at their decisions (so as to earn public sympathy) (Rear 1971:65). None of these, however, are constructive steps to close the gap between the government and the people.

Personalism

It is a common fact, though a paradoxical one, that centralization of power coexists with personalism. Personality factors are particularly conspicuous both at the top and at the bottom of the bureaucratic hierarchy, in the first case because powerholders are much less subjected to formal rules, and in the latter case because of the great need to humanize the relationship between bureaucrats and clients. The injection of personality factors into a highly centralized and formalized organization tends to make it more flexible and adaptable, as personal decisions can overcome some of the rigidities resulting from "blind" and universal application of rules. On the other hand, personalism, by giving special treatment to individuals who are able to establish some forms of special relationship or rapport with bureaucrats, also generates the danger of perverting the goals of the bureaucracy. And this danger is particularly serious at the bottom of the hierarchy because, in a system such as Hong Kong's, the contact between the bureaucracy and the people is concentrated at the policy implementation pole. This means that lower-level officials, who are charged with the task of dealing with the common people according to the letter of the law, are tempted to turn these rules to their own advantage by placing a price tag on their services. On the part of the clients, turning the process of rule application or nonapplication in their own favour by bribing lower-level officials is in general considered to be "acceptable" in Hong Kong (Lee 1977). Corruption in the lower echelons of the bureaucracy is not an infrequent happening. Nevertheless, though the bureaucratic goals are perverted by it to some extent, corruption is far from administratively debilitating in the colony, and certainly does not turn the bureaucracy into the captive of particular social forces, thus losing its political autonomy.

At the top level, the significance of personal factors has been noted by Rabushka,

> In this highly centralized, compact government, personality takes on a major role, its importance was stressed in thirty of the first thirty-one interviews I completed [with senior government officials] during the fall of 1973. (1976:2)

> Why is this government so highly personalized? The reason is that (apart from the Judiciary) all lawful power lies with the Governor; none of his staff has specific constitutional power or authority. Personality attributes thus affect the balance of actual authority between higher ranking subordinates as they run the administrative machinery of the government. (*Ibid.*: 2-3)

The administrative philosophies and goals of particular individuals at the top do occasionally result in impelling the whole bureaucratic apparatus to act in a particular direction, thus making it more adaptable to societal needs. It can easily be seen, for example, the difference between the progressive rule of Sir Murray MacLehose and that of his predecessors. Nonetheless, in view of the historical continuity and inertial stability of the Hong Kong government, which has developed with time "its own flair, *ethos* and cultural aspects" (Harris 1977:81) as well as conservatism, the injection of more flexible personality factors at the top only has a minor effect on the behaviour of this mammoth machine.

RECAPITULATION

The polity of Hong Kong is structurally dominated by the bureaucracy which is the repository of legal constitutional authority through its head, the

Governor of Hong Kong. The role orientations of the bureaucracy emphasize system-maintenance, limited government and the preservation of the bureaucracy as the only major political institution in the colony. In a general sense, the polity in Hong Kong can be depicted as a "secluded bureaucratic polity," as it is oriented towards maintaining minimal interaction with the Chinese society.

This "seclusive" posture can also be detected from the structural features of the bureaucracy and the behavioural patterns of the bureaucrats, all of which contribute to the independence of the bureaucracy from outside forces, whose contacts with the bureaucracy are mainly confined to the policy implementation pole of bureaucratic activities.

We have also noted that the bureaucracy can perform efficiently in accordance with pre-designed and well-established action plans, and that it can also act decisively. This can be attributed to the tightness of its hierarchical organizational structure, the thoroughness of its rules and codes, the professionalism of the government officials and the low level of administrative corruption. On the other hand, the adaptive capability of the bureaucracy is limited. This limitation is shown in two ways. First, the bureaucracy is constrained by its overcentralized authority and its orientation towards organizational maintenance to set and achieve new goals, and this is essential in a rapidly changing society. In other words, its transition into a more service-oriented role, particularly a role which demands more delicate skills in the handling of human relationships, is made difficult by its ingrained structural and normative features. Second, the bureaucracy has only limited capacity to play a more interventionist role in society by, for example, accommodating social forces within the bureaucratic polity through an expansion of political participation, guiding and monitoring these social forces, or putting them under a certain level of control. That is, while the bureaucracy guards its position by restricting society's participation in it and by maintaining its "seclusion" from society, it relinquishes control over social changes. This limited adaptive and penetrative capability is reinforced, obviously, by the limited resources at the disposal of the bureaucracy.

We have chosen the problem of political stability amidst economic development as the main theme of this book. With this theme in mind, it is relatively difficult to explain political stability in Hong Kong by relying heavily on the adaptability of the bureaucracy in the colony. *Theoretically* speaking, social forces unleashed by economic development should so overload the bureaucratic polity that its stability should be threatened, as it is so constrained in its ability to accommodate increased political participation and restructure itself to adjust to social change. I emphasize the term "theoretically" here because empirically the situation mentioned above has not materialized. The bureaucracy has so far not been confronted with emerging social forces which demand political participation. What all this means is that we have to look at the Chinese society carefully to see the mechanisms which restrain social forces from impacting on the bureaucratic polity and demanding political solutions. All said, the structural and normative features of the Chinese society must bear the onus of providing an adequate explanation of political stability in Hong Kong.

3. The Chinese Society I: Major Normative Themes and Utilitarianistic Familism

The Chinese society in Hong Kong is not an indigenous society with historical continuity. On the contrary, it is a "new" society formed primarily by immigrants from various parts of China, though the majority of its population came from the province of Kwangtung and only quite recently have made their decision to settle permanently in Hong Kong. In general, it can be said that the community of Hong Kong is still in its formative stages, and the public hostilities generated towards illegal immigrants fleeing to Hong Kong from China in the last several years can be considered as signs of a budding sense of community identification. Given such a social background, Hong Kong's Chinese society is a product of the mutual adjustment of an admixture of Chinese people who are divided by ethnic, territorial, dialectal and ideological identifications and who are suspicious of one another, all the while confronted with the pressing need to deal with the birthpains of a rapidly industrializing society.

While on the one hand many Chinese immigrants have brought with them social and behavioural patterns derived from the rural setting of traditional China; on the other hand, they have to adapt themselves to the exigencies of an urban and Westernizing society. Consequently, the Chinese society in Hong Kong is no faithful replica of the Chinese society on its natural soil. It is a Chinese society developed in a particular historical and geographical setting, and is geared to insuring its survival and prosperity in a far-from-benign socioeconomic environment. In building such a Chinese society, there has been an ingenious combination of typical Chinese social features and features developed in the local setting whose origin might be Chinese or foreign. All in all, however, Hong Kong's Chinese society is still very Chinese.

Our description of the Chinese society in Hong Kong is based on our theoretical need to trace the relationship between the Chinese society and political stability in Hong Kong. Consequently, it is the general characteristics of the Chinese society rather than their distribution among social groups that interest us. As a matter of fact, at the end of a meticulous statistical analysis of the distribution of the organizational and normative features in the Chinese society which is too detailed to be referred here (see Lau 1977), we are struck by the relative homogeneity of the Chinese society rather than by its internal diversity. Therefore, the Chinese people in Hong Kong share organizational and normative features which are the distinctive traits of the Chinese society in Hong Kong. Even though there are variations across educational, age, class and sex groups, these are differences in degree rather than in kind. As a result of this recognition, we feel justified that a general description of the Chinese society in Hong Kong can be presented here without doing gross injustice to the facts.

Our description of the Chinese society can be divided into four parts. In this chapter the major normative tenets of the Chinese people, which have crucial influence on their behaviour, will be delineated and discussed. Also in this chapter we shall elaborate in detail a particular cultural syndrome dominant in the Chinese society which we have termed "utilitarianistic familism." The familial ethos and the familial groups which constitute the critical elements in this syndrome are the basic features of the Chinese society which give it its identifying characteristics and structure its relationship with the polity. In Chapter 4 the social and political orientations of the Chinese people will be described, drawing on materials from both my own research and the findings of other researchers on Hong Kong. In the first parts of Chapter 5 we shall shift to a structural tack and analyze the organizational patterns in the Chinese society and its elite structure. To anticipate our findings a little bit, the Chinese society can be considered as an inward-looking, self-contained and atomistic society with apolitical orientations and low potentials for political mobilization. Such a society is a perfect complement to the "secluded" bureaucratic polity, and their coexistence as well as mutual avoidance provides a clue to the explanation of political stability in Hong Kong.

MAJOR NORMATIVE ORIENTATIONS

Three interrelated normative themes can be discerned in Hong Kong, and they exert an enormous impact on the organizational and behavioural patterns of the Hong Kong Chinese.

Emphasis on Material Values

The pervasion of material values in every facet of social life in the Chinese society of Hong Kong is easily noticeable even by casual observers. The obsession with material goods constitutes the most significant motive force in the people's working, and even non-working, behaviour. Material values are the major criterion used to evaluate the worth of things and people; and its application to the assessment of objects which in other societies are usually considered to be beyond monetary calculation is a startling phenomenon in Hong Kong. As such, money as a medium of exchange enjoys a degree of universality unmatched by any advanced industrial societies in the world; or, for that matter, by all traditional societies. In Hong Kong, the social status hierarchy can easily be converted into a hierarchy of material wealth; attesting hence to the unidimensional nature of stratification in the society. In short, material values reign supreme in Hong Kong.

A number of studies on Hong Kong have unmistakably illustrated the dominance of material values in Hong Kong. Lee, Cheung and Cheung (1979), for example, found that the degree of life satisfaction among their Chinese respondents was positively associated with the level of material well-being enjoyed by them. Furthermore, this relationship was independent of sex, age and educational status, thus attesting to its all-pervasive nature. Similarly, Mitchell reported that, compared to other Southeast Asian countries, the Hong Kong Chinese placed the greatest emphasis on "earning a lot of money" as the value which could lead to fulfillment in life (1969a, vol. 1:219). Mitchell also discovered that worries about money constituted a factor of utmost importance in generating mental strain among the Hong Kong Chinese (1969a, vol. 1:284). From another angle, Chaney, in a study of shopworkers in Hong Kong, concluded that "job satisfaction was very strongly associated with satisfaction with salary; it was also significantly associated with the existence of supplementary cash payments such as overtime pay, bonuses and the receipt of tips. In contrast, regular hours of work, monthly holidays and fixed meal breaks, the type of benefits the worker might expect to derive from working in modernized firms, were not associated with job satisfaction. Neither was satisfaction associated with the type of shop the respondent worked in" (1971:267).

The fetishism of material wealth can be easily accounted for, however. First of all, it should be noted that the immigrants coming to Hong Kong were a select group many of whom were in search of material advancement when they made their decision to move.

> The pursuit of wealth has long been a common goal in Hong Kong. It has drawn generations of businessmen from the West and from China alike. The Colony has always afforded an outlet for talent for which Kwangtung is famous. For centuries its inhabitants have been described (by other Chinese) as lovers of money, subordinating all else in its pursuit. (Hayes 1975:3)

The "infatuation for money" on the part of many Cantonese is of course understandable when it is known that compared to other parts of China, the commercialization of the province of Kwangtung was quite extensive even before it was exposed to the West in the eighteenth and nineteenth centuries. Over a relatively long period of time, the Cantonese have developed a commercial shrewdness which has drawn both envy and contempt from people in other parts of China.

The lack of traditional Chinese moral constraints on uninhibited efforts at material gain in a migrant society such as Hong Kong sets free the rampant and rapacious desire for material advancement. The absence of a gentry class, which in traditional China was the upholder of higher moral values, has removed a major obstacle for the pursuit of material values. In a colonial society, where upward social mobility through political channels is blocked, economic mobility is the only viable alternaive route of gaining prestige and status for the ambitious (Topley 1969:186-91).

The commercial and industrial nature of the colony, together with the increased contact with foreigners, makes it almost impossible for the Hong Kong Chinese to avoid being "contaminated" by these lower forms of human values. The highly visible inequality in the distribution of income and wealth, the open nature of the economy which does not allow any elite group to monopolize economic opportunities, and the material enticements diffused conspicuously throughout the colony all contribute to the cardinality of material values in the Chinese society of Hong Kong.

Short-term Time Horizon

The short-term time horizon of the Hong Kong Chinese can best be revealed in their uncontrollable compulsion to have immediate material consumption and their intolerance of delayed gratification in the future. Living under "borrowed time and borrowed place," this would appear to be perfectly normal. Yet another explanation can also be pondered: as Hong Kong has been undergoing such a breath-taking pace of economic development, and as it appears to many people, at least psychologically, that material goods of various kinds are about to be within their reach, it would take herculean efforts for the Hong Kong Chinese to resist to let their instinctive material desires be gratified immediately.

When we asked our respondents in 1977 whether they had plans for the next two to three years, 67.1% of them gave the reply that they had no plan at all. If the time period of reference was lengthened to between fifteen to twenty years, the percentage of respondents having no plan at all in mind jumped to a striking 80.4%.

Even among the economically well-off, it can also be seen that their time horizon is short.

> There is a tendency for Chinese investors in all fields to look for the maximum gain in the shortest period. A reluctance of certain people, who are not themselves entrepreneurs, to invest in industry is due partly to the fact that profits may be slow in coming. Many Chinese still prefer to invest in non-industrial property and trade because of the relatively quicker return of capital and profits.
>
> When investing in industry, the overwhelming desire of investors is to look for quick profits by whatever means present themselves as attractive in the short run rather than to look for opportunities for starting long-term investment. The financing of industries which offer quick profits may be surely speculative and undertaken by financiers who might otherwise be in the property market and

have no real intention of long-term support of the industry. (Topley 1969:220)

The general reluctance to commit resources to the uncertain long-term future is not limited to the economic realm, it is all-pervasive. Social relationships which require long-term investment in order to have their values realized are normally shunned. One underlying cause, among others, of the cultural or artistic depravity in Hong Kong can be attributed to the large amount of lead time which cultural endeavours normally require before any real achievements can be harvested. The preference for individual effort to organizational effort at pursuing goals, even though the latter way is objectively more effective in the long haul, can also be explained by the amount of time and resources the process of organizing will have to consume. This inevitably leads to a paucity of social participation among the Hong Kong Chinese.

Emphasis on Social Stability

When it is understood that the history of China in the last two centuries or so is packed with riot, rebellion, warfare, turmoil and violence, and that many Hong Kong Chinese have had the experience of fleeing as refugees from place to place during the Chinese civil wars and the war with Japan, the compelling need of the Hong Kong Chinese for a breathing space in a socially (and by implication politically) stable environment is inevitable. Even if social stability has to be bought at a price of injustice and a loss of national pride, they would have no qualms about compromising.

Aside from the historical events in the immediate past, the yearning for social and political order among the Hong Kong Chinese may also be due to an ingrained or internalized cultural aversion to aggression which can only be contained by a strong authority in society, and this has to be the government. The Chinese people are strongly dependent on public authority, whose "benign face is thus to a large degree its ability to control society's potential for conflict, to prevent *luan* [亂 disorder]" (Solomon 1971:140). On the other hand,

> the failure of public authority can then release anxieties and produce frustration and aggression. Manifestation of such aggressive behavior may in turn produce not only increased anxieties but the release of sentiments that can only complicate the reestablishment of new forms of authority. (Pye 1968:7)

Social stability definitely loomed large in the mind of our respondents. An overwhelming majority of them, 87.3%, would definitely prefer social stability to economic prosperity, if asked to choose between the two. To measure the intensity of this preference for social stability, our respondents were asked another question: whether they would still stay in a society with social stability but without much social justice. Again, 41.8% of them indicated

their willingness to stay, and only a minority were definite in their unwillingness to do so. In Hong Kong, since many Chinese people are predisposed to
preserve social stability at any costs, the implication is that they would
withdraw from activities which they perceive would lead to the disruption of
social order. Violent actions against the political order are to be avoided as far
as possible.

UTILITARIANISTIC FAMILISM[1]

The concept of utilitarianistic familism is a theoretical construct. It is
derived from a process of abstraction through which a relatively coherent set
of normative and behavioural tendencies is derived from a mélange of normative and behavioural traits displayed by a majority of the Hong Kong Chinese.
As a matter of fact, utilitarianistic familism can be considered as the dominant
cultural code in the Chinese society of Hong Kong.

Utilitarianistic familism can be defined as the normative and behavioural
tendency of an individual to place his familial interests above the interests of
society and of other individuals and groups, and to structure his relationships
with other individuals and groups in such a manner that the furtherance of
his familial interests is the overriding concern. Moreover, among the familial
interests, material interests take priority over non-material interests. Even
within the familial group, utilitarian considerations loom fairly large, especially
with regard to those familial members who occupy peripheral positions in the
group and whose affectual-ritual ties with the core members are therefore less
close. Utilitarian considerations within the familial group manifest themselves
usually in an emphasis on economic interdependence among familial members,
and in the criteria used in "recruiting" peripheral members into the familial
group. In fact, the possession of a certain amount of liberty in the selection
of peripheral members means not only that utilitarian considerations are
allowed to enter into the process, but also that the Chinese familial group in
Hong Kong is rather fluid in size, as potential peripheral members can be both
inducted into and barred from membership (occasionally membership can be
taken away even from core members or denied to potential members who
wish to marry into the family). Furthermore, achievement criteria can also be
used in the selection of new members, thus lessening the ascriptive-particu-
laristic character of membership. Structured in such a manner, the familial
group can be used in an elastic and flexible manner by the Hong Kong Chinese
to organize their own primary groups for coping with what they see as a

[1]Our discussion in this and the next sections draws heavily on Lau (1981b). I am
grateful to the National Council on Family Relations for permission to reprint portions
of the article in this book.

far-from-benign social environment.

Note that, in the definition, the concept "familial group" has been deliberately adopted, instead of the more common term "family" to represent the organizational referent of utilitarianistic familism. The choice was made because it is the author's opinion that the familial group, *included in which is the family as ordinarily understood*, is a socially relevant and significant organizational entity in the Chinese community in Hong Kong. A familial group is a group of individuals bound to each other by family and kinship ties, *as well as* by quasi-kinship ties. What is meant here is that, for some of the members, their kinsmen status is not based on blood or marriage relationships, but it is the result of being inducted into the group by the core members (who are closely related by blood or marriage ties) and thereby assigned a particular kinsmen role in the group.

To be more precise, a familial group will usually include four types of people, even though empirically speaking familial groups may not contain all of them. First, at the core of the group are those intimately related to each other, and they usually include oneself, one's parents, one's spouse and children and one's siblings. The core members, in fact, provide the cohesive force and identity of the familial group, because it is they who undertake to recruit other members into the group. The criteria for recruitment are normally set in such a way that the interests of the core members will be served by the familial group thus formed. That, of course, does not mean that they have total freedom in the choice of persons to recruit. At the very least, the potential members have the option not to join the familial group concerned. Kinship norms, which are the socially shared criteria establishing the "ideal" degree of closeness of kinsmen to one another, impose another constraint on the recruitment process. In Hong Kong, for example, one cannot behave towards one's father as if he were a more distant kinsman than one's cousin. In general, freedom in recruitment increases with movement from close relatives to distant relatives and nonrelatives. Close relatives include one's spouse's parents and siblings, aunts, uncles, nephews, nieces and grandparents of both oneself and one's spouse. It should be noted, however, that there seems to be no consensus on the exact composition of close relatives in Hong Kong. Next come the more distant relatives, who include a large pool of persons related to the core members by more remote kinship ties than those of close relatives. Lastly, nonrelatives represent an even larger pool of potential members. Since they have no direct or indirect kinship relationships with the core members of the familial group, anyone in society who comes to mind is eligible for admission into the group. The most likely to be recruited into the group, however, are close friends, persons bearing the same surname as the head of household, persons coming from the same district (and possibly speaking the same dialect) as the head of household or his spouse, and close neighbours. Both distant relatives and nonrelatives are normally considered the peripheral members in the familial group, and their membership is much less stable than that of core members and close relatives.

In Hong Kong, there is no exact word for the sort of familial group just described. The absence of such a word in the Cantonese vocabulary in Hong Kong seems to indicate the relative newness of this social phenomenon. Still, the expression "all-in-the-family" (in Cantonese, *yut-ga-yan* 一家人) would come close to what is meant, in the present context, by a familial group, even though this expression is commonly used to describe the closeness of one's relationship with others (by considering them to be members of the same family), rather than as a "sociological" term denoting a particular kind of social group.

The following sections elaborate the content of utilitarianistic familism and substantiate the description with empirical facts.

Primacy of Familial Interests

That the Hong Kong Chinese would put their familial interests above any other kind of social interests is obvious to anyone who cares to observe Hong Kong. The extremely low level of social participation among the Chinese people is one case in point. Public morality is low, and it is not uncommon to find people violating public rules or misappropriating public good to benefit themselves and their familial groups. Moral leaders and the mass media have rarely failed to turn this obsession with familial interests to advantage in their crusade to castigate the Chinese people's lack of public spirit. Moreover, in Hong Kong, it is not only the middle-aged and elderly who consider the familial group to be of overwhelming significance, but this point of view also is the norm for young adults in Hong Kong (Stoodley 1967; Chaney and Podmore 1973, 1974).

Social-Political Context as the Arena for the Pursuit of Familial Interests

Closely related to the primacy of familial interests is the conception of the sociopolitical environment of Hong Kong as a setting wherein individuals and their familial group actively pursue their own best interests. Passive adaptation to the existing institutional structure is the norm, and efforts to transform the social order are frowned upon, particularly if they lead to the disruption of social stability. Conflicts or trouble with outsiders are to be avoided as far as possible, even at the cost of some loss for the family. The government is perceived primarily as the guarantor of political and social stability, so that a peaceful environment can be created from familial operations. There is a general feeling of social and political powerlessness and alienation among the

Hong Kong Chinese. These attitudes further reinforce the primacy of the familial group and the adoption of a suspicious and somewhat hostile attitude towards society and the government.

Utilitarian Considerations in the Structuration of Intra-familial Relationships

In a general sense, the family and familial group of the Hong Kong Chinese are affectivity-charged social units, like most other families in the world. Nevertheless, utilitarian considerations have assumed enormous importance in the relationships among familial members, especially with respect to those occupying peripheral status. These considerations usually lead to an unusually strong emphasis on the norm of mutual assistance among familial members. Though services and help can be and often are extended to those members who cannot reciprocate, except perhaps for those who are core members or close relatives, in many cases such aid will be considered as a long-term investment with the hope of a pay-off in the future. Of course the existence of selfless helping behaviour cannot be entirely denied; what has been said above merely pinpoints the significance of the notion of exchange among members of the familial group, especially exchange in economic goods. After comparing Hong Kong with some other societies in Southeast Asia, Robert E. Mitchell asserted:

> The Chinese in general and the Hong Kong population in particular tend to have the lowest levels of social involvement with kin, but these populations have the highest level of economic interchange among kinsmen. (1971:40)

Mitchell's data also showed that many adults in Hong Kong saw relatively little of their parents who lived elsewhere in the colony. Of those who did not live with their parents, 26% of the men and 36% of the women said that they visited them less than once a month or that they never visited them. Those who visited their parents one or more times a week included 35% of the men and 32% of the women. At the same time, however, 65% of the married men who had a parent still living gave money to their parents, and 44% of the comparable female population also gave money to their parents (Mitchell 1971:34-35).

Similarly, the giving of non-financial goods to one's relatives is also fairly common. In Mitchell's study, 22% of the husbands and 16% of the wives had provided their own siblings and other relatives with non-financial assistance "sometimes" or "very often." Twenty per cent of the former and 16% of the latter reported giving the same assistance to their spouse's siblings and other relatives (Mitchell 1969b, vol. 2:423).

The rendering of financial assistance to one's fellow family members is also reported in middle-class Chinese families. In the middle-class families of Mei

Foo Sun Chuen, a middle-class neighbourhood, there are almost equal amounts of reciprocal aid and financial aid. According to Rosen (1976:196), the investigator of the project:

> It is no accident that there seem to be no loan companies in Hong Kong, for financial aid is still an important part of family interaction. This help may take the form of ongoing participation in rent or mortgage payments, or it may come as regular monthly subsidies to old, inferior or otherwise needy relatives.

The norm of economic obligation to one's familial members is also shared by the young adults in Hong Kong. The answers given by the young adults to two of the questions in the survey made by Chaney and Podmore (1973) are of direct relevance here. To the question "Do you think a man should help his brother with a loan, even if this deprives him and his family of something for which they have been saving for a long time?" the percentages for the respondents answering "should," "don't know" and "should not" are 81.5, 8.7 and 9.8 respectively. Similarly, to the question "Suppose your parents asked you for a loan to pay for something that was important to them, but you needed the money to pay the school fees for your children. What would you do?" the answers "lend," "don't know" and "not lend" are given by 79.9%, 12.4% and 7.7% of the respondents, respectively (Chaney and Podmore 1973:63). Similarly, in a study of labour youth in Hong Kong, Andrew Lu (1970) found that among his 551 respondents, 40.5% contributed all their monthly income to the family coffers, 28.1% three-fourths of their monthly income, and 20% half of their monthly income, thus testifying to the economic importance of young people to their lower-income families. In spite of the fact that in many ways the young adults in Hong Kong differ from their elders in their perception of family norms, the norm of economic obligation seems to have been deeply internalized (Stoodley 1967; Chaney and Podmore 1973).

Another piece of evidence bearing on the crucial significance of economic interchange in the integration of the familial group is provided by the study made by Hong (1970). In his sample of families, Hong found a widespread practice of family ownership of property. In fact, it is practised by a majority of the Hong Kong families. However, economic cooperation within the family, particularly in the form of pooling financial resources, is also popular. As this occurs in all socioeconomic strata, it is "not necessarily a consequence of economic necessities, but it can also be a manifestation of cultural values" (Hong 1970:145).

Even local leaders in Hong Kong, who are relatively well-off, are not exceptional in their stress on mutual economic obligations among family members. On the significance of filial piety, the attitudes of the local leaders in an industrial community of Hong Kong as depicted by Johnson (1971:

239) were as follows:

> Only 11 leaders (12 percent) said their children had no responsibilities to parents
> and only 16 (18 percent) said their children had no responsibilities to grand-
> parents.

and,

> Financial contributions to elderly parents are . . . perceived as an extremely
> important obligation of children (specifically sons) as are rather more common
> cultural sanctions such as obedience and respect.

Note that the evidence so far alluded to primarily concerns economic
exchange among core members and close relatives in the familial group.
Economic exchange with distant relatives and nonrelatives is much less
frequent. Among the local leaders in the community studied by Johnson, for
example,

> there was no notion that children's responsibilities extend to relatives in general
> outside the restricted parents-grandparents complex. A mere 17 leaders (18.7
> percent) saw their children as having more responsibilities to relatives, usually
> financial help, other than vague desire to maintain good relations (hao kan-ching).
> Part of this can be explained by the attenuated nature of the kinship relations of
> many of the leaders. For migrant leaders there are few relatives beyond the
> immediate family. Fictive kinship organizations, rather than institutions of
> kinship, are the forms for many kinship-type help activities. And for native
> leaders, where organized kinship units do figure in their lives, the lineage rather
> than the individual family is the focus for help and responsibilities. (1971:240-41)

To say the least, whether distant relatives and nonrelatives are able to
engage in economic exchange with the core members of the familial group is
a major criterion for their inclusion in the group. So far, no systematic study
on economic exchange between core members and peripheral members has
been undertaken in Hong Kong. On an impressionistic basis, its existence can
easily be assumed. Evidence of its existence can be cited from a study of
young workers in Hong Kong in 1978. In a sample of 373 young workers, it
was found that relatives (including distant relatives), friends and workmates
featured prominently as sources of aid whenever the need was felt by the
workers. Even though, on the whole, parents and siblings were of more
importance, in some occasions such as job-seeking, friends and workmates
were more useful (Lau and Ho 1982). If such is the situation among young
workers, more economic exchange should be expected with peripheral
members in middle-aged and older age groups.

The notion that mutual economic obligations play an important role in
structuring the relationships among family members, even to the point of
de-emphasizing the non-economic aspects, is further corroborated by the data
of the survey. Less than half the respondents stated that they maintained

close interactions with their family and other familial members, particularly in the case of close relatives and distant relatives. On the other hand, 60.5% of them indicated that they had in the past received financial and other forms of assistance from their familial members, while 73.3% of them said they had contributed financial and other help to their familial members in the past. Respondents also stated, however, that financial assistance received from and given to other relatives was very small, which means that only a few relatives had been recruited into the familial groups.

The de-emphasis on the non-economic aspects of interpersonal relationships among familial members can be illustrated again in the answers given by the respondents to a question which asked them whether they would support their close familial members if they were embroiled in trouble with others. Only 16% of them said they would definitely support their fellow familial members, 70.9% were hesitant, and 11.6% of them stated they would refuse to give them support. Except for the economic ties, then, it seems that attachments, including emotional ones, among familial members are rather tenuous among the Hong Kong Chinese.

Non-significance of the Social Status of the Family

The overriding importance of economic ties among familial members is closely related to another theme in utilitarianistic familism: the lack of significance of the family as a social status group. Put differently, the promotion of the social status of the family is no longer perceived as of much value, and the enhancement of family pride ceases to be a major motivation for an individual's behaviour. If this situation is true for the family, it applies even more to the familial group. When the respondents were asked whether they felt any obligation to promote the fame of their families in society, a substantial proportion of them (47.8%) took the rather uninvolved stance of "having some responsibility," and 30.5% of them eschewed all such obligations whatsoever. Similarly, it seems that prestige earned by someone else in their families also failed to transmit any sense of pride to the respondents. When asked whether they would feel proud because of the achievements of other family members, 63.1% claimed that they would not. These findings demonstrate the insignificance of the family (and familial group) as a status group with which one identifies. Ancestral worship, though still common to a certain extent, obviously is of small importance in integrating the family and the familial group symbolically.[2]

[2]In a survey of 3,753 married men and women in 1967, Mitchell found that 32% of husbands and 54% of wives claimed to be ancestral worshippers. These percentages were higher than those found in Taipei, Singapore, Malaysia and Bangkok (1969a, vol. 1:21). We have no way of telling the motivation involved in the practice, but

Utilitarianistic Recruitment of Familial Members and
the Vagueness of the Boundary of the Familial Group

Strong emphasis on the utilitarianistic relationships among familial group members means that the recruitment of new members and the exclusion of other qualified (by blood or marriage ties) persons are made very much easier. This ease of recruitment and exclusion applies especially to the peripheral members whose selection for inclusion into familial groups is deliberately made by the core members. Because of this flexibility of membership, the size of the familial groups can vary considerably, depending on the availability of personnel and resources and on the success of the core members in organizational expansion.

The actual sizes of the familial groups are only partially reflected in the spatial distribution of their members. The shortage of housing and the smallness of the housing units in Hong Kong inevitably lead to a spatial dispersal of the members of the families and familial groups. The 1976 By-Census of Hong Kong found that 60.2% of the Hong Kong households were of the nuclear type. Nevertheless, the physical structure of the familial groups is not indicative of their sociocultural functions and their *effective* size. As pointed out by Mitchell (1972:216):

> The fact that Chinese did not have a high proportion of large multiple-family residential units with joint or stem families is not especially significant because the residential unit is not the key to family strength and the services family members provide each other.

The compactness of the geographical area of Hong Kong means that, however dispersed the familial group members are, ties with other familial group members can still be maintained if one so chooses. In Hong Kong, an element of utilitarian rationality is deliberately adopted in the *construction* of a familial group, particularly with regard to individuals not belonging to the nuclear family.

In the process of recruitment of members into a familial group, several characteristics are noticeable. First, among individuals related to core members by blood or marriage ties, intimate kinsmen are the most important, such as parents, spouses, children and siblings. The percentages of the respondents who considered the appropriate relationships with their parents, spouses, children and siblings to be "very intimate" are 73.1, 76.5, 75.3 and 59.5,

---

impressionistic evidence and some scattered pieces of data (see for example Berkowitz *et al.* 1969:126-30) seem to show that it is basically a religious ritual inherited from the past but largely stripped of much of the symbolic meanings. In addition, ancestors might simply be propitiated in the hope that they would bestow favours upon their progenies.

respectively. As a matter of fact, one of the most important tasks of the familial groups is taking care of the elderly who are one's close kinsmen:

> Families in Hong Kong again are more likely than families in Western countries to care for the elderly. Most older married people do live with one of their children, if they have these children living locally. Bilateralism was again noted to be quite common and, furthermore, poverty plays a role but in two countervailing ways: first, the poorest of the elderly are the most likely to live with their children, but the children who have the highest earning levels are the most likely to assume this housing and financial burden. (Mitchell 1971:39)

On the other hand, close relatives and distant relatives are considered as "very intimate" only by 12.9% and 3.1%, respectively, of the respondents. As a result, close and distant relatives are not automatic members of familial groups, and, in order to be members, they have to be selected by the core members.

Second, the concepts of brother and sister are widened to include a far more heterogeneous group of people. Such people may be individuals bearing the same surname as the core members or individuals coming from the same territories and speaking the same dialects as they speak.

Third, in addition to consanguineal ties, affinal ties are usually invoked to enlist new members into a familial group. In fact, for many Hong Kong Chinese, assistance and service from one's affinal relatives are of crucial importance, and these affinal relatives are normally the most intimate ones. And this is true for the middle-class Chinese in Hong Kong. As Rosen (1976:200), who had studied a middle-class neighbourhood in Hong Kong, pointed out:

> In Hong Kong, as with residential patterns, the most glaring adaptation of the traditional kin network in patterns of socialization is the trend toward bilaterality. In almost every case where the wife had parents and/or siblings living in Greater Hong Kong, there was a good deal of visiting back and forth. This held true even when the husband's parents were living with the young couple (though the two sets of parents rarely met socially).

In addition, Rosen (1976:206) noticed:

> an increased flexibility in patterns of residence, an increased sense of choice in association with extended-family members and concomitant relaxation of the patrilineal norm, and an increased likelihood of widespread geographical dispersal that threatens to cut family ties on a near-permanent basis.

Fourth, individuals not related to the core members by blood or by marriage ties can also be treated as familial group members. In a general sense, such people are the friends of the core members. Kinship terminology in Hong Kong, however, is flexible enough to allow these friendship relationships to become relationships couched in its terms. For additional reinforcement, sworn brotherhoods and sisterhoods can also be constructed to formalize such relationships. The establishment of fictive kin relationships, most commonly in the form of adopted parents and adopted children, is a widely used strategy to co-opt friends into the familial group. How widespread the practice of adoption is in urban Hong Kong is difficult to assess, although folk impressions are that it is fairly frequent among people in all socioeconomic strata. A study (Young 1974:61) in the market town of Yuen Long, which has been undergoing rapid socioeconomic change, may give a rough measure.

> The abundant presence of [fictive kinship] ties is reflected in the fact that 27 per-cent of 460 surveyed middle school students (medium age 17) in the Yuen Long district report having at least one fictive kinsman.

Among the friends most likely to be recruited into the familial group, neighbours and workmates who can offer economic and other assistance to the core members figure most prominently. The importance of friends as potential family group members can be gauged by the fact that more of the respondents (15.8%) rated close friends as intimate to them than were those who picked close relatives and distant relatives (12.9% and 3.1% respectively).

The selectivity regarding the kinsmen with whom interaction and a feeling of closeness are desired, and the discretionary inclusion of outsiders into one's familial group through the deliberately loose and vague articulation of kinship terminology, are largely contingent upon utilitarian considerations, which are in turn dependent on the social environment of the core members. As these factors change, the boundary of the familial group will also change, and hence the composition of the familial group will forever be in a fluid and undefined condition. Nonetheless, as the anchoring point of the familial group is usually the nuclear family, social order in the Chinese society of Hong Kong can still be maintained, even though the boundaries of these familial groups overlap to a certain extent (as peripheral members in one familial group might be core members in another) and are changing with time.

Dilution of Authority Relationships and the Growth of Egalitarianism

As many members in the familial groups are recruited because of their utility to the core members, interpersonal relationships in the group tend to assume an egalitarianistic form. Of course this tendency does not mean that there is no hierarchy of authority in the familial group; at least among the adult members, patriarchalism and authoritarianism are not the only regulators of their relationships. In the working class, the status of women in the family has greatly improved. More than fifty per cent of women workers from the lower-income groups supplied at least half their family's income, according to a survey on pregnant women conducted by the Christian Industrial Council (*South China Morning Post*, October 20, 1978). Even adolescents are expected to participate in the decision-making process in the family.[3] Working daughters, for example, because of their economic contributions to the family, are able to participate in those types of decision-making having to do with themselves (Salaff 1976). Compared with families in some Western countries, it can still be said, however, that the families in Hong Kong are still quite authoritarian in tone, and parental authority is still in vogue here, though its intensity has diminished even in lower-income families.

UTILITARIANISTIC FAMILISM AS CHINESE FAMILISM ADAPTED TO A PARTICULAR STRUCTURAL SETTING

To anyone who espouses the ideal or gentry conception of traditional Chinese familism, the tenets of utilitarianistic familism would appear to be a totally different kind of familial ethos. To a certain extent, studies of Chinese family and kinship in the past can be blamed for perpetuating a monolithic, idealistic view of Chinese familism which fails to take into consideration its variations, even in rural/traditional China (Cohen 1976:227-37). Whenever variations are recognized that demand explanation, it is usually sought in the normative or cultural realm; and it is not uncommon to find that persistent appeal to cultural explanation has resulted in a failure to explain many phenomena. For example, as eminently demonstrated by Cohen, the prevalence of

[3] The trend towards conjugalism in the relationship between spouses had been described by Wong Fai-ming (1972), who focused on middle-class Chinese families. Dilution of authority relations in lower-class families has also been found. With respect to the treatment of the young, according to Robert E. Mitchell and Irene Lo, lower-class Chinese mothers "are not penetrating and permeating the entire lives of their children, and even the very young are able to make decisions by themselves; their mothers also do not closely monitor their behavior, thereby giving them further experiences of learning the world through their own unimpaired manipulation of it" (Mitchell and Lo 1968: 315). "Along with granting greater independence, parents are also letting down the generational barriers to free and open communication with their young children" (p. 316). Going one step further, the two authors considered that "the source of change in child-training practices of mothers may be related to more basic changes in the distribution of authority within families. Two changes are especially noteworthy. First, the authority of the male line, especially the father, has declined, and the mother-wife occupies a new and extremely important role in the family. Second, age as a basis for authority has radically declined in significance. This is true for siblings over [*sic*] their younger brothers and sisters" (p. 301). Accordingly, "a growing proportion of families in Hong Kong can be characterized as having egalitarian relations among their members" (p. 321). Moreover, it can also be noted that in some areas of decision-making, for example, in the choice of marriage partners, young people are able to assert more and more independence (Chaney and Podmore 1974:404-5).

joint families among ordinary peasants in Yen-liao, Taiwan, and their lack of
prevalence in many other areas easily eludes the orthodox cultural explanation.

Recent empirical studies of the Chinese family have not only "discovered"
some major patterns of variations in Chinese familism in rural settings (Wolf
1968; Pasternak 1972; Ahern 1973; Cohen 1976; and others) and in cities
experiencing the early pains of industrialization (see the evidence cited by
Lang 1946), but they also succeeded in demonstrating the utility of structural
explanations of these variations. Though these studies are still few in number,
and were conducted mainly in Hong Kong and Taiwan, they have managed to
"revolutionize" our understanding of traditional Chinese familism.

What was learned from these empirical studies is that both the organizational and normative aspects of traditional Chinese familism vary enormously
according to structural conditions. And the extent or degree of variations
differ for different components of familism. Organizational change may be
faster than change in the ideal standards of the Chinese family; and the
different components of the Chinese family may, within certain limits, vary
independently of each other. That the organization of the Chinese family can
be dissected into several components whose variations can be traced to
independent and overlapping structural factors has been vaguely recognized in
the older literature on the Chinese family. Kulp's distinctions between the
natural family, the sib, the religious family and the economic family is a case
in point (Kulp 1925:142-49); Freedman's (1961-62, 1966:44-46) differentiation between the "poor" and "rich" developmental cycles in Chinese
families is another. Its significance has only recently been grasped, and
systematic and comparative studies to elucidate it are beginning to appear.
Cohen's differentiation between the *chia* 家 estate, economy and group
represents an innovative theoretical attempt in this regard (Cohen 1970:21,
1976:58-59).

These empirical studies also show that even if it is still possible to talk
about an ideal-type Chinese familism in a rural-traditional setting, the content
of this ideal type can only be described in highly generalized terms; such
description is of limited use in understanding concrete reality. Furthermore,
ideal-typical descriptions of reality would also be oblivious to a whole range
of phenomena which do not fall within their scope, such as the incessant
interpersonal and group conflicts in the Chinese family (Wolf 1968). Lastly,
variations in the organizational patterns of the Chinese family inevitably will
also make one wonder to what extent traditional ideology of the family has
been internalized by the ordinary Chinese people, apart from those belonging
to the gentry "class."

As a matter of fact, under certain structural conditions, it is not difficult
to find that Chinese familism in a rural-traditional setting can display

characteristics which bear a close resemblance to the elements of utilitarianistic familism. Although there are not sufficient data from recent empirical studies to compare these "unconventional" manifestations of traditional familism with utilitarianistic familism point by point, it is possible to pick out some themes and make comparisons on them.

The emotional supremacy of family and kinship ties in rural China does not necessarily prevent the Chinese people from cooperating with nonkinsmen in joint ventures of mutual benefit. In the process of participation in such joint ventures, the salience of kinship based on blood and marriage ties is toned down and relationships with nonkinsmen are couched in panfamilial or pankinship terms (Pasternak 1972:128-59; Ahern 1973:249-60). The co-option of nonrelatives into the familial group with instrumental considerations under utilitarianistic familism belongs to the same class of social strategy.

Utilitarianistic familism takes a disjunctive view of familial and social interests, which means that these two interests are more or less compartmentalized; hence responsibilities towards society are not emphasized and one's obligations begin and end with the familial group. In rural China, despite cultural prescription to the contrary, social interests and social participation are usually ignored, or even downgraded. A content analysis of a sample of clan rules contained in Chinese genealogies by Liu (1959) reveals a heavy emphasis on personal integrity, family prosperity, family harmony and, by the extension of family interest, clan cohesion. Contact with people and groups outisde the kinship groups are to be held to a minimum. The purpose of the clan rules is to foster an ideal personality so oriented to family and clan that it can hardly be expected to play an active role in community life, let alone in political matters.

Though the point is not deliberately elaborated in empirical studies, utilitarian consideration is found to structure interpersonal relationships in the family in rural China. Even ancestral worship, the ritual pillar of traditional Chinese families, is not immune from it. The ritual practices in ancestral worship, the perception of one's indebtedness to the dead, and the conception of the benignness and malevolence of the dead are all, to a large extent, structurally conditioned (Ahern 1973:260-65). Closely related to the perceived significance of ancestral worship is the felt duty to upgrade the social reputation of the family and to reinforce the symbolic-affective identification with other family members. Utilitarianistic familism, in its indifference to the social status of the family, and the utilitarianistic recruitment of familial members, differ from Chinese familism in rural-traditional setting only in degree.

The orthodox view of traditional familism as dominated by undiluted patriarchal authority has also to be qualified. In fact, power and authority are differentiated, in that economic power may be in the hands of the young and competent, while ritual authority may reside in the hands of the genealogical senior. The erosion of patriarchal authority may well be pushed further when the family finds itself in a hostile and threatening environment (Baker 1968; Potter 1968).

Utilitarianistic familism, therefore, is not a qualitatively different departure from Chinese familism in rural-traditional settings. It hence must be conceptualized as an adaptation of Chinese familism to a particular set of structural conditions imposed by the urban-industrial setting of Hong Kong. And it is to these structural conditions that we shall direct our attention in Chapter 6.

4. The Chinese Society II: Sociopolitical Orientations and Behaviour

Over the past ten years or so, a number of surveys, which vary considerably in reliability and quality, on the sociopolitical orientations and behaviour of the Chinese have been conducted. While they agree on some basic themes which underlie the ethos and behavioural patterns of the Hong Kong Chinese, that they were conducted in different time periods, interviewed people in different socioeconomic groups and employed different measuring instruments makes it difficult to compare or synthesize them. Thus, in presenting the major findings from these surveys here, no serious attempt will be made to explore the intricacies of their differences or the implications thereof. What we shall do here will be to identify main themes and to subsume diverse findings under three major headings: social orientation and behaviour, perceptions of social stratification, and political attitudes and behaviour.

SOCIAL ORIENTATIONS AND BEHAVIOUR

The orientation of the Hong Kong Chinese towards Hong Kong as a society can be safely characterized as that of avoidance, which manifests itself in an aloof stance towards society, avoidance of involvement with outsiders except when instrumentally necessary, and a low social participation rate.

Aloofness Towards Society

The Hong Kong Chinese in general neither identify with Hong Kong nor are committed to it but rather tend to treat it as an instrument. Consequently, society is conceived as a setting wherein one exploits to the best of one's efforts the opportunities available so as to advance the interests of oneself and one's familial group.

When asked about the relative importance of one's own family and the society of Hong Kong, 36% of the respondents rated their own families as more important, as against a minuscule 9.6% who ranked society first. Turning to another indicator of social aloofness, 51.6% of our respondents felt no pride at all in the achievements of some of their fellow Hong Kong inhabitants, such as the one who had become the leading shipping magnate in the world. Among the middle-class Chinese, furthermore, the desire to emigrate to the advanced Western countries is fairly prevalent, though of course in practice only a small proportion of them can make it there. Among the youngsters, however, this desire to leave Hong Kong is even more intense. Being more

idealistic, people in younger age groups are more offended by the social
injustice and the lack of political opportunities in the colony. Mitchell, in a
survey of approximately 3,000 Form 5 students in Hong Kong in 1967,
found that only 23% of them opted "to stay in Hong Kong" when they were
asked the question: "If you could live anywhere today, where would you
prefer to live?" (1969c, vol. 2:338) Judging from past experience, however,
we can expect that most of the youngsters will change their mind when they
reach adulthood to conform to those attitudes held by their elders.

After a content analysis of the films produced in Hong Kong, Jarvie came
to the conclusion below which reflects the general aloofness towards society
as held by the Hong Kong Chinese:

> To generalize dangerously, before the 1970s, the vast bulk of films made in Hong
> Kong had nothing whatsoever to do with life in Hong Kong. That is to say, the
> realities of such life, and the problems people had to cope with, were never the
> integral basis from which proceeded plot, character development, action, and so
> on. (1977:90)

The avoidance of the existing society and the seeking for refuge into an
unreal world was underscored by the same author in another passage:

> We notice persistent avoidance of modern times in any truly recognizable form;
> we see that many films are set in an at best vaguely specified part of China at an
> unspecified (but post (1911)-revolutionary) time . . . , and the family or the
> criminals are vaguely located; where people in trouble—bullied by family
> members, or seriously ill, or star-crossed in love—do not know what action to
> take, where to turn. All these patterns tell us perhaps a society that has lost its
> bearings, does not know where it is, still less where it is going, is unable to take
> command of the tide of events. Individuals appear helpless victims of family,
> political, or business tyrants, social customs, disease. As a consequence, they hark
> back to a China where things were clearer, more stable, more understandable
> (oddly, this includes a China being attacked by the Japanese, when in fact chaos
> reigned); a China that many of them don't even recall at first hand, except perhaps
> as children; but rather a China described to them by refugee parents as a sort of
> good time that, when lost, resulted in disruption and flight. It goes without saying
> that cultural nostalgia and selective memory ensure that this former world is
> purely imaginary. What is significant is its sociological function: it serves to
> explain who and where and what people were before, as a standard to judge the
> present, as a future to which to aspire. (Jarvie 1977:93-94)

On the other hand, nevertheless, this affective and identificational aloofness towards the existing Hong Kong society is coupled with an instrumental
attachment to it. It is interesting to note that as a place to make a living,
Hong Kong is highly regarded by the Chinese people, and that explains why,
among our respondents, 52.7% of them would still prefer to remain in Hong
Kong even if opportunities emerged elsewhere. Yet, at the same time, they
did not entertain any desire to try to improve it to suit their cherished

"ideals," if there were any. This dualistic attitude towards the Hong Kong society characterizes the social orientation of the Chinese inhabitants, and it might be that these attitudes are useful in enabling them to adapt to a place like Hong Kong, which they live in but fail to identify with, with such a high level of success.

The conviction that Hong Kong is a land of opportunity tends to ameliorate feelings of alienation and provide hope for material gain among a majority of the Chinese inhabitants, irrespective of age. In this respect, the opinion of the younger generation is of crucial importance, as they are the ones who are in the process of striving for success or are about to do so. Mitchell's study of Form 5 students in 1967 provided the lowest estimate of availability of opportunities in Hong Kong, compared to others. Yet, in response to the question "How much opportunity is there in Hong Kong for you to be a success in your career?" still 69% of the students queried said "some, but not too much," while 15% felt that there was "quite a bit" and 12% thought there was "little or none" (1969c, vol. 1:82). As time moves on, the image conjured up looks brighter. In the early 1970s, Chaney and Podmore found that, among their 1,123 young adult respondents, 62.7% agreed with the statement that "Hong Kong is truly a land of opportunity and people get pretty much what they deserve here" (1973:60). While Chaney and Podmore's sample consisted of a cross-section of the young adults in Hong Kong, the survey of Lau and Ho on a sample of young workers in 1978, a majority of them under thirty-five years of age, found that a striking 60% of them believed that Hong Kong offered opportunities for upwardly mobile common people (1982).

In view of the overriding emphasis on material values by the Hong Kong Chinese, the perception of Hong Kong as a place where ample opportunities are available for these values to be realized reinforces the instrumental attachment of the Hong Kong Chinese to the colony.

Avoidance of Involvement with Outsiders

Suspicious attitude towards outsiders and distrust of them have long been a recognized cultural feature of the Chinese people, which have their roots in a peasant society where relatively self-contained life confined to small geographical areas was the rule. Given the Chinese abhorrence of conflict and aggression, we find the coexistence of intense emotional attachment among people in small groups, and cold, impersonal postures towards those who are outsiders.

> Given this set of perceptions and emotional concerns, China's difficulty in becoming a well integrated national society is understandable. Reluctance to face up to points of dispute and avoidance of contact out of fear of aggression fragment

the society into suspicious family groupings. . . .

There is an all-or-nothing quality about this style of social relations: either the full trust and reliance characteristic of "dependency," or apprehension and avoidance of outsiders. Extending the range of social transactions beyond a close circle of known and trusted individuals is unlikely when there is an expectation that one will be cheated, or where the striving for personal interests seems to lead to violent conflict. (Solomon 1971:103)

When asked whether conflict with outsiders should be avoided as far as possible even if damage to oneself and one's family resulted, 82.2% of our respondents answered yes. This indicates that even though familial interests are of enormous importance, these still do not justify overt conflict with outsiders. Unless the stake at hand is so large that conflict avoidance would mean serious impairment of these interests, the familial group is anxious to avoid conflict as far as possible. Furthermore, our respondents not only set stringent standards for themselves with regard to conflictual entanglement with outsiders, they also applied these standards to judge the behaviour of others. Fifty-six per cent of them declared that they would not approve of the behaviour of those people, who, in safeguarding their own familial interests, engaged in social conflict, and, as a result of the enlargement of this conflict, put other people's interests in jeopardy. Social stability, to reiterate, was very much in the mind of our respondents, and they would not countenance socially disruptive activities on the part of others, even though these activities might be justified by their own familial interests. The findings here seem to imply that many Hong Kong Chinese, even though believing everybody is entitled to pursue his own interests, still expect others to observe certain rules of the game, the function of such observance being to ensure an adequate quantity of social stability in society, without which everyone's private interests will be endangered.

In Hong Kong this avoidance attitude towards others has produced a relatively "cold" society in which concern with the well-being of others is low. Sherry Rosen had found such a society in the middle-class district called the Mei Foo Sun Chuen:

The actual atmosphere within the Mei Foo is one of aloofness, a wariness and even mistrust of one's neighbors that is more characteristic of the Simmel-Wirth interpretation of urban life-styles than it is of suburban attitudes. Residents and non-residents alike are quick to explain that Mei Foo residents have come in search of privacy, and are more concerned with "minding their own business" than with creating a community spirit. (1976:28)

Another piece of evidence on the tendency to avoid outsiders by the Hong Kong Chinese is provided by Angela Kan. In her study of a sample of lower-income residents living in public housing estates, she found that more than a half of them had not attempted to mediate in the fights and quarrels between their neighbours nor had acted as mediators in such events (1974:58-59). In the same spirit of avoidance, 66.7% of her respondents agreed with the statement that it was best if everybody would mind his own business (*Ibid.*: 60). Furthermore, 48.4% strongly agreed, and 46.5% agreed, that the residents living in the housing estates were manifesting the attitude of "sweep up the snow at one's own doorway and don't bother with another's frosty roof" (*Ibid.*: 61). Such attitudes of non-involvement definitely are not conducive to cozy relationships among neighbours.

Mitchell also found that the Hong Kong Chinese had low involvement with their co-workers, their neighbours and their friends. More shockingly, compared to other Southeast Asian countries, the Chinese society of Hong Kong was marked by the lowest social involvement with others on the part of its people (1969a, vol. 2:490). Only 37% of the Hong Kong respondents saw their co-workers socially once every two weeks or more often. Only 42% saw their neighbours socially two to three times a month or more, and only 12% of them considered that a neighbour was one of their best friends. In the same vein, Hong Kong women were found to be outstanding in Southeast Asia for their lack of friends. Men were also the extreme for all the male populations surveyed. Forty-four per cent of the women interviewed, in contrast to 12% of the Indian women interviewed in Singapore, said they had no close friends. Twenty-one per cent of the Hong Kong men, in contrast to 7% of the Chinese men in Malaysia and 7% of the Thai men in Bangkok, gave the same answer (*Ibid.*: 481-88). With regard to the low neighbourliness among the Hong Kong Chinese, Angela Kan came to the same conclusion. Generally speaking, among the residents in the public housing estates she studied, the overt expressions of social relationships among neighbours were extensive in only casual activities, such as greeting, chatting and allowing children to play together as well as in occasional exchanges, such as visiting and helping each other. However, in terms of affect, less than half of the respondents could be described as having an "intense" relationship with their neighbours, "intense" being measured by Kan by the knowledge of their occupation, industry and ethnicity, and familiarity with their families (1974:28).

On the other hand, that a certain amount of interaction with outsiders is allowed provided utilitarian interests are thereby served can be demonstrated by the answers given to a question which asked the respondents whether they would still keep some outsider as a friend if his personality was defective in many respects but he was in a position to help their families in one way or another. Aside from the non-committal answer of "it depends," it is evident that more of our respondents (38.9%) would still prefer to befriend that person, compared to those (32%) who would not do so.

Such an attitude would lead us logically to expect that involvement with outsiders would be actively sought after only if an individual is in trouble and if other people's assistance is desperately needed. In fact, this is the case in general, but not quite. In Kan's study of lower-class people living in public housing estates, it was true that in personal and family crises, such as when small children or sick persons needed someone to take care of them, neighbours rather than relatives and friends were likely to be approached. Nevertheless, the high percentages of people not seeking any help even during times of financial crises or emotional disturbances from their neighbours still revealed the prevalence of reserved attitudes with respect to outsiders when affection and emotional attachment were entailed. Moreover, in crises or under conditions of poor security around the housing block, even though the residents were theoretically expected to face them as a group, the data of Kan still showed a prevailing atmosphere of unconcern and non-cooperation, which is astonishing (1974:28-29).

In Mei Foo Sun Chuen, the middle-class residents were more capable of cooperating with outsiders in times of crises, but their involvement was segmental and temporary:

> Accordingly, Mei Foo residents have virtually made a religion of non-participation in the new community. Efforts by the local kaifong neighborhood association to recruit new members from the Mei Foo population have been in vain, as have been attempts by the government to set up centers in the village [sic] where citizens can come forward and present ideas for the anti-crime and anti-litter campaigns. The gracious new community center, which opened in 1973 in Stage II, has remained in excellent condition largely because of almost total lack of use. (Rosen 1976:29)

> There is one area in which Mei Foo residents do participate, so to speak, and that is in terms that relate to the protection and upkeep of their property and privacy. (Ibid.: 30)

> The dispute of the Management versus the residents, which began some five years after the Estate was opened [i.e., in 1972], provides the single piece of evidence that Mei Foo residents can in fact be organized into participation when the stakes are felt to be sufficiently high. (Ibid.: 30)

> Even though the battle of the fee increases brought residents together, if only for a matter of months, it brought them together over an issue that was ultimately one of private self-interest rather than of community concern. Even so, the residents could not channel their interests into one unified front, but rather allowed their force to be weakened by factionalism. (Ibid.: 37)

Low Social Participation

An aloof attitude towards society and the distrust of outsiders, together with the emphasis on the familial groups, are followed by a low rate of participation in voluntary associations. Our 1977 survey showed that only 19.6% of the respondents had joined voluntary associations of any kind. Even among that 19.6% who joined, it is possible that many of them, particularly those who joined trade unions under the promptings of their workmates, were far from being active in their membership. As can be seen from Tables 4.1 and 4.2, among the joiners, those who had joined two voluntary associations or fewer amounted to 89.8%.

TABLE 4.1

Number of voluntary association memberships claimed
by respondents who have joined voluntary associations

Number of voluntary association memberships	N	Percentage
1	75	69.4
2	22	20.4
3	4	3.7
4	1	0.9
5	4	3.7
6	1	0.9
7	1	0.9
Total:	108	99.9

TABLE 4.2

Among joiners, number of voluntary associations
joined by types of voluntary associations

Type of voluntary associations joined	Number of voluntary associations joined							
	0	1	2	3	4	5	No answer	Total
Clan/district associations	79	24	4	—	—	—	1	108
Economic associations	67	35	3	2	—	—	1	108
Political associations	104	3	—	—	—	—	1	108
Community associations	92	14	1	—	—	—	1	108
Religious associations	90	15	—	—	2	—	1	108
Recreational associations	85	16	4	1	—	1	1	108
Social welfare associations	100	6	1	—	—	—	1	108
Total:	617	113	13	3	2	1	7	

Among the voluntary associations joined, many were closely connected with quasi-familistic relationships (such as clan and district associations), with the requirements of one's job (e.g., trade unions), or with one's personal needs (e.g., religious associations and recreational associations). Voluntary associations which were primarily concerned with social or community well-being could attract only meagre participation.

As for the reasons given for joining voluntary associations, 55.6% of the respondents claimed that it was to serve their own interests and those of their families, while only 22.2% of them had the interests of society or community in mind.

When we compare the social participation rate of the Hong Kong Chinese with that of the United States, the former appears to be strikingly low. In the case of the United States, Jack Rothman, after an extensive survey of litera-ture in this area, concluded, "Most adults are members of voluntary associa-tions" (1974:283-304). One of the typical study in this area is a study by Babchuk and Booth (1969). They interviewed a representative cross-section of persons aged 21 to 63 in a Midwestern state. It was found that 84% of their respondents belonged to at least one voluntary association.

The participation rate does not seem to increase even when participation is actively solicited by organizations to promote the well-being of the members themselves. Community organizations deliberately set up in poor neighbour-hoods fall into this category. A case study of a community development project in a district of Hong Kong called Sau Mau Ping found that few men participated in the project of the Block Mutual Help Association, and that female membership predominated in the Association and also in the youth group, despite the fact that the two fieldworkers in the project were male. Even among females and youths, the participants were only a minority in the district (Riches 1973a:73-74). Another study of four community centres in four districts of Hong Kong came to the same conclusion. It was found that the registered membership of the community centres expressed as percentages of the populations of the districts served and the resettlement estates im-mediately adjacent to the centres was extremely small (Riches 1973b:38). People with a high participation rate, the most catered to as members by these community centres, were those between the ages of 14 and 19. Indeed if one also takes into consideration the percentage of young persons within the 6 to 13 age groups who were centre members, a picture emerges of the community centres performing merely the role and functions of youth centres, thus distorting the original intention of the community organizers (*Ibid.*: 42).

Even among young persons, though they are more enthusiastic joiners than their adult counterparts, one of the most important reasons for their partici-pation is an instrumental consideration to take advantage of the recreational facilities these organizations have to offer, or to learn a skill which they can capitalize on in the job market. When it comes to trade unions, which are reputed to be politically oriented towards either of the two Chinese governments, the aversion of young persons towards them is explicit. In their study of young adults in Hong Kong, Chaney and Podmore found that

> only 2% of the whole sample reported that they were members of a trade union (47.5% of all respondents were normally employed). While another 17% said they would join if there were one available, nearly 18% said they "didn't know", whether they would join or not, and 65% said they definitely would not. Of course these figures are rather unrealistic as they include many respondents who were not working. However, enthusiasm for collective action was even lower amongst workers than amongst the overall sample.... The percentage who say they would definitely not join a trade union rises to 69% amongst those who were working. Of those who were members just over half said they were satisfied with their union. (1973:46)

When asked about their opinion towards trade unions, 63.6% of them disagreed that trade unions should be involved in politics, while 67.4% agreed that trade unions should only concern themselves with the social lives of their members (*Ibid.*: 60). The abhorrence of politics by the young adults is manifestly evident here, and explains their low participation rate in trade unions.

PERCEPTION OF CLASSES AND CLASS CONSCIOUSNESS

In a highly commercialized and industrialized society where an emphasis on material values is prevalent, it is not surprising to find that the basis for class division is perceived to be wealth. Nevertheless, people also perceive a class of officials because of the dominance of the bureaucratic administration in the colony. On the whole, however, the preponderance of wealth as the criterion of social class categorization is unmistakably clear.

> For the greater part of the community genealogical background in China or within Hong Kong is of little importance in the determination of status or class. While some positions have in the past tended to be reserved for members of "Hong Kong families" it is possible for individuals to obtain considerable status on the basis of their own ability to amass wealth.... Opportunities for the accumulation of wealth are further enhanced by government measures: taxation is low, public security is good and there are few legal restrictions to impede the development of business and industry. (Topley 1969:190)

Moreover, the importance of wealth is, in many cases, not even diluted by the negative implications of some non-material criteria associated with the way wealth is accumulated. What it means is that either the people, when attributing a class label to a particular person, usually do not consider the ways whereby wealth is amassed to be relevant, or that even if wealth is

obtained through devious or illicit means, a person will still be accorded a
high status provided he is willing to devote part of his wealth to socially
acclaimed uses.

> Generally speaking rich people who made money by socially disapproved means
> can gain status and respect if they are accepted by the influential members of
> community. Most people like to associate with the wealthy in Hong Kong and
> they are likely to be accepted if they later transfer to respectable business and use
> their money in ways approved by Chinese society. There will usually be people,
> however, who continue to hold them in contempt behind their backs. Those
> whose fortunes are based on dubious activities of forebears operating when there
> was greater legal laxity are not likely to meet with any social disadvantages. I have
> heard Chinese boasting about the known or suspected illegal practices of their
> ancestors. (Topley 1969:205)

In view of the theoretically fine gradations in which wealth can be divided,
it is not particularly surprising to find that in Hong Kong, there is no universal
agreement on the number of classes in the society. When we also consider
that objectively speaking, the distribution of income and wealth in Hong
Kong is highly unequal, the fact that this objective reality is not reflected in a
dichotomous conception of the class structure is intriguing. In 1976, 1,239
respondents in Kwun Tong, an industrial community in Hong Kong, were
asked in a survey what they thought were the number of social strata in Hong
Kong. The results are shown in Table 4.3.

TABLE 4.3
Perceptions of number of strata in Hong Kong

Number of strata	N	Percentage
1	28	2.2
2	158	12.2
3	311	24.1
4	273	21.1
5	204	15.8
6	73	5.6
7 or more	48	3.7
Don't know	173	13.4
No answer	25	1.9
Total:	1,293	100.0

Source: Social Research Centre (1976:131).

The ways of classifying social classes used by the same respondents are
similarly diversified and reveal a lack of consensus on the class structure of

Hong Kong:
  (1) Purely stratified by scholarship/talent (1.5%);
  (2) Scholarly/talented (High) vs. Immoral (Low) (0.3%);
  (3) Scholarly/talented (High) vs. Lower working class/jobless (Low) (2.0%);
  (4) Scholarly/talented (High), Economically active (Middle) and the Immoral (Low) (0.7%);
  (5) Economically active (High) vs. Jobless/outlaws (Low) (1.0%);
  (6) Socially contributive (High) vs. Discontented (Low) (0.5%);
  (7) Directly involved in productive work such as labourers (High) vs. Not directly involved in productive work such as government officials (Low) (0.2%);
  (8) From high to low are: those having political/administrative power such as government officials, those having power at work such as industrial/commercial managers/executives, those under supervision such as clerical staff, and those who are powerless in all respects (10.8%);
  (9) From high to low are: government officials, businessmen, clergymen, labourers and beggars (1.2%);
  (10) From high to low are: the wealthy and authoritative, government officials, those engaged in industry/commerce, labouring people living in difficulties (4.0%);
  (11) From high to low are: government officials, workers in various occupations, immoralists/criminals (2.9%);
  (12) Government officials (High) vs. Criminals (Low) (0.2%);
  (13) Purely stratified by occupational prestige (3.9%);
  (14) Those in high positions (High) vs. Criminals (Low) (0.7%);
  (15) From high to low are: entrepreneurs, workers in various occupations, labourers/jobless (6.6%);
  (16) From high to low are: government officials and entrepreneurs, elites and the prestigious, workers in various occupations (3.8%);
  (17) From high to low are: prestigious professionals, workers stratified by occupational status (4.6%);
  (18) From high to low are: prestigious professionals, workers in various occupations, outlaws/criminals (2.2%);
  (19) From high to low are: elites and the prestigious, government officials. workers in various occupations and the jobless (2.0%);
  (20) From high to low are: elites and the prestigious, senior staff in organizations, junior staff in organizations, labourers, the jobless and the outlaws (3.3%);
  (21) Purely stratified by wealth and income (16.5%);

(22) From high to low are: the rich, employers, workers stratified by occupational status (3.6%);

(23) From high to low are: the wealthy, the educated, the poor and the ignorant (1.2%);

(24) From high to low are: the wealthy and good, the poor and good, and the bad (1.2%);

(25) Purely stratified by districts and housing types (2.2%).

And, for one reason or another, 22.8% of the respondents gave no answer to the question (Social Research Centre 1976:132-33). Another interesting piece of finding is that when asked to assign a class label to themselves, 35.4% considered themselves as belonging to the "working class," while the other assignments were scattered haphazardly across a wide spectrum of labels (*Ibid.*: 134).

A careful perusal of the findings presented above would lead to several observations about the conception of social class in Hong Kong. First, there is no general consensus as to the class structure, only a conceptually fragmented picture of social class. Second, underlying more than half of the classification schemes employed by the people are the dimensions of wealth and income, though other criteria such as political or administrative power, educational achievements and "morality" are occasionally inserted to complicate the general scene. Third, many of the "conceptual schemes" are non-exhaustive, which is to say that they do not cover the whole populace. They hence tend to represent what the people regard as the most important ingredient of success or failure in Hong Kong. Fourth, closely related to the previous point is that in some classification schemes, individual status or class categories are based on different criteria, thus resulting in a juxtaposition of several class categories which are strictly speaking non-comparable. Finally, the fragmented conception of class structure tends to impede the formation, at least in an ideological sense, of two polarized and antagonistic classes, or the possibility of class conflict. In short, social classes as structural forces in shaping inter-personal relationships and political actions are relatively insignificant in Hong Kong.

When social relationships are viewed primarily in pecuniary terms, when social mobility is seen as a result of wealth accumulation, when opportunities for upward mobility are seen as available, and when the wealthy are admired as people who have earned their success through cunningness or individual striving, then class consciousness and class antagonism would be low. Our study of a group of young workers in Hong Kong had also borne out this point. The wealth and status of the rich were not seen to result from a process of economic exploitation which deprived the lower strata of their rightful share. To probe further, we asked our respondents whether they would agree that a man in Hong Kong had to divest others of their possessions in order to get rich (Lau and Ho 1982). The responses given underscored the point that to the workers the principle of zero-sum economic game did not hold in Hong Kong. In all, 91.2% of them did not agree with the statement, and only 4.8% agreed with it. Feelings of antagonism towards the rich were extremely weak. Paradoxically, it is probably the rich who are more conscious of their class position and are more inclined to see their relationship with the working and lower classes in "conflict" terms. In a study of leaders in the industrial community of Tsuen Wan, Graham Johnson found that the "Tsuen Wan leaders were more likely to express attitudes of class conflict in abstract contexts of class interests rather than the commonsense context of employers' treatment of employees" (1971:247). "Whereas 58 percent argued that the interests of workers and capitalists did coincide and that cooperation rather than conflict ought to guide economic relations, it might be possible to argue ... that this represents a 'Confucian ethic' at work. But equally 40 percent ... suggested a 'conflict' response" (*Ibid.*: 247). And the leaders were more prone to say that there was inequality of opportunity in Hong Kong (*Ibid.*: 251).

In a certain sense, Hong Kong workers can be depicted as a type of privatized worker as conceptualized by David Lockwood. One of the characteristics of a privatized worker is that he is strongly motivated to view social relationships in pecuniary terms. Based on this conception, he does not think of a society divided up into either a hierarchy of status groups or an opposition of classes. His model of society is one in which individuals are associated with, and dissociated from, one another less by any type of social exchange than by the magnitude of their incomes and possessions (Lockwood 1975:23-26). As a result,

> power is not understood as a power of one man over another, but rather as the power of a man to acquire things; as purchasing power. Status is not seen in terms of the association of status equals sharing a similar style of life. If status is thought of at all it is in terms of a standard of living, which all who have the means can readily acquire. It may not be easy to acquire the income requisite to a certain standard of living and hence qualify for membership in a more affluent class; but given the income there are no other barriers to mobility. (*Ibid.*: 24-25)

One more indicator which reflects the harmonization of class relationship in Hong Kong is the congruence between the behaviour of the upper-strata people and the role expectation of them held by the lower classes. In our survey, the young workers were asked what responsibility did the wealthy people had, in their opinion, to help the poor. Only 8.3% of them considered that the wealthy had a great responsibility. Even though another 56% regarded the rich as having this responsibility, the statistic indicates more that the workers expected the rich to be charitable in accordance with Chinese custom than that they were insistent that the rich be held responsible through some kind of mandatory charity. Given a generally low expectation for the rich, the data show that our respondents were not disappointed. Even though none of them thought that wealthy people had demonstrated great willingness to help the poor, still 19.9% thought that they were willing to do so, and 36.5% detected some degree of willingness among them (Lau and Ho 1982). These findings seem to indicate that the charity works of the wealthy, in addition to enhancing their fame and reputation, do have the side effects of allaying class animosity.

When such delimited conceptions of the role of the upper strata are coupled with a general belief that these role expectations have been more or less fulfilled, it would not be surprising to find that our young worker respondents would explain their current livelihood primarily in terms of their individual efforts and the resources they could mobilize from their familial groups. When asked who should they depend on for help when in difficulties, the findings were, however, somewhat puzzling. When the possible sources of help were presented to them one by one for consideration, it was found that 75.3% of the respondents considered that fellow family members should be relied upon. As for relatives, friends, voluntary associations and charity societies, government and someone with "face" (prominent individuals), the figures were 64.6%, 70%, 65.6%, 67.9% and 34% respectively. What this suggests is that at the attitudinal level, except with those with "face," all these sources were theoretically important for resource procurement. At the behavioural level, however, it was found that the government, voluntary associations and charity societies were seldom approached for assistance. In addition, we had also found out that there were apparently unmet needs in the lives of the young workers (but the condition of need nonsatisfaction was somehow quietly tolerated), the underutilization of these sources of help is quite difficult to comprehend. One way out of this interpretive dilemma is to treat this evidence as reflecting a dimly-held expectation which had been learned from the mass media or other channels of information, yet had not really been seriously held or internalized. Alternatively put, it seems to us that the actual expectation for the wealthy and others are much lower than the one given to us (*Ibid.*).

To further buttress our interpretation of these idiosyncracies in the data, let us consider other information in connection with the study of young workers. When requested to explain the low socioeconomic status of the poor people in Hong Kong, 11.3% of the respondents attributed it to "fate," 38.6% explained it in terms of indolence of the poor, and 22.8% used the broad category of "Hong Kong society" as the causal factor. When further queried as to their opinion on the means available to the poor people if they were to improve their livelihood, 81.2% chose "one's own efforts," 4.3% picked "one's children's achievements," 5.1% would rely on the "unification of the poor people to fight for their rights," while 2.4% opted for "help from the government" (*Ibid.*).

Incidentally, the same line of reasoning can be found in the social leaders. When asked the reasons for the inequality of opportunity in Hong Kong, 52% of Tsuen Wan's leaders picked "lack of education," 23% "lack of influence," 9% "luck," 4% "laziness," and 2% "lack of money" (Johnson 1971:252). As to the factors which determined success in Hong Kong, the same group of respondents emphasized individualistic ones. Thus, 6% mentioned "luck and pull," 31% "hard work and study," 21% "both equal," 3% "both, luck higher" and 39% "both, diligence higher" (*Ibid.*: 252). Similarly, when asked to explain why people were poor, 29% attributed it to "lack of education," 18% to "poor inheritance," 15% to "laziness," 4% to "too many children," 3% to "bad habits (gambling, opium)," 5% to "fate" and, what is most enlightening, only 14% to "the economic system" (*Ibid.*: 254).

Hence, both workers and social leaders explain individual success or failure by means of individualistic factors. The system as a whole is rarely blamed for its role in posing as an obstacle to the mobility of individuals. The attitudes displayed here fall in line with those expressed in association with utilitarianistic familism, both of which evince non-systemic ways of perceiving things. They function to reinforce the tendencies of system-avoidance and social passivity.

The lack of working class solidarity in Hong Kong and workers' relative passivity (as indicated by the low rates of work stoppages in the past decades) are well-known facts. However, this objective passivity does not seem to square too well with the data on perception of class action on the part of the young workers. It seems that at least at the attitudinal level our respondents were sympathetic to the interests of their fellow workers, as they claimed that they would be willing to participate in class actions to further their common interests. When presented with a hypothetical situation in which the poor people had already organized themselves to fight for their rights, 46.6% of the respondents said they would join them, while 13.4% were hesitant. Another illustration of identification with one's fellow workers was that 65.7% of them would prefer to see their neighbours buying new colour television sets while they themselves were not able to do so, than to see an unknown wealthy man earning several million more dollars. This finding is quite important when we take into account the fact that many workers would normally choose as their reference group their fellow workers, particularly those living close by, and making comparisons with them. Thus, 79.1% of our respondents indicated that they themselves would derive satisfaction when they, upon comparison, knew that many people in Hong Kong were doing less well than themselves (Lau and Ho 1982). Culling these data, our respondents seemed to be quite aware of some common interests between themselves and other Hong Kong workers. Nevertheless, this awareness might not necessarily be deep-rooted, and it has so far only rarely been converted into overt behaviour. Moreover, when taking into consideration their attitudes towards the upper strata, these common interests did not seem to be defined in such a way that antagonism towards the wealthy would automatically ensue. Finally, two caveats are in order. First, as our respondents are young workers, they did not necessarily represent the attitudes of their older counterparts. We are confident that the latter would endorse attitudes more conservative and traditional, and more averse to any forms of collective action. Second, there is also the possibility that our respondents were deliberately giving "false" responses to their interviewers, who were university students, in order to "convince" them that they were adopting "progressive" attitudes. Nevertheless, both points cannot be corroborated by hard empirical evidence, for they are unfortunately unavailable.

POLITICAL ATTITUDES AND BEHAVIOUR

The political culture of the Hong Kong Chinese presents a paradox which is somewhat difficult to disentangle. It seems to consist of a hodgepodge of disparate elements which are both positive and negative towards the political system wherein the people find themselves. This confusion in the political culture reveals in general the confusion among the Chinese themselves as to what to expect from the government, how to relate to it, and what is their role in the political system. What it all boils down to is that the system is both liked and disliked, accepted and rejected, evaluated favourably and unfavourably. Nevertheless, if a catchword has to be found to describe the political culture of the Hong Kong Chinese, we might well use the word "political aloofness." They assign a relatively delimited role to the polity, they depend on the government to execute this role, and they want to keep themselves uninvolved. Alternatively put, they have a strong need for an authority to serve as the bulkwark for a stable society, yet they fear relationships with that authority with which they have unavoidably to maintain in one way or another. This dilemma of political authority presented to the Chinese constitutes the two faces of authority to them:

> Government's benign face is thus to a large degree its ability to control society's potential for conflict, to prevent *luan*. (Solomon 1971:140)

> The second face of public authority is perceived in the glaring image of a rapacious tiger, stirring all those concerns about the harshly punitive and manipulative use of power which were acquired early in life. (*Ibid.* : 141)

This ambivalent attitude towards political authority consequently creates a sense of anxiety in the contacts with it. To avoid anxiety and to allay fear, delimiting the role and function of the government and to avoid having anything else with it as far as possible are the optimal solutions. And these tendencies are eminently represented in the political culture of the Hong Kong Chinese.

Definition of the Role of Government

The primary role of government in society is largely conceived to be that of maintaining social stability, and it is understandable as Hong Kong has been a haven for Chinese immigrants who fled from war and hunger in the mainland in the past one and a half centuries. In my 1977 survey of adult Hong Kong Chinese, 57.3% of them regarded the major responsibility of the government as the performance of this duty, in comparison to the 10.5% who would place the construction of a democratic and egalitarian society on the top priority list of governmental responsibilities. As long as the government can maintain social stability it will be accepted, and the level of political frustration among the Chinese will be held within controllable limits. However, for the Chinese to be satisfied with the government, it seems that more may have to be done by it, as 50.5% of the respondents maintained that they did not consider the government to be good, as, aside from the maintenance of social stability, it had done few other things.

One of the most important of these other things is service delivery, and it is particularly emphasized by the younger generations. Even on this aspect, however, the expectation is still rather low, and is far from the types of "aspiration explosion" plaguing other parts of the world. Though we have no data here to throw light on the types and amounts of services that have to be provided by the government in order to satisfy the Chinese people, I would guess that they expect services which are beyond their capability and which are deemed to be essential for a decent livelihood. For example, since land sales are monopolized by the government, public housing plays a prominent role in the real estate market. For services available through the primary resource networks, centring on the familial groups, the Hong Kong Chinese are extremely reluctant to substitute government help. Furthermore, so far they have forborn unmet needs without translating them into radical political or social actions (Lau and Ho 1982).

In our study of 1978, young workers were asked whether they felt that the government had the responsibility to take care of the common people.

Only 19% gave the clear-cut answer of "great responsibility," while another 71.8% picked the answer of "responsibility" and 3% that of "no responsibility." These respondents seem in favour of more public services but not insistent upon getting them. Moreover, a majority of the Chinese do not seem willing to initiate political action to "demand" them from the government.

In view of this relatively low expectation of the government, and taking into consideration that law and order have largely been maintained and the government has in the last decade or so stepped up the process of service delivery to the poor and disadvantaged (however inadequate the services are), the attitude of our respondents (the young workers) to the government is fairly favourable. Thus, 0.3% of them thought the government had shown great willingness to take care of the common people, 37.5% considered it to be willing, and 32.2% felt that the government had at least shown some willingness to do so. In general, the government's performance so far is in conformity with our respondents' role expectations of it (Lau and Ho 1982).

There is a diffuse tolerance of the political system by the Hong Kong Chinese. My 1977 survey showed that 81.6% of the adult respondents would like to have the status quo maintained, 13.6% did not care and only 0.7% were reluctant to see the status quo maintained (Lau 1977:199). In his interviews with 254 Chinese residents in Hong Kong in 1966-1967, Hoadley found that, in response to the question "Are you satisfied with the form of government Hong Kong has at present or would you prefer Hong Kong to be governed by an assembly elected by the people?" only 22% opted for an elected assembly; 21% expressed satisfaction with the status quo; and 51% answered "don't know." On a question about the future of Hong Kong, 29% wished to remain linked to Britain; 7% wanted to become part of mainland China; 12% wanted independence from both; and 52% had no opinion (1970: 212).

Nevertheless, their attitude towards the status quo or existing governmental system is not highly supportive. Among the respondents of Hoadley's survey, "about half of those *with* opinions expressed negative orientations toward the police, the Government, and the possible representativeness of the Legislative Council, that is, toward the system, the outputs, and its inputs. Only about one-quarter of all respondents appear positively oriented toward inputs exemplified by free criticism of police and an elected assembly. Regarding orientation toward the system, less than one-third openly favor continued British presence, again with one-half expressing no opinion" (1970:213). The fact that Hoadley's survey was conducted during the most "turbulent" years of Hong Kong's postwar history might have produced more negative replies from the respondents, and hence might have underestimated the support given to the system as a whole. However, even bearing this in mind, it can still be said that the Hong Kong Chinese tolerate the system rather than actively embrace it.

Similarly, among the younger generation, support for the status quo is prevalent, even though they have a lot of grievances against the system. Among the students in The Chinese University of Hong Kong, for example, there was substantial positive feeling for the existing governmental system (*Ibid.*: 216). Mitchell (1969c, vol. 1:343-44) also found that among the Form 5 students he had interviewed, only 15% were specifically concerned with changing the existing form of government, and they were more inclined to prefer a wider role for the government in the manufacturing and educational sectors. However, it is also found that, in response to the question "In general, how well do you think that Government understands the needs of the people in Hong Kong?" only 9% of the students felt that the government understood these needs very well. An additional 20% felt it understood these needs fairly well, 56% said "not too well," and 15% thought that the government did "not at all" understood these needs. Most students felt that they were in disagreement with the government, although only 14% said they "strongly disagree" with the government, 55% simply "disagree," whereas 31% either "agree" or "strongly agree" (Mitchell 1969c, vol. 2:344-45). In view of the fact that students everywhere harbour anti-system feelings in varying degrees, the political attitudes of the students in Hong Kong are, by comparison, far more moderate. And they are more obsessed with their own future careers, occupations and achievements than with social or political affairs. In short, Hong Kong's students are in the main privatized individuals (Mitchell 1969, vol. 1).

Political Powerlessness

Under the general rubric of diffuse tolerance of the existing form of government, it is also possible to locate a pervasive sense of political powerlessness among the Hong Kong Chinese. This facet of the political culture of the Chinese people is the most reported item in the studies which I have come across, and this serves to underscore its significance in the political life of the colony.

Under a bureaucratic polity, it is easily understandable that the Hong Kong Chinese should feel that they are powerless to decide on public policies which affect their livelihood. However, whether the state of powerlessness is one which is accepted as an immutable fact of political life, and hence is accepted with resignation, or one which is considered as gross social injustice that has to be eradicated, we have no way of telling. Based on my personal experience, I consider the former interpretation more plausible. Under the heavy yoke of bureaucratic officialdom in traditional China, where the common people were treated as inferior subjects, the Chinese had developed a non-participatory parochial political culture. Furthermore, in the Chinese political culture, there is a diffuse fear among the people of assuming responsibility in decision-making and of developing innovative social ideals. This reinforces the reluctance to exert one's political will, and makes subordinating oneself to hierarchic authority a voluntary act.

> The tradition of filial or loyal dependence on those with power develops in a subordinate the sense that neither authority nor responsibility can be shared; they are only delegated or acquired indirectly within a superior-subordinate relationship. Hence a passivity, a reluctance to take initiative or to be critical—what the historian Balazs has termed a "panicky fear of assuming responsibility"—becomes the safest course for avoiding the harshness of authority. (Solomon 1971:116)

> The propensity to fear disorder and to seek predictability, the drive for conformity and the comfort of well-defined norms, the great capacity for energetic activities and the desire to avoid the risks of personal responsibility in decision-making, the belief in hierarchic authority and the fears about conflicting authorities—all combine to make the Chinese enthusiastic and effective participants in organizations that are hierarchic in form. (Pye 1968:175)

The sense of political powerlessness takes two forms. First, it involves a low sense of political efficacy. Political efficacy means the feeling that one's individual political action does have, or can have, an impact upon the political process, i.e., that it is worthwhile to perform one's civic duties (Campbell *et al.* 1954:194). When 1,065 ordinary respondents in Kwun Tong whom King interviewed were asked what they thought they would do about it if there were a government regulation which they believed was unjust, only 14% of the respondents claimed they could do something about it, while 81.9% of them thought that there was nothing at all they could do to change the situation (King 1972:16). The sense of political efficacy of the social leaders in Kwun Tong was not much higher. Among the twelve heads of organizations interviewed by King, four of them said they could do "something" about an unjust government regulation, six admitted that they could do "very little," and two said "nothing at all" (*Ibid.*: 17). The same sense of political powerlessness among the Hong Kong Chinese was reported in my study of 550 of them in 1977. As many as 91.1% of them felt that they had no power to change the society of Hong Kong. Furthermore, an even higher percentage of them, 96.7%, maintained that they had no influence whatsoever on the formulation of government policy. These findings indicate that not only the sense of political efficacy is low among the Hong Kong Chinese, but also that most of them are not aware of any possible forms of interest articulation or interest aggregation, not to say interest representation, at the governmental level. The government appears to be a distant and invulnerable entity which in many ways controls their fate. It is beyond their capability to do anything about it. In this sense traces of a subject political culture, to use the term of Almond and Verba (1965), seem to be apparent, and adaptation rather than active intervention appears to be the guiding principle regulating the relationship between themselves and the government.

Despite their general sense of powerlessness, we can still detect a fairly strong desire among the Hong Kong Chinese to exert influence over the government, as can be seen from the fact that 58.5% of the respondents in my 1977 survey expressed such a desire. Similarly, a poll conducted by the Reform Club on the Hong Kong residents found that half of the adults in the survey were in favour of having elected members in the Legislative Council, including 14% who were strongly in favour. Only 2% were against the idea, while 48% were indifferent (*South China Morning Post*, November 30, 1977). Nevertheless, it is extremely difficult to make sense of these findings, as it is not uncommon in surveys to find that when respondents are hypothetically offered something which they do not currently have, they would normally be inclined to take it. But that of course does not mean that when the "good" is not forthcoming, they would take action to get it. What it all boils down to in the current context is that when asked whether they would like to have the right to vote, it is highly improbable that the Hong Kong Chinese would verbally turn down the offer. To ascertain the extent to which the "need" for political influence is real, some additional in-depth questions have to be asked, which we do not have here. Then there is also the problem of what to use the political influence for, once they are given it. It could be in the direction of the commonweal of society, or it could be in the direction of satisfaction of one's own familial interests, or minimizing the negative effects of government policy on these interests. Taking into consideration the meanings which all our available data happen to bring out, the latter possibility seems to be the more likely to materialize. If such is the case, wide dispersion of power in Hong Kong might result in a mobilization of partisan and parochial interests, which is detrimental to social and political stability, especially in a society where the degree of mutual suspicion is high.

Another dimension of powerlessness relates to the perceived responsiveness of the government which is thought to be low. On the other hand, the Hong Kong Chinese at least feel a certain measure of freedom in discussing "politics" which others without having to worry about the reactions of the government, even though they do not think that their opinion will carry much weight with the bureaucracy. The findings of Hoadley are relevant here, even though they were obtained in the atypical year of 1966-1967 and hence would underestimate the *actual* freedom of speech felt by the people.

Interviewers invited responses by 254 Chinese residents to the question, "Do you
think that people in Hong Kong are free to criticise the actions of the Hong Kong
police force without fear of punishment?" Only 27 per cent of respondents said
yes, while 40 per cent refused to answer. Of the remaining 33 per cent who
answered no and volunteered supplementary comments, only one respondent
indicated any actual experience with the police. The others, presumably basing
their answers on "common knowledge" rather than experience, thought that
criticism in a British colony was illegal, that the police would interfere with one's
business establishment, that "the Government has a right to do anything," and
that Chinese people are afraid of Government officials. (1970:212)

The survey conducted by King several years later on the people of Kwun
Tong discovered a much improved picture. Among his respondents, 41.3%
felt moderately and/or strongly that it was perfectly free to talk politics with
others. Only 6.2% of the respondents felt that they were not free to do so.
Still, two qualifications with regard to these findings need to be noted. First,
there was a relatively high percentage (18.6) in the sample giving no answers
to the question presented to them. According to King, there was a significant
number of people in Kwun Tong who simply did not want to talk about the
word "politics," even though this word had been "skilfully" taken out of the
questionnaire. Second, in the actual question, the words "public affairs"
instead of "political affairs" were used. And it is possible that these nonthreatening words elicited a more favourable response from the people (1972:
9-10). Overall, therefore, the timid avoidance of "politics" is still a prevalent
phenomenon in Hong Kong.

That the Chinese people felt that the government was not responsive to
their needs was also reported by King, and this time it was the social leaders
who were asked the questions. Some 399 heads of local organizations were
asked how they saw government officials' reaction to their opinions and
suggestions. The figures showed that leaders in Kwun Tong had a fairly low
expectation of consideration and responsiveness from government officials.
Only 11% and 17.5% respectively felt that their opinion and suggestions
would be given serious and moderate consideration by government officials,
while 41.6% of them said "depends" and 13.6% expected them to be totally
ignored (*Ibid.*: 12). If such are the views of local leaders, by extrapolation,
the perceived responsiveness of the government by the common people
should be even much lower. When it is recalled that many of the young
workers studied by Lau and Ho (1982) were relatively satisfied with the
performance of the government thus far, the conclusion would most likely
be that if the government is to be considered to be "responsive," it is because
it has "responded" to the needs of the people by anticipating them, and
not because it is "forced" to be responsive by public pressure. Anyway,
the prerogative to initiate actions still resides with the government, which

decides on the kinds and quantity of public opinion that have to be taken into account.

When we take into account the traditional political culture of the Chinese, wherein the compartmentalization of polity and society is endorsed, the relatively low degree of responsiveness of the government does not seem to be particularly detrimental to the operation of the colony, provided that the government can anticipate some of the salient needs of the people and take actions to meet them. The proper pattern of relationship between the polity and society in traditional China was eminently captured by Pye in the following passage:

> The lack of recognized linkages between the polity and the society presented the most acute problem at the point where the formal reach of government came to an end at the outer limits of the bureaucracy. At this point local officials were supposed to go no further than to offer a sympathetic ear to private complaints, informally adjudicate or mediate disputes among citizens, and accept a tolerant live-and-let-live attitude toward private activities as long as they did not result in any demands upon the state. (1968:20)

> Most importantly, it was assumed that all the most important relationships for the society lay either within the activities of officials or in the complete privacy of the family at home. (*Ibid.*: 25)

A kind of "render-unto-Caesar-what-is-Caesar's" philosophy is imbedded in Chinese political culture. Unless the government fails to perform what it is expected to perform or makes gross encroachments upon society, grievance against the government will be kept within safe bounds.

Political Knowledge

One of the distinctive aspects of the political culture of the Hong Kong Chinese is active search for knowledge about the political world in which they are living. And this greatly contrasts with their general political aloofness. In general, the Hong Kong Chinese seem to be moderately informed about the events taking place in Hong Kong and elsewhere. In terms of their knowledge about governmental institutions and the logic of operation in the government, however, they are much less informed. This might be attributed to the fact that most of the media of political information in Hong Kong carry mostly international and local news, while structural analysis of decision-making within the government and the operations of the government are not frequently published, as they are largely unavailable for public scrutiny.

A study of the mass communication patterns in Hong Kong had been done by Charles Allen in 1970. It involved, among other things, questionnaire interviews with 3,000 Chinese. Some of the pertinent findings with respect to the amount of political knowledge the Chinese had are the following:

(1) 84.5% of the respondents had read at least one daily newspaper in the day before the interview.

(2) 85% had read at least one daily newspaper in the week before the interview.

(3) 48% liked the local news best, and 36% liked news in general best, in the daily newspapers they had read. (Note that there is overlapping between these two figures.)

(4) Average amount of time spent in reading newspapers: 39.4 minutes.

(5) 46% had read at least one magazine in the month before the interview.

(6) 40% claimed that they liked news best on radio.

(7) 51% reported that they heard news on radio the day before the interview.

(8) 58% had television sets at home; and 43% of the respondents said that their favourite TV programme was news.

(9) 41% of the respondents got their news from newspapers; 36% from radios and 22% from televisions. (1970:17-33)

Other studies on this topic arrive at similar conclusions. Thus, King found that, among his 1,065 respondents in Kwun Tong, 42.5% followed the accounts of public and government affairs "from time to time," and 6.6% followed it "regularly." In comparison to other countries, like the U.S.A., Britain, Germany, Italy and Mexico, the proportion of people in Hong Kong who followed politics regularly (6.6%), or, in other words, the "attentive public," is relatively low; while the percentage of people who followed politics from time to time was rather high. King also interviewed fifteen civic and governmental leaders about their view on the ordinary people's concern for current affairs, ten of them said "moderate," one even said "very great," but none said "very low" (1972:6). My 1977 survey likewise found that as many as 62.7% of the respondents claimed that they paid close attention to local affairs.

The compartmentalization of cognitive political involvement on the one hand and attitudinal and behavioural involvement on the other among the Hong Kong Chinese is not difficult to comprehend. Under a bureaucratic polity which meets the people primarily at the policy implementation stage and in a society where everyone is engrossed in the pursuit of familial interests, a fair amount of knowledge about the policy content and activities of the government is essential if one's familial interests in a changing society are to be safeguarded or promoted. The acquisition of political knowledge is not for the sake of facilitating political participation, but for the purpose of enabling oneself to adapt better to one's social and political environment.

Perception of Government Officials

The attitudes of the Hong Kong Chinese towards the government officials are ones of envy, fear, respect, abhorrence, avoidance and aversion. The educational gap that divides the bureaucrats as a group and most of the Chinese populace generates misunderstandings and distrust. The overcentralization of power in the government is conducive to much red tape which mars the relationship between the officials and their clients, producing an atmosphere of impersonality which is deeply detested by a people who lay stress on "human sentiments." The condescending attitude of many officials in no way mends soured relationships. And the efforts of both parties to "humanize" their relationships on many occasions have bred corruption, which is mostly found in areas where direct contacts between officials and their clients are made, notably among policemen and other street-level bureaucrats. To make matters worse, the traditional Chinese attitudes towards lower officials, who are seen as the stooges of an exploitative and distant state, are not conducive to hospitable relationships with bureaucrats. All in all, the structural setting where contacts between bureaucrats and the people are established does not call for harmonious relationships between them.

The Information Services of the Hong Kong government, in cooperation with Survey Research Hong Kong, conducted a survey on the people's relationship with the government in 1973. Some of the findings are quite pertinent to the points raised in the last paragraph:

(1) The general picture which emerged of the lower-level employees of the government was very clear. They were perceived as moderately hard-working and efficient, sometimes not as polite to the public as they should be, and in some cases corrupt.

(2) Of the sample taken (the size of the sample was not reported), 24% citicized the police for corruption, while 14% alleged corruption in government hospitals; 22% of the respondents claimed that policemen "cannot or don't fulfil their duties."

(3) About the hospitals, "there were reports of rudeness mainly from doctors, then from nurses, and finally from the amahs." Of the complaints, 23% referred to visits to a government doctor, 17% alleged that they had been "scolded by a nurse," 12% were complaints involving hospital attitudes over babies and births, and an astonishing 13% referred to improper treatment while visiting patients in hospitals. On corruption in hospitals, "the main complaint was the extraction of tips or tea money, principally by the amahs. This was alleged by people visiting friends in order to get in the wards as well as patients themselves."

(4) With the police, "the major single type of complaint was of rudeness

when going into a police station to report something. Five percent (all aged 15-19) claimed that they had been treated rudely when being stopped and searched in the streets. A further 4 percent (aged 20-24) claimed to have been beaten up, or a relative had."

(5) Of the respondents having personal contacts with the police, 22% reported that they had witnessed corruption, mainly what would be described as petty corruption. Asking for "black money" or bribes from hawkers, pak-pai (illegal taxi) drivers, mini-bus drivers, gambling-stall operators, mahjong players, traffic offenders, were all mentioned. It was conservatively estimated that about 110,000 people had experienced corruption from the Hong Kong police principally in a petty form. The report was reassuring, however, in its confirmation of the fact that whatever the complaints made about the police and their manners towards the public, serious crimes (excluding drugs, prosti-tution and gambling, one guesses) got dealt with despite bribery: "There were reports of more serious types of corruption by a few respondents. These were the 4 percent who said they had to pay money when reporting to the CID [Criminal Investigation Department] and 2 percent who reported they had to pay money to find a missing person." In view of the constant barrage of public attacks on the police, the proportion of serious complaints about misbehaviour by the police was remarkably low.

(6) Immigration Department staff "seem to be rude to people . . . when they are applying for re-entry permits." With the Post Office, "practically all cases of rudeness happened . . . when sending a parcel or buying stamps." Much more serious than the instances of corruption and lack of helpfulness mentioned so far were the allegations about the Fire Services. They were accused of "demanding money to put fires out." (Quoted from *Far Eastern Economic Review*, June 25, 1973.)

For the most part, the ordinary people lack the means and the capability to deal effectively with street-level bureaucrats. In traditional China, common people usually tried to shield themselves from government officials by means of "buffers" or intermediaries—normally the gentry—whose social status and education could command respect from officials and hence took the stridency out of the cacophonous relationship between the two parties. In Hong Kong, as we shall see in the next chapter, the intermediary structure is weak. Under such a condition, to avoid having contacts with bureaucrats as far as possible, either through "self-help" activities or to make do with shortage of services, is the only way to relate oneself to the bureaucratic polity.

Since the establishment of the ICAC (Independent Commission Against Corruption) by the Governor in 1974, bureaucratic corruption has declined. If a survey were done today on the attitudes of the Hong Kong Chinese towards the bureaucrats, they would score higher points on their honesty and courtesy. On the other hand, their condescending stance towards their clients and the over-rigid application of administrative regulations probably has changed too much. If anything, the removal of "corruption" as a means to "humanize" bureaucrat-client relationships might even aggravate their impersonality and discourage people who can afford it from approaching the bureaucracy for help. Improvement of the relationships between bureaucrats and clients thus would call for efforts which would subject the bureaucrats, particularly street-level bureaucrats, to some form of client control. And this can certainly be done even if the basic features of the bureaucratic polity remain unchanged.

Political Participation

Findings on the attitude and behaviour in connection with political participation of the Hong Kong Chinese are highly fragmented, and they would preclude any attempt at piecing together a systematic picture of the phenomenon. Nevertheless, the thrust of the findings is unmistakably clear: political participation is usually shied away from by the ordinary people, and the middle-income residents are not much better in this respect.

My 1977 survey found that an overwhelming majority of the respondents, 88.5%, had not had any discussion of public affairs at all with government officials and social leaders, thus indicating the large communication gap between the government and the governed. In fact, aside from the dearth of institutionalized and even non-institutionalized channels of participation in the colony, the sense of citizen duty of the Hong Kong Chinese does not seem to demand much political participation. According to King's study of Kwun Tong residents, only 12.7% of the respondents had an orientation towards the self as an active participant, while 23.9% showed rather an orientation towards the self as a passive subject in the system. Moreover, 63.4% of his respondents either did not know how to exert political influence or had no interest in doing so (1972:14-15).

The social leaders studied by King evinced a diffuse commitment to political participation *in principle*. But when queried about specifics, they did not seem to have ideas about what to participate *for*. The question of "How do you think the ordinary people should participate in the local community affairs?" was asked thirteen local leaders in Kwun Tong by King. All of them unanimously answered that the ordinary people should "actively participate" in local community affairs. This information would definitely indicate that the leaders had an orientation towards the self as an active participant. However, other evidence somewhat contradicts the previous characterization. Among 346 heads of factories, 67 or near 20% of the total gave no opinion on what degree the government should control industry. And among 94 doctors, 43 or near 46% of the total did not give an opinion on whether or not the government should exert more control on medical practices of Western-trained physicians. According to King, these figures suggested that a significant number of the leaders were either ignorant of or lacking a definite orientation towards the input object or towards the self as an active political participant (1972:15).

In my opinion, these seemingly contradictory findings, as well as some others which we have encountered in the past, are not that difficult to make sense of. On the one hand, they show that many of the Hong Kong Chinese have been influenced by modern democratic ideas, which can be found in bits and pieces in textbooks, newspapers, and even in the speeches of government officials. On some occasions, Hong Kong has even been dubbed as an exemplar of "democracy" in Asia, and this is usually rationalized on the grounds that the residents in Hong Kong are able to enjoy a degree of freedom unmatched by many other places on the continent, even though this, in a theoretical sense, has nothing much to do with a democratic political system. The rhetorical use of democratic terms is very common in the colony, even though few people are really dedicated to them or take them seriously. On the other hand, it is utilitarianistic familism, social aloofness and political passivity that are deeply rooted in the objective structural factors found in Hong Kong, and are continuous with the traditional cultural ethos of the Chinese people. Under these cultural themes, the Hong Kong Chinese are handicapped from thinking in terms which transcend the immediate and parochial confines of themselves and their familial groups. In general, the Hong Kong Chinese are prone to think in concrete, piecemeal and short-term ways, relating to things which are directly and immediately experienced and which affect their individual and familial interests. They are not used to thinking in systemic terms or in terms of common interests, as this would require them to take into consideration a large bulk of information on different sectors of society and at different levels of abstraction, couch them in a long-term perspective, and to balance them in such a way that the long-term interests of each sector will be best served. In addition, this kind of thinking will demand the forging of logical and empirical linkages among the disparate elements going into the reasoning and conceptualizing process. If they are forced to think in terms of common interests, they not infrequently will simply have their partisan interests enlarged, as though "what is good for themselves will also be good to society as a whole." Consequently, a diffuse support for democratic ideals and an actual incapacity to see them through are the distinctive traits of the Chinese populace in Hong Kong.

The same incongruence between attitude and actual behaviour is also evident in the case of the young workers studied by Lau and Ho (1982).

A "participatory" attitudinal stance seemed to prevail, but it was seldom substantiated by explicit actions. When asked whether they had taken any action in the past to express their disapproval of a governmental policy which adversely affected their interests, 88.5% of them gave a negative answer. And, among the 7.8% of those who had taken actions, most of them were concerned with trivial matters (e.g., physical conditions in the buildings, noise pollution, etc.), and the actions taken were extremely mild (e.g., writing to newspapers, going to see the government officials concerned). At the attitudinal level, conversely, they seemed to be more "activistic." For example, 46.9% of them claimed that they would take action in the future if they were adversely affected by government policies. When queried as to the kind of action they had contemplated, about 56% of them refused to answer, which indicate that they were still unclear about the channels through which to express their opinions to the government. Among those who gave definite answers, 34.5% would opt for personal contact with the government officials in charge; 22.4% would file complaints through the mass media; 8.5% would seek help from the mutual-aid committees in their buildings and from other kinds of non-governmental organizations; 7.3% would petition to the Governor and other high-level government officials; 6.7% would ask for help from the Urban Council or the UMELCO (see also Chapter 6); and 3% would make public statements or air their complaints to TV, radio and newspaper reporters. Almost all the actions contemplated involve particularistic relationship between the complainant and the government, and collective action against the government is conspicuous by its absence. And, to what extent these contemplated actions will materialize even if the conditions would demand them were ripe is anyone's guess.

Voting in the Urban Council Elections

Until 1982, the Urban Council is the only public body which includes elected members who are voted into office by a small franchise. (Here I exclude the village representative system in the New Territories from discussion because of its limited significance to Hong Kong as a whole). The elected members, twelve in total, constitute half of the membership of the Council, the balance of the membership being appointed by the government. Over the years, the number of eligible voters has expanded. However, even up to 1973, the true maximum possible number of eligible voters is probably less than 600,000 (Miners 1977: 177). The Urban Council is only held responsible for a narrow array of functions related to environmental public health, recreation and amenities and cultural services. Consequently, it has never been a "heavy-weight" in the political arena of Hong Kong, and it is even contemptuously tagged as the "garbage Council" by many Hong Kong residents. Despite its political insignificance, the fact that it contains elected members has drawn attention to the voting patterns in its elections, which provides some indicators of political participation of the Hong Kong residents. Analysis of the voting statistics, however, is fraught with difficulties. The poor voter turnouts are often alluded to as an indicator of the political apathy of the Hong Kong Chinese. But, in view of the political light-weightedness of the Council, it can also be interpreted as the result of the eligible voters' shying away from a futile political exercise. The latter explanation is oftentimes used by critics of the government to support an argument which calls for an opening up of the seats in the more prestigious Legislative Council for election. Up to the present moment this request has not been heeded by the government. My own standpoint is that the voting patterns in the Urban Council elections do reflect to some extent the political orientations of the Hong Kong Chinese. And, unless some conditions have changed, even elections for higher-level "political" offices will not draw a high rate of voter turnout. One of the major reasons for believing so is that Hong Kong so far does not have strong political parties or strong leaders (with strong popular mass bases) which can offer inducements to the voters, canvass them and push them into the voting booths.

Table 4.4 gives the voter turnouts in selected years of the Urban Council elections.

TABLE 4.4
Voter turnouts in Urban Council elections

Year	Registered voters	Votes cast	Percentage voting
1963/65	25,932	5,320	20.5
1965/67	29,529	6,492	22.0
1967/69	26,275	10,189	38.8
1969/71	34,392	8,178	23.8
1971/73	37,788	10,047	26.6
1973/75	31,284	8,674	27.7

Source: From the *Annual Departmental Reports of the Commissioner of Registration of Persons.*

In Urban Council elections, the registered voters are only a small proportion of the eligible voters, who in turn represent a small percentage of the total adult population. Moreover, the actual voters are only a minority in the population of registered voters. The low voter turnout rates are vivid indicators of the political apathy of the Hong Kong Chinese. If it is true that the voter turnout rate is contingent upon the eligible voters' perception of the decision-making power attached to the elected offices, then the small number of eligible voters who did take the trouble to vote should do so because they believed that they were voting into office candidates who could wield influence over important matters. But such is not the case. Hoadley had interviewed 155 Chinese adults chosen by interval sample from the South Kowloon section of the 1967 *Final Register of Voters*, and the findings provide some data on the attitudes of enfranchised individuals. Fully 80% of the respondents said they had no interest at all in the election campaign. However, 86% could recall hearing about the elections in two or more ways (newspapers, radio, TV, handbills, candidate visit, etc.), so most voters were at least aware of the campaign and the impending election. Forty-four per cent professed to have a favourite candidate and named that candidate for the interviewer; again, this indicates that voters were informed. And 57% of the respondents scored either three or four out of four on a "citizen duty scale" constructed by Hoadley. The actual rate of voter turnout was 38.8% for the eligible and registered population.

> Why was the turn-out so high [in comparison with previous elections] when the interest, as measured not only by the survey but also by press coverage and level of compaign activity, was so low? The high citizen-duty scores are on clue; apparently those individuals who were registered felt some obligation to the *system* of elections. When asked "What did voting in the election mean to you, personally?" the modal answer (32 per cent) was "to do my duty, to be a good citizen" or in words to that effect. Equally frequently (31 per cent) voters responded that they voted to elect a good man, or a good representative who would work for the people's benefit. A third popular response, related to the first, was "to exercise my right to vote" (15 per cent).
>
> Another indicator of attitudes toward inputs and the self as political actor is the answer to the question, "What is the purpose of elections in Hong Kong?" While 24 per cent of respondents volunteered no answer, and while another 24 per cent answered that elections were useless, a farce, or a Government show, the majority was more positive. Forty-four per cent stressed the fact that the election gave citizens a chance to participate in Government, to express opinions, to feel closer to Government, and to gain practice for eventual self-government. Another 8 per cent stressed instrumental features of the election: that it might lead to better Government policy, that it would stimulate public service, that it would lead to improved community conditions, or that it was just good in some unspecified way. (Hoadley 1970:214)

To the extent that a preponderance of the registered voters viewed their registration or voting as the result of their non-instrumental political values, they were not deterred from doing so by the limited power of the Urban Council. To extrapolate the matter further, it seems to me that those eligible voters who fail to register do so *not* because they consider the Urban Council too powerless, but because they do not share the values of those who do register, values which are non-parochial and non-instrumental in character.

And these values are incompatible with the values—utilitarianistic familism, social aloofness and political passivity—which we find are hallmarks of a majority of the Hong Kong Chinese. Consequently, the low voter registration and turnout rates are not surprising. The small number of registered voters who seem to espouse "modern citizen values" would be the exception that proves the rule. It is worth mentioning, moreover, that the eligible voters are mostly middle class in status. If anything, the poor voter registration and turnout in the Urban Council elections underscore the political passivity of the middle sector in Hong Kong, and its inability to play any supervisory role over the bureaucratic polity. In fact, the middle-class Chinese so far have displayed a degree of political quiescence comparable to that evinced by the strata below them.

RECAPITULATION

To recapitulate, this and the previous chapters delineate the parameters in the normative orientations and structural arrangements of a fragmented and atomistic Chinese society. This society has in the past been made up of sojourners and has only recently obtained a settled population. Therefore, discontinuity in the composition of membership is its distinctive trait, and it explains the relative futility of a historical approach to the understanding of this society in its present form.

The Chinese society is largely apolitical, and the major orientation of the Chinese people is diverted away from the political realm towards the sphere of the economic wherein the goods which the Hong Kong society is able to promise are supposed to reside. The cardinal importance attached to material values, the short-term time horizon and the emphasis on social stability (which encompasses political order) are the three attitudinal poles which undergird the behaviour of the Hong Kong Chinese. They are pervasive in the normative/behavioural syndrome of the Chinese people which I have dubbed "utilitarianistic familism." Under the umbrella of utilitarianistic familism, instrumental concerns loom large in the construction of the familial groups, the articulation of familial goals and the manipulation of interpersonal relationships.

To a people so immersed in the frenetic search for private gains, the larger society and the bureaucratic polity appear to be generally remote and elusive, except when they are seen as instrumentalities to familial interests. The minimal involvement of the Hong Kong Chinese in social and political activities is natural consequence.

These apolitical and asocial attitudes find reinforcements in the resourcefulness of the familial groups to cater to the mundane needs of the Chinese populace, thanks to the economic prosperity which Hong Kong so far has been able to create. This vibrant economy has further dampened the possibility of class conflict by implanting in the mind of the ordinary people the conception of an expanding-sum economic game, in which all players will benefit, though differentially. Consequently, instead of being perceived to be antagonists, the affluent in society are posited as models for envy and emulation. In the same fashion, other potential lines of division are expediently brushed aside so that familial interests can be maximally served amidst social stability and economic prosperity.

5. Linkages between the Bureaucratic Polity and the Chinese Society

The elemental organization unit of the Chinese society in Hong Kong is the familial group, which constitutes the primary focus of identification of the Chinese people. It is also the core of a primary resource network within which resources and services are exchanged, and through which many of the salient needs of the Hong Kong Chinese are met. Relatively speaking, of course, familial groups are of lesser importance to those who enjoy higher incomes, and hence are more resourceful than those whose lower incomes make it imperative that they engage in reciprocal exchanges with their familial intimates. Nevertheless, inasmuch as the bulk of the Hong Kong Chinese are in the lower income categories (because of the inequitable distribution of income), the significance of familial groups in the structure of the Chinese society cannot be exaggerated. Even for those with higher incomes, the continual tenacity of familial ethos would preclude a wholesale extrication of themselves from familial groups. Evidently, Hong Kong can be said to be an atomistic society, comprising a large conglomeration of familial groups whose relationship with one another and with the bureaucratic polity is minimal and infused with mutual suspicion.

As we have already seen before, in juxtaposition with the atomistic Chinese society is a bureaucratic polity, with its deliberately delimited role conceptions and penchant for the maintenance of its political autonomy. One of the major characteristics of this "secluded" bureaucracy, which has serious repercussions for its relationship with the Chinese society, is that it lacks both the desire and the capacity to "penetrate" into the Chinese society and mold it according to its wishes. Consequently, linkages between the bureaucracy and the Chinese society cannot be established by means of a series of administratively controlled mechanisms which have the explicit purposes of regulating the behaviour of the populace and mobilizing their resources to supplement those provided by the administration. Such mechanisms are commonly found in many of the administrative states in other parts of the world. Other common linkage devices such as political parties, electoral systems, legislatures packed with elected politicians and patron-client networks are conspicuous in Hong Kong by their absence. Even though both the bureaucracy and the Chinese society display attitudes and behavioural patterns which would minimize their involvement with one another, it cannot be denied that in a relatively industrialized society such as Hong Kong linkages between the two parties have to be forged if smooth governance is to be accomplished. The overriding obsession of the government with law and order, coupled with the fact that the provision of a battery of basic services to the populace is one of its major functions, would mean that contacts with the Chinese society is unavoidable. Information about the attitudes and behaviour of the Chinese people, and their evaluation of the government and the services it delivers are essential to policy-making inside the bureaucracy. Furthermore, through some forms of linkage, the bureaucracy would of course like to obtain a certain amount of political support and willingness to abide by the rules it has set down for society. On the part of the Chinese people, some linkages with the bureaucratic polity are also deemed to be indispensable if for no other reasons than to exert influence on it so that more favourable public policies can be obtained, or that the rough edges of unpopular policies be smoothened out.

In Hong Kong, the linkage between the bureaucracy and the Chinese society is achieved through three main channels: intermediate organizations, the Chinese elite and officially-sponsored linkage devices. Empirically speaking, however, the three channels are interrelated. For instance, the Chinese elite is involved to a large extent in both the intermediate organizations and the officially-sponsored devices. There is no doubt about it that these mechanisms do serve to integrate the bureaucracy and the Chinese society to a certain extent, and hence facilitate communication between them. Nevertheless, by and large these mechanisms are weak. Their major function, as seen from empirical evidence, is to form a pipeline through which information can flow between the bureaucracy and the Chinese society. But in the performance of this function, these pipelines are far from satisfactory. Not only are they deficient in maintaining a steady and adequate flow of information in both directions, they are also ineffective in bringing the opinion and desires of the vast bulk of the Chinese populace to bear upon the decision-makers in the bureaucracy. As a result, these mechanisms are largely the means whereby the decisions and wishes of the government are unilaterally transmitted to the Chinese society, though because of the weakness of these mechanisms, the recipients of these messages constitutes but a small portion of the Hong Kong Chinese. All in all, the existence of these mechanisms have not contributed much to the integration of the bureaucratic polity and the Chinese society, nor have they involved the Chinese society into the decision-making process in the government. The defectiveness of these linkage mechanisms is a major characteristic of the minimally integrated social-political system of Hong Kong.

Before discussing the arguments raised in previous paragraphs, let me point out that when I speak about the low degree of linkage between the bureau-cratic polity and the Chinese society, by "Chinese society" I mean the vast bulk of the Chinese populace in Hong Kong. There is no need to belabour the point that there is a highly inequitable distribution of opportunities of access to the bureaucracy among the Hong Kong Chinese. For the Chinese elite, access to the government is made much easier by their social status, their exclusive clubs and associations, and their personal acquaintance with high-ranking government officials. For the majority of those in middle-income groups and for almost all of those in lower-income groups, however, access to the government is much more difficult. The middle-income groups, who are the beneficiaries of the post-World War II economic boom, and are enjoying a comfortable and continually rising standard of living, can be considered to be the staunch supporters of the status quo. The relative lack of access to the bureaucracy does not necessarily lead to political dissent or dissatisfaction. Since our focus in this book is on the problem of political stability in Hong Kong, both the Chinese elite and the middle-income groups can be said in general to be reliable stabilizing forces. Therefore, as the Chinese people in the lower-income groups constitute the majority of the populace in Hong Kong, their relationship with the bureaucracy and the implications of this relationship for political stability in Hong Kong constitute the focus of analysis in this chapter.

THE CHINESE ELITE AS LINKAGE MECHANISM

Since the Chinese elite plays a prominent role in both the intermediate organizations and the officially-sponsored linking devices in Hong Kong, an investigation into its composition and its structural location in the social-political system is a prerequisite to an understanding of the relationship between the bureaucratic polity and the Chinese society.

As a backdrop for the analysis of the role of the Chinese elite in Hong Kong, a slight digression on the Chinese gentry in traditional (mainly late imperial) China would be helpful. In a certain sense, traditional China can be likened to Hong Kong in that there was also a juxtaposition of a bureaucratic regime and a society composed of a multitude of familistic and quasi-familistic groups. In such a social-political context, the role of the Chinese gentry as an intermediary between the bureaucratic state and the people was critical to the maintenance of political stability. This intermediary role of the gentry was widely recognized by both the officialdom and the people alike, and the gentry as a group was socialized into this role through long periods of Confucian education and participation in the elite culture of the society.

In retrospect, it can be said that the effectiveness of the Chinese gentry as an intermediary linking the state and the society hinged upon several factors. First, Confucianism inculcated into the Chinese gentry both a sense of

obligation to the state and to the common people, and with a sense of
duty to harmonize the relationship between the two. With regard to the
common people in particular, the gentry invariably adopted a paternalistic
and protective posture. Even though there is no denying that their material
interests were eminently served through their intermediary role, still the
responsibility to look after the interests of the underlings in the face of
bureaucratic arbitrariness was strong among them. Second, the function of
mediation was made possible by a similarity of outlook between the officials
and the gentry. As a matter of fact, there was a constant interchange of
personnel between the two groups. Officials in their retirement would be
reverted to the gentry status, while there was always hope for the gentry to
enter into officialdom. The similarity in outlook, ethos and interests greased
the interaction between the officials and the gentry, and facilitated joint
participation in the solution of problems which afflicted particular areas or
particular groups of individuals. Third, and most important, the Chinese
gentry was an integral part of the local societies in which it found itself. The
status and effectiveness of a particular gentry member was contingent upon
the recognition and support of his constituents, who might at the same time
be his fellow *tsu* 族 (clan) members and his village or district co-inhabitants.
In a general sense, except for the upper-level gentry members, most of the
gentry members based their power and influence on particular geographical
areas. It was as recognized leaders of local groups that the gentry introduced
themselves to the officials. The ability to mobilize support behind them gave
them a certain degree of political independence which the officials had to
take into account. Dependent on the officialdom for recognition and bureaucratic positions as they were, it was still true to say that as a result of their
"rootedness" in the people, the gentry as a group could command concessions
and respect from the imperial bureaucracy.

As Hong Kong is a society of migrants in search for economic and political
security under British rule, the Chinese gentry as a political group does not
exist. The efforts on the part of the colonial government in the early years of
Hong Kong to attract Chinese personalities with respectable status to settle
down in Hong Kong came to nought. This failure is not difficult to understand.
Given the anti-material stance of the Chinese gentry, the burgeoning commercial city of Hong Kong was seen by them as the sanctuary of the corrupt
forces of a mercantile and materialist West, and was thus objectionable.

Under the historical and structural conditions of Hong Kong, it is inevitable
that the Chinese elite who rose to prominence were based largely on economic
power, with a small portion of them grounding their status on the mastery of
Western knowledge. With the development of Hong Kong, the composition of
the Chinese elite became more differentiated, but it is still true that the

economic elite constitutes the most important and influential part of the Chinese elite.

Carl Smith, in a study of the Chinese elite in Hong Kong in the 1841-72 period, traced its emergence in a concise manner:

> [In the first decade, the elite] was recruited from a few successful contractors and builders, several government servants, compradores of foreign firms, and Chinese Christians attached to military groups.
>
> The second decade of Hong Kong's history was marked by an influx of population and capital caused by disturbed conditions in South China created by the Taiping Rebellion. This influx turned into an exodus when hostilities began between the British and Chinese in 1857. But war brought more compradores to Hong Kong as foreign firms moved down from Canton.
>
> In the third decade there was a revival of trade, and a growing merchant class provided its share of elite. By the end of the 1860s a clearly defined elite group had established itself, providing leadership for the Chinese community. (1971:74-75)

Since the nineteenth century, the rise to prominence of the economic elite continued unabated. The postwar economic boom and the shift of Hong Kong from an entrepôt to an industrial city have given rise to an industrial/ entrepreneurial elite who as of now are the dominant economic elite in this Chinese society.

Viewed from one angle, because of the relative recency of Hong Kong as a British colony and the absence of an entrenched indigenous Chinese elite before the imposition of British rule, it can be said that the Chinese elite have never consolidated into a highly organized and exclusive power group. From another point of view, however, the compactness of the colony and the intimate business and social connections among the elite members foster common outlooks and interests reinforced by inter-marriage among a few core elite members and their offspring. Since wealth is the primary criterion for entry into elite status, the Chinese elite as a group cannot deny it to those who are able to "make it" in Hong Kong, even though those who managed to accumulate their wealth several generations earlier would tend to look down upon the upstarts who have yet to learn the cultural styles befitting elite status. Despite the fine distinctions within the Chinese elite and the intense economic competition among them, the fact that they are similarly located in the social structure of Hong Kong would mean that in general they share a common orientation towards the bureaucracy, and towards policy priorities. In short, the Chinese elite in Hong Kong are a distinctive interest group in itself (Davies 1977).

What is the intermediary role of the Chinese elite? In order to answer this question two tendencies in the relationship between the Chinese elite and the social-political system of Hong Kong have to be studied, and the result of the working of these two tendencies is a weakening of the Chinese elite as a linkage mechanism between the government and the common people. First, the Chinese elite play an increasingly conspicuous role in rendering service to the government, thus serving a para-administrative function in the bureaucratic polity. As such they are being co-opted into the bureaucratic polity by the government through a variety of appointments to serve in public bodies.[1] The co-optation of the Chinese elite is intended to serve basically two purposes: One is to legitimize the political system, a process described as "the administrative absorption of politics" by Ambrose King:

> By this we mean a process by which the government co-opts the political forces, often represented by elite groups, into an administrative decision-making body, thus achieving some level of elite integration; as a consequence, the governing authority is made legitimate, a loosely integrated political community is established. (1975:424)

Another purpose is to solicit information, on technical matters and on the Chinese society, from the Chinese elite so as to improve administrative decision-making. Since the Second World War, with the growing complexity of the industrial society, the ability of the Chinese elite to render professional and technical advice to the government has become increasingly important in obtaining official recognition of elite status. Before the Second World War, it was those Chinese elite members who were deeply involved in the organizational life of the Chinese society and were recognized as its leaders who were picked out for consultation and recognition by the government. In the words of

[1] The Chinese elite co-opted by the government represents a narrow sector of the Chinese society of Hong Kong. Take the Unofficial Members of the Legislative Council as the example. With a few exceptions, they are men of wealth. According to the computation by Ambrose King, "among the Chinese Unofficial Members, prior to 1964, over 90% are from 'established rich' families and are among the small circle of elite in the Chinese community. After the mid-1960s, another category of persons has been rising— the 'new rich,' representing the ever-increasing industrial force" (1975:426). Another study of the Hong Kong elite co-opted by the government, which included both Chinese and non-Chinese elites, came to similar conclusions:
"The employers and business voices that are heard in government circles come from firms which are either [large] or which are non-manufacturing concerns occupied in banking, accounting, stockbroking or import/export businesses. These circles contribute 95.4 per cent of the members of the tribunal panels, 37 per cent of the members of the educational boards, 66.4 per cent of the membership of the thirteen general committees, and 52.9 per cent of the voices on [the Executive Council, the Legislative Council and the Urban Council.] In brief, they command a two-thirds voice in advice and policy ratification. In comparison, the voice even of the charitable organizations is small and . . . that voice is in no way 'independent' of the business world. Organised labour and Hong Kong's many low income groups have a pathetically small voice, negligible in advice and information and wholly absent in decision making." (Davies 1977:63)

Lethbridge, "they were chosen only *after* they had worked themselves up through a Chinese system of influence and power, understood and accepted by the Government itself. Even before a Chinese reached the Legislative or Executive Council, he was vetted [*sic*] by his own community" (1969:82).

The second tendency is that the gradual extension of official recognition to the Chinese elite based on individual achievements and expertise drives elite members away from those intermediate organizations which in the past had played a significant role as an intermediary between the government and the ordinary people, which increasingly suffer from a shortage of leadership talent. In the prewar period, one of the ways to convert economic power into social status, and subsequently official recognition, is to obtain leadership positions in those Chinese voluntary associations which engaged in philanthropic and self-help activities as well as served as intermediaries between the government and the Chinese society. This processes of status mobility had been lucidly described by Lethbridge:

> To achieve high status, usually a function of wealth for the Chinese in Hong Kong, for the higher reaches of the civil service were closed and there was no native gentry class, a Chinese had to "buy" himself into various social positions by displays of munificence and . . . by participation in a wide range of charitable and welfare organizations known to the Chinese community. To achieve high status a Chinese had, therefore, to prove himself by public works. . . .
> It follows that prominent Chinese in Hong Kong were prominent firstly because they were rich; but that with wealth a number of prestigeful positions became available. The rules of the game were well known to socially mobile Chinese and the system was . . . a Chinese adaptation to the peculiarities of a colonial regime. This should be noted that the acquisition of wealth was more important in Hong Kong than in China proper, for Hong Kong has never been a mere microcosm of the homeland. There are some differences in social organization between the two. (1969:84-85)

There are two other reasons for the diversion of attention of the Chinese elite away from those intermediate organizations which have both in the past, and, though in a much diluted form, at present linked the government and the common people. One of these will be discussed in greater detail in the next section, and it involves the gradual weakening of these organizations in the last few decades or so. The erosion of their social prestige, resource and membership bases makes them no longer attractive targets for elite involvement, particularly to those who are more ambitious. The gradual abandonment of them by the government itself would also convince the Chinese elite that affiliation with them would be a fruitless endeavour if the goal is to obtain official recognition of elite status. Another factor is the gradual weakening of the Confucian ethos among the Chinese elite. Compared to the Chinese elite in the past, the postwar generation of Chinese elite is much

more individualistic, Westernized, professional and rational in their orientations. If they are to have organizational affiliations, they would usually choose
the professional and business associations, and the charity or philanthropic
organizations with Western origins, which are of much higher prestige than
those traditional Chinese organizations which are now in decline. As
organizations catering to the interests of particular groups whose memberships
are homogeneous in terms of social class and education, professional and
business associations play at best a marginal role in linking the bureaucracy
and Chinese society. The same can be said for philanthropic/civic organizations such as the Lions Club and the Rotary Club.

What all this leads to is that, in the postwar period while the Chinese elite
is being co-opted in growing numbers into the bureaucratic polity, at the
same time it ironically is increasingly detached from the ordinary Chinese
people. In the past, when the Chinese elite was more involved in "cross-class"
intermediate organizations, its relationship to the sub-elites was much closer.
These sub-elites had much less prestige in the Chinese society, but their
leaders were closer to the people, since they were in charge of the day-to-day
running of the intermediate organizations. Consequently, they were able to
play a more effective role as an intermediary. Nowadays, the three parties are
no longer organically linked together, thus creating a serious communication
gap among the various hierarchical levels within the Chinese society. Because
of the ineffectiveness of the Chinese elite as a mediating mechanism, the
compartmentalization of the bureaucratic polity and the Chinese society
becomes more acute.

In a context of organizational detachment of the Chinese elite from the
Chinese people, it can be argued that some functions of mediation between
the government and the Chinese society can still be performed by the elite. In
fact, the "representation" of the interests of the Chinese society before the
administration is still considered important by the elite, and on some
occasions individual elite members act with this purpose in mind. But even if
the intention is still sincere, the actual execution of the mediation role under
a condition of organizational detachment is fraught with difficulties. One is
the organizational vacuum lying between the elite and the Chinese people
which inhibits the flow of information between them. A consequence of this
is that the elite lack sufficient and reliable knowledge about the attitudes and
behavioural patterns of the people. Contacts between them are extremely
rare. Our research on the young workers in Hong Kong showed that social
leaders (someone with "face") were the least significant channel through
which help was to be sought (Lau and Ho 1982). Similarly, the study of the
residents of Kwun Tong by Choi Ching-yan showed that more than fifty
per cent of the respondents did not know of any leader who could be of help

when something drastic happened in the community or did not consider that any leader who could help existed (Social Research Centre 1976:135).

Another factor dampens the effectiveness of the Chinese elite even if they attempt to play the intermediary role is the overwhelming dominance of the bureaucracy in the political arena. Inasmuch as the Chinese elite members are co-opted into the bureaucratic polity individually by the government, they are dependent on it for official recognition. To an individual elite member, official recognition of elite status is of enormous symbolic importance in enhancing his overall social status and prestige in the Chinese society. And, if he is an industrialist or merchant, official recognition is also a very important asset in establishing business connections.

Given this dependency on the bureaucracy, any attempt to confront it directly by raising radically dissenting voices will be discreetly suppressed by the elite themselves. Besides, the basic orientation of the Chinese elite towards political stability and economic prosperity is a powerful restraining force in itself. Consequently, vigorous articulation of interests in behalf of the common people and against the interests of the government is relatively rare, and an atmosphere of harmony between the government and the Chinese elite prevails most of the times. The general submissiveness and extreme moderation of the co-opted Chinese elite and their consequent timidity in addressing serious social issues are oftentimes castigated by newspaper editorials and independent researchers (Rear 1971:75-81; *South China Morning Post*, April 4, 1971).

The asymmetrical relationship between the co-opted Chinese elite and the bureaucracy is also evident in the arena of public decision-making, wherein the former play largely a marginal role. Even though the advice and opinion of the Chinese elite might be attended to by government officials, the latter monopolize the prerogative to make the final decisions. The lack of powerful mass bases on the part of the Chinese elite seriously reduces their stature in the eyes of the officials, and weakens their ability to press demands upon the government. The decision-making processes in the advisory committees,[2] which are set up by the government with the express purpose of tapping the expert opinions of the elite (both Chinese and non-Chinese), show vividly the dominance of the officials. For one thing, personalities with sharply critical views of the government and its policies will be adroitly excluded from membership in these committees. Another thing is that government officials seated in these committees are generally intolerant of criticisms from the unofficial members there. The editorial of the *South China Morning Post*

[2]In 1978 there were about 90 statutory councils, boards or committees, about 50 permanent non-statutory bodies with unofficial members and 16 permanent non-statutory bodies with official members only, numbering about 156 in all, with a total membership of perhaps ten times that figure.

on November 4, 1978, for example, quoted some harsh comments on these committees from Miss Lydia Dunn, an Unofficial Member of the Legislative Council. "Unfortunately," she said, "some committees are chaired by officials whose minds are made up, who cannot accept any form of criticism and who, as a consequence, are suspected—rightly or wrongly—of not being prepared to recommend for appointment to their committees anyone who is known to be a critic." This phenomenon of administrative authoritarianism can also be noted in the following evaluation of the advisory committees from John Walden, the Director of Home Affairs. This evaluation is distinctive not only in its candidness, but also in the fact that it should come out from a high-ranking government official:

> I sit on a number of these [statutory and non-statutory advisory committees, councils and boards] and if they are typical then it seems to me that there is a great deal of room for improvement both in the way they are operated and in their coverage of the field of government policy making, planning and decision making.
>
> There are important government committees on which the public has never been represented, there are statutory committees that are used to rubber-stamp government decisions and there are departments exercising powers which would be better exercised with unofficial advice but which do not have an advisory committee.
>
> The appointment of unofficial members as chairmen of committees, the nomination of a proportion of unofficial members by reliable organisations instead of by government selection, the holding of committee meetings after normal office hours so as to make it easier for busy people to attend, monitoring the quality of papers tabled for discussion, are some obvious ways of improving the system that have never been seriously explored. (1980:6)

INTERMEDIATE ORGANIZATIONS
AS LINKAGE MECHANISM[3]

The Chinese people are renowned for their voluntary organizational capabilities. Through establishing voluntary bodies to cater to their social and cultural problems, the Chinese in Hong Kong, since the ceding of the place to the British, have demonstrated their ability to maintain social peace and a decent level of social well-being among their fellows. Not uncommonly, these voluntary associations were able to expand their functions both to come to grips with larger-scale social problems (like the Po Leung Kuk which helps girls and young women needing care and protection (Lethbridge 1978:71-103)) and to assume the political function of mediating between the Chinese

[3] Portions of the material in this and the next sections are derived from Lau (1981a). I want to thank the University of California Press for granting me the permission to reprint portions of the article.

people and the alien British authorities. In the latter function, the Tung Wah Hospital is a case in point. The functions of the Tung Wah in the past were never purely medical. In fact, in conducted a variety of philanthropic activities, and served as the unofficial "government" of the Chinese community in the eyes of both the British colonial authority and the Chinese government (*Ibid.*: 52-70). Through these intermediate organizations and their leaders, the interests of the Chinese were heard, and, to a certain extent, taken care of by the colonial administrators. And the Chinese leaders of these organizations were "seldom afraid to press vigorously their own points of view and that of the Chinese community as a whole" (*Ibid.*: 82).

The *de facto* autonomy of the Chinese community, under the control of a cohesive layer of prosperous Chinese businessmen and social notables, was deliberately encouraged by the British authorities before the Second World War. This autonomy was further enhanced by the right granted to the Chinese to operate a private police force of their own (the District Watchmen) (*Ibid.*: 104-29). The reliance of the British colonial administration on the indigenous organizations of the Chinese for administrative and political purposes had in fact segregated the Chinese community from the colonial government. The Chinese leaders provided the link between the two on the one hand, and mobilized resources within the Chinese community to take care of its own needs on the other. Under such an arrangement, depoliticization and political peace were maintained. Furthermore, the unrelenting fluidity of the Chinese population and their low sociopolitical aspirations, coupled with the authoritarian nature of Chinese leadership, ensured that political issues, if any, seldom spill over beyond the boundaries of the Chinese community.[4]

The decade immediately after the restoration of British rule in Hong Kong at the conclusion of the Second World War witnessed the virtual indispensability of intermediate organizations in the colony. The massive influx of Chinese refugees into Hong Kong, the gloomy economic and employment conditions, the wide-ranging social problems awaiting remedies, and the meagreness of resources in the hands of the government aggravated the urgency to mobilize and channel societal resources and initiative to cope with the "crisis." Moreover, the unpreparedness of the colonial government to tackle problems of such magnitude, and the inexperience of the understaffed bureaucracy schooled so far in classical laissez-faire doctrines reinforced the urgent need for voluntary efforts. In that decade, there was a proliferation of intermediate bodies of various kinds. They included community organizations like the Kaifong Associations (neighbourhood organizations), and non-territorial

[4]The most important demands for political participation taken place in Hong Kong before the Second World War were initiated by British merchants and entrepreneurs (Endacott 1964b:104-29).

organizations based on ascriptive and functional ties, such as clansmen associations, district associations and chambers of commerce (*shang hui* 商會). In many chambers of commerce, ascriptive ties in the forms of district and dialectal connections loomed very large in spite of their supposedly general nature.

All these intermediate organizations served the Chinese community in a variety of ways: welfare provisions for the needy, job referrals, political representation, education, physical accommodation of new immigrants, recreation, financial aid, legal and administrative assistance, reinforcement of group solidarity, cultural preservation and the conferral of status to those serving as leaders. A majority of the Chinese elite were involved in the activities of these organizations, primarily as honorary or actual leaders, thus conferring upon these organizations the status of *bona fide* organizations of the Chinese people. "Only the extremely wealthy are unlikely to belong to *huis* [organizations], and even a very rich man may join one of these peculiarly Chinese co-operatives on occasion as a means to help a friend in need of a loan" (Burton 1958:7).

Take the Kiangsu-Chekiang Provincial Association as an example. It was one of the most important organizations of this kind at that time in Hong Kong, because approximately 200,000 refugees from the Shanghai area poured into Hong Kong at the time of the Communist takeover of China, and these people were a long way from home. It had a membership of 8,000 men, almost all of whom were successful businessmen. Among the refugees, about 15,000 of them (almost all ex-soldiers) had absolutely no relatives or friends to help them, and hence most of the Association's requests for aid came from this group. The Association served also as an informal employment contact office, through which the refugees were found employment in many cases in the industrial enterprises of their fellow Shanghainese (Barnett 1953:5-6).

The aggregate efforts of these organizations contributed in no small measure to the integration of the new immigrants into the urban society of Hong Kong. The dependence of many ordinary people on these organizations for service provisions subjected them to the informal control of these organizations and their leaders in one way or another. Though it was necessarily true that many Chinese people were apathetic to these organizations and did not participate in their activities, their structural and functional viability could not be denied. Their functions in organizing the Chinese community and in linking it up with the larger political order by serving as intermediaries were in hindsight well-nigh indispensable.

To the government, these organizations served basically two main purposes. On the one hand, they served as administrative ancillaries, supplementing the administrative work of the bureaucracy. For example, the Kaifong Associations in the 1950s played a prominent role in the arbitration of family conflicts which abounded in these difficult times. In addition, these organizations served as relatively effective mechanisms whereby the Chinese community could be brought under some measure of administrative control. Through the Secretary for Chinese Affairs, the government maintained some forms of regular contact with many of these organizations, and through these contacts tried to obtain information on the Chinese society and transmit the intentions and policies of the government to the public.

> The Secretary for Chinese Affairs is, except in regard to the special responsibilities of the Public Relations Officer, the Governor's main channel of direct communication with the Chinese people of Hong Kong. In this capacity he is also responsible to Government for helping to assess trends in Chinese public opinion, for advising on Chinese customs or beliefs, and for assisting in the presentation of official policy to the Chinese public. Generally, the Secretary for Chinese Affairs should also advise on any aspect of relationships between government departments and Chinese residents.
>
> For the better discharge of his responsibilities the Secretary for Chinese Affairs is required to maintain and as far as may be practicable improve his relationships and direct contacts with lawful Chinese societies and traditional organizations in Hong Kong. (*Annual Report of the Secretary for Chinese Affairs*, 1958-1959:1)

In the last fifteen years or so, the decline of these organizations as functional intermediaries between the government and the ordinary people was a well-known phenomenon to the government, the general public, and the organizational leaders themselves. One of the indicators of this decline is their decreasing importance in the eyes of government officials, who were increasingly reluctant to contact them or treat their leaders as "spokesmen" of the Chinese society. Another indicator is the diminishing role of the organizational leaders in the moulding of public opinion in the Chinese community. While their activities and functions were still reported in some newspapers, they were no longer able to catch the eye of the public. As empirical research on the recent development of these organizations is scanty, the conditions conducive to this long-term decline process can only be surmised.

In the case of the Kaifong Associations, the process of decline can be illustrated by the shrinkage of their active and passive membership, the depletion of their financial resources, the failure to recruit young and dynamic leaders, and the inability to execute many of the functions which formerly constituted the mainstay of their performance. The incessant bickering among the Kaifong leaders themselves further detracted from the internal solidarity of a movement whose very survival was already in serious jeopardy (Wong 1971, 1972a, 1972b).

A glance at the financial status and activities of a representative group of

Kaifong Associations in 1978 will throw light on the moribund conditions of these organizations.[5]

The Aberdeen Kaifong Association
Major services provided (and recipients): funeral expenses contributory scheme (228), emergency relief (10), medical service (21,000) and primary education (160). Budget: HK$350,000. Major sources of revenue: membership dues and donations. Number of membership: 3,200. Estimated active membership: 100.

The Chai Wan Resettlement Kaifong Welfare Association
Major services provided (and recipients): kindergarten (160), medical service (9,125), emergency relief (700) and funeral expenses contributory scheme (3). Budget: HK$60,000. Major sources of revenue: membership dues, charges/fees and donations. Number of members: 4,000 families. Estimated active membership: 150.

Cheung Sha Wan Kaifong Welfare Association
Major services provided (and recipients): assistantships (3) and funeral expenses contributory scheme (40). Budget: HK$60,000. Major sources of revenue: membership dues, donations and contributions for specific purposes. Number of members: 1,200. Estimated active membership: 120.

The Chuk Yuen Cottage Area Kaifong Welfare Advancement Committee
Major service provided (and recipients): financial aid (1,800). Budget: HK$18,000. Major sources of revenue: membership dues and donations. Number of members: 300. Estimated active membership: 250.

The Mongkok Kaifong Association
Major services provided (and recipients): medical service (15,000), loan services (nil), emergency relief (200) and funeral expenses contributory scheme (2). Budget: HK$200,000. Major sources of revenue: membership dues and donations. Number of members: 13,000. Estimated active membership: 150.

The Shamshuipo Kaifong Association
Major services provided (and recipients): medical service (12,000), scholarships (no data), emergency relief (1), primary education (1,000) and new year gifts (500). Budget: HK$140,000. Major sources of revenue: membership dues and donations. Number of members: 1,200. Estimated active membership: no data.

---

[5]Data on the intermediate organizations were collected by Dr. Ho Kam-fai and myself, with the help of two research assistants, in the summer of 1978. Officers of the organizations were interviewed on the phone about conditions in their organizations.

The Tai Hang Sai Kaifong Welfare Association
Major services provided (and recipients): medical service (10,000) and funeral expenses contributory scheme (120). Budget: HK$40,000. Major sources of revenue: membership dues, charges/fees, donations and contributions for specific purposes. Number of members: 2,300. Estimated active membership: 100.

The Tsimshatsui Kaifong Association
Major services provided (and recipients): medical service (31,300), primary education (no data) and emergency relief (2,000). Budget: HK$83,000. Major source of revenue: donations. Number of members: 2,600. Estimated active membership: 520.

The Wan Tau Hom Resettlement Kaifong Welfare Association
Major service provided (and recipients): material relief (130). Budget: HK$24,000. Major sources of revenue: membership dues and donations. Number of members: 500. Estimated active membership: 130.

The Yaumati Kaifong Welfare Advancement Association
Major service provided (and recipients): medical service (8,000). Budget: HK$50,000. Major sources of revenue: membership dues and donations. Number of members: 1,200. Estimated active membership: 150.

When we take into consideration the fact that the populations supposedly served by these Kaifong Associations range from several tens of thousands to several hundreds of thousands, the figures presented above are depressing. Moreover, a lion's share of the tiny budgets of these organizations was earmarked for the upkeep of physical equipment and for employee emoluments.

In a study of the Shek Kip Mei and Tsz Wan Shan Housing Estates, two lower-class residential areas, Angela Kan found that more than 90% of the residents there did not make use of the services provided by their Kaifong Associations. Among the reasons given by the respondents, it is revealing to note that "don't know of its existence," "no time" and "no interest" were the most frequently cited (1975:30). Similarly, in a study of Kwun Tong in 1976, C. Y. Choi found that when asked to give the names of three Kaifong leaders in the community and the organizations they represented, 94.9% of his 1,293 respondents failed to give any answer (Social Research Centre 1976:135). These scattered pieces of evidence forcefully attest to the obscurity of these community organizations in the areas where they are located.

The mediating role of the Kaifongs, even in their prime, was performed only moderately effectively. Based on interviews with a group of Kaifong leaders in the late 1960s, Aline Wong found that the majority of her respondents believed that the government's policy towards their Kaifongs was, in general, supportive. But this was only a small majority (55%). Of the remaining number of leaders, a few (3%) said outright that the government was not supportive at all, while another 3% were bitter about the whole business, accusing the government of making use of the Chinese to "rule" the Chinese. On balance, the proportion of leaders thinking that the government's attitude had been unfriendly was almost as much as the proportion of leaders thinking the opposite. Upon further probing, it was found that in general, the opinions of the Kaifong leaders were seldom solicited by the government, apart from the representation which the leaders made to it on their own initiative. Even in the matter of Kaifong representations, it was not certain how many of the leaders' suggestions had been taken into consideration by the government. It was not surprising therefore that some of the Kaifong leaders became rather disillusioned with the government's attitude towards their organizations. An important reason for their disillusionment lay in the fact that the government seemed to be rather reluctant to recognize their service to the community. In the matter of receiving honorary titles, for example, the Kaifong leaders had a small share. In fact, only 15% of the leaders in Wong's sample had ever received honours from the government. And, among the total of 126 Unofficial Justices of Peace, only four were Kaifong leaders, two of whom were included in her sample (1972a:157-60).

The predicament of the Kaifong Associations is shared by a predominant majority of other traditionalistic Chinese voluntary associations. The following presents the financial and membership conditions of a representative group of them in 1978:

(1) Clansmen Associations

Au, Ou and Au-yeung Clansmen's Association

Major service provided (and recipients): emergency relief (nil). Budget: HK$20,000-30,000. Major sources of revenue: membership dues, donations and rent. Number of members: 400. Estimated active membership: 300.

Chow Clansmen Association

Major services provided (and recipients): scholarships (45) and funeral expenses contributory scheme (15). Budget: HK$60,000-70,000. Major sources of revenue: membership dues and donations. Number of members: 1,200. Estimated active membership: 130.

Chung's Clansmen Association

Major services provided (and recipients): funeral expenses contributory scheme (3) and scholarships (5). Budget: HK$13,000. Major sources of revenue: donations and contributions for specific purposes. Number of members: 650. Estimated active membership: 300.

Fung Clansmen's Association

Major services provided (and recipients): scholarships (15), funeral expenses contributory scheme (17), emergency relief (nil) and clinic (200). Budget: HK$56,000. Major sources of revenue: membership dues, donations, contributions for specific purposes and rent. Number of members: 1,200. Estimated active membership: 100.

Lai Shi Relationship Association

Major services provided (and recipients): funeral expenses contributory scheme (30), assistantships (15) and emergency relief (nil). Budget: HK$5,000. Major sources of revenue: membership dues and donations. Number of members: 1,300. Estimated active membership: 700.

Lee Clansmen's Association

Major services provided (and recipients): funeral expenses contributory scheme (3) and emergency relief (2). Budget: HK$30,000. Major sources of revenue: membership dues, donations, contributions for specific purposes and rent. Number of members: 800. Estimated active membership: not available.

Leung Clansmen Association

Major services provided (and recipients): funeral expenses contributory scheme (21), scholarships (34) and emergency relief (nil). Budget: HK$70,000. Major sources of revenue: membership dues, donations and contributions for specific purposes. Number of members: 1,000. Estimated active membership: 450.

Ngan's Clansmen Association

Major services provided (and recipients): funeral expenses contributory scheme (6) and scholarships (15). Budget: HK$25,000. Major sources of revenue: membership dues and donations. Number of members: 500. Estimated active membership: 300.

Pang Clansmen Association

Major services provided (and recipients): medical aid (nil) and relief for funeral expenses (2). Budget: HK$12,000. Major source of revenue: donations. Number of members: 700. Estimated active membership: 20.

Hong Kong Sin Clansmen Association

Major service provided: nil. Budget: HK$4,000. Major sources of revenue: membership dues and donations. Number of members: 180. Estimated active membership: 40.

Hong Kong Szeto Clansmen Association

Major services provided (and recipients): scholarships and assistantships (4) and funeral expenses contributory scheme (14). Budget: HK$20,000.

Major sources of revenue: membership dues, donations, contributions
for specific purposes and rent. Number of members: 1,000. Estimated
active membership: not available.

Tam Clansmen Association
Major services provided (and recipients): scholarships (6), funeral
expenses contributory scheme (2) and emergency relief (nil). Budget:
HK$30,000. Major sources of revenue: donations and rent from proper-
ties. Number of members: 1,700. Estimated active membership: 35.

(2) District Associations and Chambers of Commerce

Chiu Chow Merchants Mutual Assistance Society
Major services provided (and recipients): distribution of winter clothing
(7,000), emergency relief (1,000), clinic (11,000) and funeral expenses
contributory scheme (no data). Budget: HK$200,000 (including
HK$160,000 for the welfare department). Major sources of revenue:
membership dues, donations and others. Number of members: 500.
Estimated active membership: 100.

Chiu Chow Residents' Public Association
Major services provided (and recipients): scholarships (10) and funeral
expenses contributory scheme (no data). Budget: HK$72,000. Major
sources of revenue: membership dues, donations and contributions for
specific purposes. Number of members: 3,000. Estimated active
membership: 400.

Chung Shan Commercial Association of Hong Kong
Major services provided (and recipients): emergency relief (110),
funeral expenses contributory scheme (6), and clinic (720). Budget:
HK$30,000. Major sources of revenue: donations and rent from proper-
ties. Number of members: 5,000. Estimated active membership: 100.

Hong Kong Hok Shan Association
Major services provided (and recipients): funeral expenses contributory
scheme (12), assistantships (23) and primary education (2,000). Budget:
HK$30,000. Major sources of revenue: membership dues, donations
and rent. Number of members: 1,600. Estimated active membership:
1,300.

Kwangsi Province Natives Association
Major services provided (and recipients): funeral expenses contributory
scheme (3) and scholarships (30). Budget: HK$20,000. Major sources
of revenue: membership dues and contributions for specific purposes.
Number of members: 600. Estimated active membership: 300 (?).

Ng Yueh District Association
Major service provided (and recipients): funeral expenses contributory scheme (13). Budget: HK$12,000. Major sources of revenue: membership dues, donations and contributions for specific purposes. Number of members: 2,000. Estimated active membership: 40.

Hong Kong Pan U District Association
Major services provided (and recipients): funeral expenses contributory scheme (24) and emergency relief (nil). Budget: HK$50,000. Major sources of revenue: membership dues, donations and contributions for specific purposes. Number of members: 550. Estimated active membership: 400.

Hong Kong Po On Po Chung District Association
Major services provided (and recipients): scholarships (37) and funeral expenses contributory scheme (85). Budget: HK$18,000. Major sources of revenue: membership dues, donations and contributions for specific purposes. Number of members: 1,200. Estimated active membership: 500.

Sam Sui Natives Association
Major service provided (and recipients): scholarships (210). Budget: HK$40,000. Major sources of revenue: contributions for specific purposes and rent from properties. Number of members: 2,000. Estimated active membership: 40.

Sun Hing Residents' Association
Major services provided (and recipients): scholarships (60), funeral expenses contributory scheme (37), emergency relief (3) and loan (nil). Budget: HK$40,000. Major sources of revenue: membership dues and rent. Number of members: 1,200. Estimated active membership: 80.

Sun Wui Commercial Society of Hong Kong
Major services provided (and recipients): funeral expenses contributory scheme (2) and emergency relief (nil). Budget: HK$54,000. Major source of revenue: rent from properties. Number of members: 1,800. Estimated active membership: 50.

Tung Koon District Society
Major services provided (and recipients): scholarships (12), funeral expenses contributory scheme (100) and emergency relief (no data). Budget: HK$70,000. Major sources of revenue: membership dues, charges/fees, donations and contributions for specific purposes. Number of members: 4,000. Estimated active membership: 1,000.

Even these dismal figures most probably have exaggerated the actual performance of these traditionalistic organizations, especially with regard to
membership and finance. At the present moment, these organizations are
really inward-looking organizations bent on self-preservation. Most of the
Kaifong Associations, in catering to their need for organizational maintenance,
have gradually shifted from charity work to organizing educational, recreational and training activities which are revenue-generating. Their function as
a political intermediary between the government and the ordinary people is
no longer significant. In the same vein, the clansmen, district and commercial
associations have entered into profit-making activities which serve to financially underwrite their continual existence as organizational entities.

The current structural conditions of these organizations can be gleaned from
those of the Waichow Hakkas, whose district associations are among the largest
in Hong Kong. A rare study of these organizations by Hsieh Jiann (1979, 1980,
1981) contained a number of highlights on their structural characteristics,
and I believe that these characteristics are not confined to them alone:

(1) A substantial proportion of the officials in these organizations were
    engaged in the construction industry, and they actively provided job
    opportunities to their fellow Hakkas. In a certain sense, these organi-
    zations took on the character of trade guilds.

(2) There was a large leadership stratum in these organizations. The proli-
    feration of both actual and honorific official titles in these organiza-
    tions testified to the status-conferral functions of organizations of this
    kind. This also constitutes a means to enable these organizations to
    attract prominent individuals into the organizations.

(3) As of 1978, almost all of the leaders in these organizations were lesser
    figures in the Chinese society. Individuals with society-wide status and
    prestige failed to turn up in the leadership structure. And there was no
    reason to believe that these lesser figures managed to maintain constant
    or regular contacts with the Chinese elite in Hong Kong.

(4) 95.4 per cent of the leaders were born in Mainland China. This showed
    that traditionalistic organizations in Hong Kong were largely the
    organizations of the immigrants. As these people began to settle down
    in Hong Kong, these organizations would suffer a process of decline.

(5) Over the years, this large organizational complex of the Waichow
    Hakkas had experienced a metamorphosis process from one executing
    bona fide traditional self-help and mediating functions to one whose
    main concern is financial solvency and the immediate interests of its
    dues-paying members.

To generalize further, organizations similar to those of the Waichow Hakkas which are much smaller in scale should be facing even greater hurdles in their quest for survival. Compared to the Kaifongs, the function of these organizations as political intermediaries is even more negligible. Even in their heyday, their connection with the colonial authorities was fragile. Their deterioration will inevitably bring out their final abandonment by the government.

As the aging of leadership and membership, financial insolvency, and shortage of dynamic leadership continue to haunt these traditional organizations, sooner or later they will become the property of history.

It is not difficult to discover the reasons for the decline of these intermediate organizations in Hong Kong. Firstly, industrialization and value changes in Hong Kong have gradually rendered traditional voluntary organizations both ideologically unattractive and functionally redundant. The rise of the standard of living of the general public has reduced the demand for private welfare. The identification of most of these organizations with traditional Chinese values and with the Nationalist regime in Taiwan naturally undermines their appeal to the new generation of Hong Kong Chinese, who are becoming more Westernized and "a-nationalist."

Secondly, the assumption by the government, on ever larger scales, of the responsibilities for delivering educational, social and financial services to the disadvantaged in society has inadvertently weakened these organizations as welfare institutions. Joining these organizations is no longer deemed to be imperative even by the most needy, with the exception perhaps of the elderly whose funeral needs are compelling. Moreover, their role as administrative ancillaries in the delivery of government services has also been downgraded as the government increasingly relies upon its own officials to do the job.

Thirdly, with particular relevance to the Kaifongs, locality feelings among the ordinary people have gradually attenuated. Large-scale internal population movements (stemming from the construction of public housing estates in outlying areas) and the recency of the planned communities are not breeding grounds of locality identification. Hong Kong is in essence an atomistic society where identification with larger collective units by the people is minimal. Neighbourliness among the Hong Kong Chinese is strikingly low, and community spirit is hard to locate (Kan 1974). These factors, plus an increasing population density and an accelerated diffusion of high-rise buildings as the modal residential accommodations among the ordinary people, which have their own complex managerial and physical problems, make the Kaifong Associations appear to be oversized and unwieldy organizational monsters.

Fourthly, in a modernizing urban society like Hong Kong, urban welfare problems have so changed in nature that global solutions involving substantial resource investments and coordination of efforts by the government are required, and the government is the only agency with the necessary authority and means to undertake these herculean tasks. In the process of centralizing decision-making in areas which in the past were marked by confusion, official neglect and decentralization, traditional organizations have to be relegated to oblivion. Even organizations of this kind which are structured on a society-wide basis, such as the Tung Wah Hospital and the Po Leung Kuk, have to take on a new role, however reluctantly, as the agency of the government, and act in accordance with its strategic demands.

Fifthly, the co-optation of increasing numbers of the Chinese elite into the central decision-making processes of the government, as has been mentioned earlier, thus makes them unavailable for leadership positions in these traditional organizations. What is more disastrous, from the "linkage" point of view, is that the upper-level Chinese leaders are no longer organically joined to the lower-level Chinese leaders such as those found in traditionalistic organizations. Consequently, the value of these lesser elite members as political intermediaries drastically depreciates.

Finally, at least attitudewise, the new generations of Hong Kong Chinese are more politically vocal and articulate. The submissive deference of traditionalistic leaders to government officials and their general political docility are to them obnoxious and anachronistic features.

The decline of these intermediate organizations has manifold effects on Hong Kong. The least serious one is its impact on social welfare, as economic growth enables the familial groups to get access to increasing amounts of resources to meet the needs of the ordinary people. The social welfare and other service programmes of the government play a supplementary and increasingly significant role in alleviating the social pains generated by rapid industrialization. The more serious outcome lies in the political realm. The peculiar situation in Hong Kong is that these organizations are the only organizational links between the government and the ordinary people. Devices such as mass political parties, trade unions[6] and political patrons or

[6]The weakness of the trade unions in Hong Kong is a distinctive feature of the colony. "If we compare 1961 with 1971, years in which we have census data available, the number of adult workers in full-time employment increased from 925,700 to 1,281,360 and the proportion of full-time workers who were paid-up members of a trade union increased from 12.8 per cent to 13.1 per cent. That is, the unions just managed to keep pace with the rapid expansion of employment but failed to strengthen their position significantly" (England and Rear 1975:87). Inordinate fragmentation as a result of political, territorial and craft distinctions is both an identifying characteristic and an inhibitory factor of trade union development in Hong Kong. The political weakness of trade unions and the instrumental attitude towards trade unions on the part of the Hong Kong workers have turned them into *de facto* voluntary welfare agencies. As a result, trade unions are a comparatively insignificant force in the realm of industrial relations. Several factors can be adduced to explain the weakness of trade unions in Hong Kong.

"strongmen"[7] which in many developing countries serve as political intermediaries are not found in Hong Kong. The decline of these organizations in
practice aggravates the problem of "linkage," thus increasingly isolating the
government from the people. To say this is definitely not to idealize or
romanticize the role played by these organizations in prewar Hong Kong. In
the earlier era, the less complex nature of the society, the less important
service-provision role of the government, the higher level of political passivity
of the Chinese populace, and the lesser objective need for the government and
the people to establish closer relationship all suggest that the need for linkage
then was less than it is now, when all the above-said conditions have changed
quite a bit. Even if all the intermediate organizations whose decline we have
depicted were to regain their former vitality, I would still very much doubt
their ability to serve as a viable and effective link between the government

---

"First, the mobility of the labour force in [the manufacturing industries] —itself in part
a form of protest about working conditions—hinders the development of stable workers'
organizations. Secondly, the victimization of trade union activists is a severe deterrent to
organization." Thirdly, the "political nature of the unions is often given as a reason for
their failure to attract more members. . . . There is no doubt that the unions' political
character is repellant to a labour force which contains a high proportion of political
refugees who have no wish for further entanglements" (*Ibid.*: 99). The "political nature"
of the unions here refers to their political attitudes towards the Communist regime in
China and the Nationalist regime in Taiwan. Fourthly, "most unions in the Colony are
organized from the top down, rather than as grass root expressions of organized and
continuing discontent with working conditions. The quality of leadership has always
been important for unions but never more so than when still in their formative stage.
The quality of leadership in Hong Kong leaves much to be desired" (*Ibid.*: 99). Moreover,
the diluted sense of class consciousness among the Hong Kong workers, the availability
of opportunities for social mobility through individual strivings, the fluidity of the labour
market, the persisting paternalistic relationships between employers and employees, and
the operation of ascriptive and particularistic ties (e.g., ethnicity, regionalism) within the
working class are powerful factors militating against the rise of trade unions as a potent
political force in Hong Kong.
    [7]Individuals with "face," who in other places take the forms of patrons, political
brokers, *caudillos*, political party influentials, etc., and play crucial mediating roles, do
not appear in Hong Kong. The absence of the traditional gentry in an immigrant society
means that persons who can claim traditional authority to bolster their intermediary role
are not to be found. The lack of a politically significant and individually lucrative
electoral system in addition deprives the common people in Hong Kong of a leverage
with which to engage in reciprocal exchange with those resourceful personalities who
seek public offices through soliciting or "buying" votes from the disadvantaged (e.g., a
classic case is the urban political machines in the U.S.A. in the early twentieth century
and the Congress Party in rural India today). Moreover, geographical mobility and the
complexities of urban problems would also preclude the formation of durable patron-
client networks, even when an electoral system is there. This would discourage powerful
persons from investing in these "risky" and uncertain political enterprises.

and the people. Their decline would simply make the situation even worse, and the search for "modern" alternative linkage devices more urgent.

It is doubly unfortunate that the other voluntary associations, many of them are organizations of the "modern" type, largely fail to serve the mediating function. In a certain sense, it is uncontestably true that the Chinese people are remarkable in their organizational ability. Voluntary organizations of various genera run into several thousand in Hong Kong. Nevertheless, as we have already seen in Chapter 4, the Hong Kong Chinese have only an extremely low social participation rate. Consequently the scenario in the voluntary organization field can be portrayed as one of fragmented pluralism, with many of these organizations leading only a marginal existence. Moreover, a preponderant majority of these organizations are formed to cater to specific and narrow interests, and this is notably true for those professional organizations and "expressive" organizations which deal with recreation, tension-release and various forms of sociability. By and large, "modern" voluntary organizations are inward-looking entities, playing only a peripheral role in the political arena of Hong Kong.

On the other hand, it is not fair to say that they play no political role at all. With respect to matters which have direct relationship with them, these organizations and their leaders may get in touch with the government in an advisory or liaison capacity. On occasions where the policies or lack of policies of the government provoke public clamour, some of these organizations may add their voice to it by issuing public statements, thus contributing to the formation of public opinion in Hong Kong. Still, on the whole it can be said that though some of the "modern" voluntary associations in Hong Kong manage to play the role of interest-articulator and interest-aggregator on behalf of the Hong Kong Chinese, they play it only infrequently, occasionally and in an *ad hoc* manner. Moreover, they play it in the capacity of public opinion carrier or promoter, and not from a position of strength based on organizational linkages with the general Chinese populace. As such, they can never substitute for linkage devices which can structurally integrate the bureaucracy and the Chinese society and integrate them in such a manner that both parties can affect each other in a regular and effective fashion.

The weakness of the mediating mechanisms and the "compartmentalization" of polity and society have also left the Hong Kong government on the two horns of a political dilemma. While it has no intention of forgoing the political autonomy it has so far jealously guarded or of tearing down the "compartmentalization" of the polity and society by means of involving the Chinese society into the political arena, it still needs to gather sufficient and reliable information on the Chinese society as a prerequisite for efficient administration. And this need for information is increasingly felt as the government plays an enlarged role in service delivery, and as administration of an industrial society is becoming a more and more complex matter. Without sacrificing its decision-making autonomy, two kinds of tactics have so far been adopted by the government to deal with the problem of information collection, and, as a corollary to it, to exert some moderating pressure upon popular aspirations. It is also expected that these tactics will enable the government to anticipate the behavioural tendencies of the Chinese people which might have political implications, so that public policies can be so modulated as to pre-empt undesirable political consequences and to allow the government to take on the visage of a responsive authority. One of these tactics is to officially sponsor the formation of citizen organizations, and the other is to establish official linkage mechanisms. Both of them are responses to the gradual emasculation of the traditionalistic organizations as mediating devices, and both of them, as the results so far reveal, are not impressively successful, even from the government's point of view. This section will discuss the first tactic, while the next one will take up the second one.

It is not irrelevant to say that government officials in Hong Kong are patently distrustful of and apprehensive about strong local organizations, which might be infiltrated by subversive and criminal elements. Their unwillingness to allow political considerations to infringe on the supposedly efficiency-oriented administrative process makes substantial delegation of resources and decision-making power to the grass-roots levels impossible. Furthermore, the government may not be incorrect in looking with disdain the ineptitude of local leadership which has thus far been displayed, and leadership talent is in critically short supply particularly in the socioeconomically homogeneous public housing estates, which accommodate a substantial proportion of the Hong Kong Chinese.

Since the early 1970s, the government did begin to initiate local organizations in the form of Mutual Aid Committees (MACs). The appearance of MACs was largely an "accidental" phenomenon, and represented a spin-off from the officially-inaugurated campaigns to clean up Hong Kong and to fight violent crime. These campaigns were efforts on the part of the government to get the people mobilized to fend for themselves in those mundane matters affecting their localities. If successful, these campaigns would form the basis of sustained self-help activities by the people themselves. They would presumably lessen the administrative burden of the government, which is increasingly faced with resource strains, and contribute to general community well-being. In retrospect, the accomplishments of these campaigns in terms of concrete results and the mobilization of people are rather disappointing, and the campaigns immediately lost steam as soon as the government left the scene. However, the campaigns have induced the government to realize the utility of grass-roots organizations in injecting some cohesive cements into an atomistic society and to assume some functions previously performed by the bureaucracy. This realization prompted the government to launch the MAC movement with much fanfare and publicity.

> The Mutual Aid Committee Scheme was launched in June, 1973. The aim was to bring about the spirit of neighbourly co-operation in the management of multi-storey buildings enabling owners and tenants to work together to improve security and cleanliness in them. The Mutual Aid Committee is a simple form of organiza-tion which can be set up with a minimum of formality.
>
> In this connection, the Governor-in-Council on 26th May, 1973 amended the Schedule to the Societies Ordinance so as to dispense with the requirement for the Mutual Aid Committees to register as societies provided that they were approved by either the Secretary for Home Affairs or the District Commissioner, New Territories. The initial approval was up to 31st March, 1974.
>
> 79 Community Organizers were recruited to assist and to promote the aims of this scheme. These officers worked on evenings, Saturdays, Sundays and public holidays when meetings of tenants and owners could be conveniently convened. They visited multi-storey buildings and estates with a Liaison Officer of the department, explained the benefits of mutual aid.
>
> A Steering Committee on Mutual Aid Committees and Building Management was set up in Headquarters in order to solve problems encountered by field staff and also to co-ordinate the work of City District Offices in this endeavour.
>
> By the end of 1973, a total of 1,214 Mutual Aid Committees had been set up in various buildings and residental groupings, with a total membership of some 110,380 households. Crime prevention, though being the initial concern, was by no means the sole preoccupation of these Committees, which were also involved in the "Clean Our Building Campaign." (Director of Home Affairs 1973-74:6)

The respective numbers of MACs and household membership increased to 1,636 and 188,022 at the end of 1974, and 2,061 and 266,601 at the end of March 1976. This miraculous proliferation of MACs took place at the expense of constructing the necessary conditions for organizational vitality, notably in the areas of management and resource deployment. Leadership ineptitude and passivity of membership are major inadequacies hampering the effective functioning of these bodies.[8] The functions allotted to the MACs by the government were few, and they were mainly responsible for promoting the spirit of neighbourly cooperation in the management of multi-storey buildings, and enabling owners and tenants to work together to improve security and cleanliness in them. The MACs were granted few resources and authority by the government, which was determined to restrict their functions and

---

[8] Casting an attentive eye on the possibility of the infiltration of "bad elements," including triads (a secret society engaging in criminal activities) into the MACs, the government is always on the alert to restrain the activities and power of the MAC leaders. This bespeaks of the ambivalent attitude of the government towards local leadership in Hong Kong.

organizational scale. Consequently, mergers and the formation of federations among MACs were discouraged, thus seriously limiting their potential effectiveness as community organizations. Operating under such restrictive conditions, it is small wonder that the MACs failed to earn the support and active participation of their members and constituents.

The MAC movement, however, reveals the relationship between the bureaucracy and the Chinese society in Hong Kong. There is a large halo of ambiguities about the functions of the MAC and its location in the social-political system of the colony. These ambiguities reflect on the one hand the indecisive stand of the government towards local organizations. The government seems to waver between treating the MACs as intermediate organizations with some "political" functions and confining their activities to a narrow range of trivial responsibilities with no political overtones. On the other hand, the MAC leaders and the Chinese people tend to overestimate the importance and status of the MACs and consider them to be a sort of "bridge" between themselves and the "distant" bureaucracy. The comments on the MACs by a number of social leaders reported in the *South China Morning Post* after five years of their existence tended to revolve around their supposedly "political" functions:

The Director of Sau Mau Ping's Young Workers Centre, Sr. Theresa Dagdag, was commenting on reports which accused the Government of either blocking or failing to promote people's participation to politics.

Meanwhile, the Public Housing Rent Policy Action Committee, which is composed of 55 organizations of which more than 30 are Mutual Aid Committees, declared that many MAC leaders are disillusioned with the way things are run at present, particularly with the strict control exercised by the City District Office.

In a speech on Sunday, the Chairman of the Hongkong Christian Industrial Committee, Dr. L. K. Ding, accused the CDOs [City District Offices, see pp. 150-51] and MACs of being obstacles to genuine participation.

The Director of the Hongkong Council of Social Services, Mr. Y. F. Hui, said the success of the CDO scheme depends on the Government's willingness to listen to true representatives of the people and not "yes men." . . .

As for pressure on the MACs from the CDOs, a spokesman for the Public Housing Rent Policy Action Committee, Mr. Lai Tin-yue, said two MACs have withdrawn from the committee after it had publicised their support.

"We suspect it is due to pressure from the CDOs," Mr. Lai said.

"From our past experience, we know and accept the fact that whenever MACs supported issues of public concern, which may not be within the provisions of Government policies, they would receive pressure from their CDOs." . . .

According to informed sources, one of the latest efforts to frustrate the MACs is carried out in Kwai Shing Estate, Block 10.

The Government is planning to set up a sheltered workshop there, and the MAC wants to do a survey to collect the residents' opinions on the subject. However, they were told by the New Territories Administration that it was none of their business. (April 18, 1978)

The public's "misunderstanding" of the purposes of the MACs spurred a retort and clarification from the Director of Home Affairs the next day:

As for the MACs, Mr. Walden said they were never intended to be used for political purposes.

"The idea was to get people together to solve common problems within their own buildings. They were not intended as evidence of grassroot democracy in a political sense," Mr. Walden explained.

"We don't encourage MACs to group together because by so doing they might be involved in the game of politics and tend to be diverted from the original objective and instead try to gain political power and prestige," he said.

Besides being a channel for disseminating Government information and collecting public feedback, the CDOs are used to monitor effects of Government policies on the people and to assess the kinds of services they need.

"We are still at an embryonic form of people's participation which is informatory rather than policy-making. Of course there is room for more public participation in policy formulation but that wasn't the original intention," Mr. Walden said. (*South China Morning Post*, April 19, 1978)

This verbal exchange between the social leaders and the Director of Home Affairs is enlightening in a number of ways. First, it demonstrates the salient need for linkage between the bureaucracy and the Chinese society and the need is perceived by both parties. Second, the imputation of different meanings to the MACs by the government and the society attests to the "communication gap" between the two. Third, both the government and the people are prone to attribute political motivations to the behaviour of each other. This shows that a cloud of mutual suspicion hangs over the interaction between them. Finally, it demonstrates that the Chinese society is more prepared to exert some forms of influence on the government than the latter is willing to grant. All in all, the "compartmentalization" of polity and society is increasingly felt to be intolerable by the Chinese, and to a lesser extent, by the government too.

Being sponsored and controlled by the government, and without a supportive mass base, the MACs cannot be considered as effective community organizations performing service delivery and integrative functions. The promotion of the MAC movement, whilst reflecting the importance attached to voluntary organizations by the government, is in the main a kind of effort at administrative penetration. Judging from current results, however, this penetrative attempt is made hesitantly and is devoid of notable achievements.

OFFICIAL LINKAGE DEVICES

The linkage devices installed by the government to deal with the "communication gap" between itself and the Chinese people arising from the "intermediary vacuum" take variegated forms, ranging from the creation of a high-level post of Secretary of Information, paying more attention to the Chinese press, particularly its editorials,[9] shoring up the mass media facilities in the hands of the government, to the establishment of organizational linkage mechanisms. Because of their relative importance, I shall concentrate only on the last of these.

The riot in 1966 exposed the "communication gap" between the government and the Chinese society in dramatic clarity. The turmoil of 1967, though instigated by external forces, nevertheless brought to the attention of the government that a sizeable proportion of the Chinese populace were not informed of the government's policies and intentions and were amenable to

[9] On the surface, the press in Hong Kong looks like an awesome political force which should be capable of playing a mediating role. In 1980, "Hong Kong has a flourishing free press with 114 newspapers and 326 periodicals catering to a high readership market. ... Some 350 copies of newspapers are printed for every 1,000 people in Hong Kong. Only Japan exceeds this figure with 490 copies to every 1,000 people" (*Hong Kong Annual Report*, 1980:164). In actuality, the proliferation of newspapers and other printed media and the ensuing cut-throat competition among them are one of the causes of their political impotence. Being commercial enterprises catering to the interests of their readers, it is more befitting to say that it is the readers who influence the press along rather than the reverse. Exotic news items are oftentimes the ingredients captivating the attention of the readers. Eroticism and sensationalism, not to say downright vulgarism and pornography, are the key to survival for many small newspapers and magazines. Even among the more important newspapers, there is a conspicuous absence of attempts at providing contextual, systematic and historical analyses for a meaningless and bewildering morass of scattered and simplistically-handled news items. Without doubt the newspapers are not solely to be blamed for this state of affairs. The practice of the government to indulge in secrecy and its unwillingness to release critical information for public consumption are also to be blamed. In order not to overly castigate the press in Hong Kong, it should be noted, albeit the mythology created by the press to the contrary, for the most part the press has not played a politically formidable role even in a country like the U.S.A.:

> "The bland tone of the press is not the consequence of a powerful and continuing restraint of a fourth estate eager to exercise its prerogatives under the constitutional guarantee of the press. Newspapers and magazine publishers are generally of the conservative classes themselves. Moreover, most of them operate on a thin resource base and cannot afford to assume risks—or to generate anxieties in the minds of their bankers. Pressure does not need to be brought upon them to keep them safe and sane; they are not often bribed or coerced, for they do not have to be. Yet the principle of control of the deviant at the margin applies from time to time as individual papers get out of line. The sources of control include advertisers, those who appear to be able to carry out threats to boycott circulations, and, on occasion, politicians." (Key 1961:381-82)

If such is the situation in the U.S.A., it is doubly true in Hong Kong. The press in Hong Kong is less fortunate than its counterpart in the U. S. in that it cannot seek refuge in constitutional guarantees. The powerful hand of the government is a factor which has to be incessantly borne in mind.

distorted anti-system appeals, though they were not subsequently converted
into anti-system actions.

One of the most important administrative innovations adopted by the
government immediately after the suppression of the riots was the setting up
of a number of City District Offices in the urban areas of Hong Kong, each of
which was headed by a City District Officer (CDO). Through the CDOs, the
government hoped to fabricate new official channels of access for the ordinary
people, and in due course to bridge the communication gap between itself
and the governed. The directive of the Governor to the CDOs featured the
following task assignments:

(1) "By developing the widest possible contacts with associations and individuals
in your district, you should aim to supplement with personal explanation Government's output of information through the mass communication media. . . .
Through your familiarity with the district and with the problems and needs of the
people, you will be in a special position to advise on public opinion and local
needs."

(2) "One of your most important tasks is to arouse the interest of residents in the
affairs of their district, to focus their attention on community problems and to
encourage them to contribute constructively to their solution."

(3) "An equally important aspect of your work will lie in helping individuals with
their problems."

(4) "In performing the role described above, your most important asset will be an
intimate knowledge of your district and the people in it."

(5) "Remember that it is not sufficient for those who benefit directly to be aware
of what has been done for them. It is also of great importance that the people of
Hong Kong generally come to value the services of C.D.O.'s, even though they
may not need them themselves. This means you must ensure that publicity
coverage is regular and responsible."

(6) "Remember that nobody owes you a living. The office is paid for by the tax-
payers and we must ensure that it renders services of value considerably in excess
of the cost. If this is not so, the money could be put to better use in other services."
(Selected from the Secretary for Chinese Affairs 1969.)

The reality, however, falls far short of these lofty and idealistic statements.
In the first place, without conferring executive power over other departments
in the government to these "political officers," they were doomed from the
start as functional official intermediaries. The constant shift of personnel in
and out of the City District Offices precluded the possibility of forging viable
and stable ties between the CDOs and their constituencies. The fact that
officials were assigned to fill the CDO posts only temporarily would mean
that open confrontation with other departments, to which they might subsequently be transferred, on behalf of the interests of the people would be
difficult to imagine. It turned out that after a number of years in operation
these administrative bodies served mainly to unilaterally transmit information
and decisions from the government to the people, and to collect information

on the latter for consumption by the former. Upon evaluation, both functions have not been carried out. As agencies representing the interests of the people *inside* the administration, the CDOs were on the whole failures.

After studying the functioning of the CDO in Kwun Tong at close range, the observations of Ambrose King perhaps come close to reality:

> The CDO has not been as successful in its "information input" as in "information output." Despite its efforts to reach people in the street, it has thus far not been very successful in penetrating the masses in a structured way, although it has been fairly successful in securing the views and attitudes of local leaders towards government policies and actions before they are put into effect. (1975:436)

King's remark in the last sentence however has to be qualified somewhat, for the local leaders approached by the CDOs represent only a narrow spectrum of leadership in the localities. Another statement by King is more to the point:

> In analyzing the ... political function of the CDO, political socialization and recruitment, we must bear in mind that generating a favorable and supportive attitude and behavior toward the Government was one of the basic reasons for the inception of the CDO Scheme. The CDO, as the political agent at the district level, is not aiming at political mobilization of the populace; in fact, it is trying to depoliticize the political process. In short, the CDO Scheme is primarily concerned with social stability rather than with social change. (*Ibid.*: 437)

Furthermore, the increasing scales of urban and social problems have rendered the CDOs inappropriate mechanisms for the solution of these global problems, which demand attention from the top level of the government. This structural incapacity is a major cause of the low stature of the CDOs in the mind of the public at large and recently even by the government itself. One of the results of the lowered standing of the CDOs within the government is their failure to compete for experienced officials to staff CDO positions. According to the *South China Morning Post*, "half of the City District Officers have less than four years of experience and at present no satisfactory answer to this has been found" (November 1, 1976). In a bureaucracy where the effectiveness of an official depends very much on his administrative rank, the lack of high-level officers in its camp was a heavy blow to the viability of the CDO Scheme.

Aside from the CDOs, two other official channels of access of imputed significance are the ward offices of the Urban Council and the UMELCO Office (Office of the Unofficial Members of the Executive and Legislative Councils of Hong Kong). The former are run by the elected members (elected on an extremely limited franchise) of the Urban Council, which is responsible mainly for sanitation, sports and cultural activities, and the provision of some urban services. The latter is deliberately set up by the government as an alternative to the stillborn ombudsman scheme, which has the potential of posing serious threats to the hegemony of the bureaucracy. Both bodies are designed to deal with complaints and representations from the general public. In the case of the ward offices, issues lying within the domain of the Urban Council might have the chance of resolution, as the Council at least has its own allotted resources to get some things done. In the case of the UMELCO Office, on the other hand, even though it is granted the right to information from the government, the right of access to government officers, and the right to challenge the action taken by government departments, these rights by themselves are not sufficient to enable the UMELCO Office to impose its will upon government officials. Consequently, most of the positive achievements of the Office, which are not impressive at all, are due to the goodwill and cooperative attitude of some government officials, and the Unofficials' deliberately refraining from pressing issues on government officials which are threatening and embarassing in nature.

In general, what is evident from the figures released by the ward offices and the UMELCO Office is a low level of utilization of their services by the general public, and their inability to resolve the major problems afflicting those who sought help from them.

Since its introduction on November 1, 1965, the Urban Council Ward System, with its ten ward offices, has seen an increasing volume of cases brought under its attention. The following figures represent the number of cases received in the period 1968-1978:

TABLE 5.1
Case brought to the ward offices

Year	Number of cases
1968	2,792
1969	3,047
1970	6,020
1972	8,754
1974	8,435
1976	11,060
1978	10,294

Source: Compiled from the *Monthly Reports on the Work of the Urban Council and the Urban Services Department* (Hong Kong: The Urban Council, 1968-1978).

Taken in all, the volume of cases brought to the attention of the elected Urban Councillors is small, which bespeaks of the low level of salience of the ward offices as a means of problem-solving for ordinary people. However, when compared to the CDOs and the UMELCO, the elected Urban Councillors are more likely to be approached by the ordinary people because of their reputed outspokenness and their more critical stance towards the government (Hoadley 1968:179-92). Nevertheless, the relative insignificance of the Urban Council as a political institution in Hong Kong also puts a stranglehold on its utility as an intermediary. An editorial in the *Hong Kong Standard* on July 28, 1966 pointed out the weaknesses of the ward offices:

> There can be little doubt that part of the recent criticism directed against the Urban Council Ward System stems from a misconception about the role played by Councillors in these wards.
>
> The population has been told on a number of occasions that these Councillors serve as Ombudsmen.
>
> An Urban Councillor cannot compel any Government Department to provide information.
>
> He can only invite the head of the Department to look into a matter and give him an explanation. And he has to be satisfied with the answer he receives, whether or not it really gives any satisfaction.
>
> He does not have the staff to deal with a large number of complaints, he does not have the facilities to examine their legal and technical aspects, and he does not have the background or experience to perform effectively the functions of an Ombudsman.
>
> He cannot investigate on his own, he can only suggest that the Department or Departments concerned carry out investigations.

Turning to the cases brought to the attention of the ward offices, it is not startling to find, given the serious shortage of housing in Hong Kong, that more than half the cases were related to housing needs. They accounted for 61.6%, 57%, 62.7%, 52.3% and 45.3% of the total number of cases in 1970, 1972, 1974, 1976 and 1978 respectively. The balance were related to problems of hawkers, markets, legal aid, police behaviour, social welfare and water supplies. What is staggering is that a predominant majority of the complaints and requests brought to the ward offices fell outside the scope of activities and hence outside the authority of the Urban Council. In 1974, 1976 and 1978, for instance, the proportion of cases falling under the aegis of the Urban Council (meaning that the ward offices could at least take some actions) were 12.1%, 14.1% and 14.8% respectively. Evidently, these figures reflect the ignorance of the ordinary people about appropriate channels of lodging complaints and filing representations. But the thrust of the matter is that most of them, who had mustered enough initiative and "courage" to make the attempt at influence, had to be sent away frustrated and disillusioned.

In the words of the government, the purpose of establishing the UMELCO Office was "to promote closer relationships between the Unofficial Members of the two Councils and members of the public, who were invited to call at the office to put forward their views on any matter of public interest or to lodge individual complaints against Government department" (*Annual Report of the UMELCO Office*, 1971:1). Like the cases of the ward offices, cases related to housing and resettlement were the modal cases brought to the Office, though they usually accounted for less than half the total number of cases, being 20% in 1970-71, 38% in 1971-72, 35% in 1972-73, 35% in 1973-74, 27% in 1974-75, 25.5% in 1975-76 and 23% in 1976-77. In numerical terms, the volume of cases dealt with by the Office was rather small, ranging from 834 in 1970-71 to 3,169 in 1977-78. Again, like the ward offices, though slightly better, the proportion of cases dealt with which were classified as Type A cases (those where the complaints were fully rectified or the clients' requests met in full) was not encouraging. The rest of the cases were either classified as Type B cases (those in which some degree of advice, information, explanation or assistance was given) or Type C cases (those in which UMELCO was unable to help because the complaint was found to be unjustified or because of action taken by the government department was in accordance with the approved prevailing policy). The proportions of Type A, Type B and Type C cases in selected years are listed below:

TABLE 5.2
Cases completed by UMELCO (in percentage)

Year	Type A	Type B	Type C
1970/71	25	46	29
1971/72	31	39	30
1972/73	29	42	29
1973/74	26	47	27
1974/75	22	57	21
1975/76	22	58	20
1976/77	21	60	19

Source: Compiled from the 1970-1977 issues of the *Annual Report of the UMELCO Office*.

From these figures, it appears that the UMELCO Office is essentially a mechanism for the transmission of official information and informal advice, falling far short of being a device for solving the problems of the ordinary people. In this sense, its self-declared mission of intermediary between government and people is largely unrealized.

Understandably, besides the above-mentioned channels, other channels of interest representation are available in Hong Kong. As enumerated by John Walden, Director of Home Affairs, they are: advisory boards and committees, informal contacts with individuals or groups through city district offices in the urban areas, petitions by individuals to the Governor or his officers, public statements, commissions of inquiry, contacts between government departments and their customers, letters to the editors of newspapers—particularly in the English papers—ring-in programmes on the radio, public affairs programmes on the TV and radio, and green papers on public policy (*South China Morning Post*, September 25, 1979). To the man in the street, most of these channels are beyond reach, either because of the obstacles posed by literacy requirements and political sophistication, or because of their time-consuming nature. That the official channels of access to the government cannot function to integrate the ordinary Chinese into the political and administrative system is beyond doubt.

6. A Minimally-integrated Social-political System

An autonomous bureaucratic polity, an atomistic Chinese society and weak links between them are the three principal structural features of Hong Kong. Because of this, Hong Kong can be characterized as a minimally-integrated social-political system in which the polity and the society are only minimally integrated. The choice of this clumsy term is unfortunate, as a crisp depiction of Hong Kong has yet to be found. As such, the term "minimally-integrated social-political system" is mainly suggestive and illustrative, for it fails to bring out in detail many of the specific aspects of the nature of Hong Kong as a social-political system located in a particular structural-historical context. To say the least, the bureaucratic empires of the past, colonial societies, patrimonial political systems and bureaucratic-authoritarian societies are all characterized by a low integration of polity and society, even though they are found in different historical times or are situated in different structural contexts.

In order to spell out the distinctiveness of Hong Kong's "minimally-integrated social-political system," this chapter will lay bare its salient features and the conditions which underlie their emergence and maintenance. Because the volume of arguments and descriptions to be covered in this chapter is fairly large, unavoidably they must be handled in a schematic though systematic manner. Except for those crucial points where substantiation by empirical evidence is called for, a general and relatively abstract treatment is chosen. Some of the points covered have been briefly touched upon in the last five chapters. It is time here to bring them together so that their relationship with one another can be more easily discerned.

NATURE OF A MINIMALLY-INTEGRATED SOCIAL-POLITICAL SYSTEM

As a minimally-integrated social-political system, Hong Kong displays the following features:

(1) Both the bureaucracy and Chinese society are wary of their autonomy and integrity, and are always on guard against intrusions or encroachments from the other side. In addition, both of them are reluctant, except when extremely necessary, to tamper with the affairs which are deemed to be within the jurisdiction of the other party. Obviously, this delineation of the basic posture of the bureaucratic polity and the Chinese society is highly simplistic, but it nonetheless brings out in sharp focus the fundamental

characteristic of a minimally-integrated social-political system—the "boundary-maintenance" orientation of both the bureaucratic polity and the Chinese society. The "boundary" between the bureaucratic polity and Chinese society of course includes numerous items, such as the forms of division of labour between them, the relative amount of societal resources (including political power and economic goods) to be allocated between them, the amount of societal information and its distribution, so on and so forth. Nevertheless, to the bureaucratic polity, its "boundary" is largely defined in political terms, and is couched in the form of a monopolization of the political arena. As a result, in Hong Kong the bureaucratic polity and the political arena are almost coterminous. Concretely put, this means that aside from the bureaucracy, other political institutions which would enable non-bureaucratic "outsiders" to acquire or exercise political power are either non-existent (such as political parties) or so weak that it would be a misnomer to apply the term "political institution" to them (such as the voluntary organizations). Consequently, if political power is to be procured, it has to be done *through* the bureaucracy, rather than *outside* of it. Acquisition of political power by means of over-throwing the bureaucracy is undoubtedly possible, but it would be considered "illegitimate" under the extant circumstances in Hong Kong.

To the Chinese society, "boundary-maintenance" by and large falls into the social and cultural realms. This means that the Chinese people in Hong Kong are jealous about preserving their customs, mode of thinking, habits, mores, lifestyles and patterns of social organization, things which constitute the cultural and social heritage of the Chinese people. The conservatism of the Hong Kong Chinese and the lingering feelings of cultural superiority needless to say underlies this "boundary-maintenance" ethos. In fact, if Chinese nationalism can be said to exist in Hong Kong, it assumes the form of cultural nationalism rather than political nationalism. This posture of the Hong Kong Chinese does not pose any threat to the political dominance of the bureaucracy; on the contrary, it complements it and enables both of them to coexist peacefully. What it demands from the bureaucracy is that the social and cultural heritage of the Chinese people be respected, and that the polity has no "right" to interfere with it, not to say to transform it in accordance with the prescriptions of some kinds of "apocalytic" ideologies.

(2) That the bureaucratic polity and the Chinese society can coexist peacefully hinges on the fact that in reality both of them do not attempt to intrude into each other's "territory." Granted the fact that Hong Kong is a relatively industrialized society where some forms of contact between the polity and the society are not only unavoidable, but necessary (the enforcement of contract in commercial undertakings is a good example in this connection), serious attempts to change the boundary between the two are

not encountered because both the bureaucratic polity and the Chinese society lack the will, the perceived need and the means to do so.

For the bureaucratic polity, the original and major purpose of acquiring Hong Kong from China in the first place continues to be the promotion of economic activities. To change the Chinese society in accordance with Western social and political philosophies is out of the question. The doctrines of laissez-faire and social non-interventionism are in practice guarantees against tampering unnecessarily with Chinese affairs. The search for law and order in the colony so that trade and commerce can prosper freely would call for the preservation of a Chinese society which is stable and relatively well-organized. Thus, it is imperative that the traditional structure, particularly the leadership and authority structure, of the Chinese not be disrupted, for fear that unpremeditated attempts at restructuring it would unleash destabilizing forces beyond the power of the British to control. The adoption of a diluted form of "indirect" rule—allowing the Chinese to mind their own business while relying upon Chinese social leaders to supply the government with information about the Chinese society—is the strategy. But the fine distinction between indirect rule as practised in Hong Kong and indirect rule as practised in former British colonies must be underscored. In the latter case the intention of resource extraction from the indigenous populace loomed very large, whereas in Hong Kong the maintenance of social stability is the major concern.

The British also see no perceived need to intrude into Chinese society. The ability of the Chinese to maintain order among themselves and their voluntary, though maybe somewhat reluctant, withdrawal from the political arena (hence posing no challenge to the British monopoly in this field) and the limited functions performed by the government make intervention unnecessary. Unlike other independent countries, the fact that Hong Kong politically is a dependent colony means that many of the functions performed by the Hong Kong government, as a non-sovereign government, are not needed or, if needed, are performed by the British government in Whitehall. Limited government inevitably results in limited contact between it and the Chinese society. Consequently, the bureaucratic polity and Chinese society share a "short" boundary. A short boundary is conducive to a high degree of separation between the two as interactions between them are thus circumscribed.

Even if the bureaucratic polity were to intervene into the Chinese society, it lacks the means to do so. As a laissez-faire government, the resource base of the bureaucratic polity is small. Moreover, it lacks the organizational penetration into the Chinese society to allow it to mould it in accordance with the government's wishes. Coercive means are out of the question. Not only would coercion destroy both stability and the human initiative needed for an industrial society heavily dependent on foreign trade and investment, it would also draw the unpredictable wrath and reaction of the Communist Chinese regime which, under normal circumstances, does not interfere with the government of Hong Kong.

That the Chinese society lacks the will, the perceived need, and the means to intrude into the bureaucratic polity is equally self-evident. The general political apathy of the Chinese people, which can be traced to their political culture, precludes any serious effort at acquiring political power and dominating the political arena. Moreover, it should be noted that to the Hong Kong Chinese, "political freedom" does not mean freedom to participate in political decision-making, but freedom *from* political oppression. It is this need for "political freedom" which drove many of them to Hong Kong in the past, though of course the economic motive was the most important factor. To the Chinese, bureaucratic power and hegemony are the givens with which one must live. They desire to minimize the incursions of bureaucratic power into their daily lives. Unless conditions are so unbearable that they have no alternative but violent political actions, the Chinese people will remain politically quiescent.

Embracing the ethos of utilitarianistic familism, which is engendered by the implanting of traditional Chinese normative, organizational and behavioural patterns onto the particular Hong Kong setting, the Chinese people in Hong Kong are able to meet many of their mundane needs arising from urban living through their primary resource networks, at the core of which is the familial group. Admittedly, not all Chinese people are involved in familial groups because of the absence of kinsmen and many of these familial groups are poorly organized and endowed with limited resources. Still, it cannot be denied that familial groups are the basic constituent unit in the Chinese society in Hong Kong. The low level of dependence on the government for the supply of resources to meet daily needs results in a situation where the bureaucratic polity is not salient as a channel of resource acquisition. As such, Hong Kong furnishes a prototypical case of the "social accommodation of politics." Low political salience and the ability of the Chinese to solve many of their problems jointly ensure that social issues, if any, are rarely pushed into the political arena for resolution or translated into political issues demanding redistribution of political power. A normative corollary to this is that individual or familial failures most of the time are explained away in individualistic or fatalistic terms, thus leaving the polity unscathed and insulating it from possible attacks from society. One more point that should be noted is that the limitations in the power of the government and its dependency on the British government (and to a lesser extent on the reactions of the Chinese government) are also known to the Chinese people, which sufficiently convinces them that it would be futile to press the government hard on many issues as they are beyond its power. Consequently, drastic political action would only be counter-productive, as it would lead either to the breakdown of social and political order, the precariousness of which necessitates the dominance of the bureaucracy, or it would lead to a Communist takeover after which Hong Kong would lose its value as a flourishing economy to both the British and the Chinese governments. Both these eventualities are haunting scenarios.

Even if the Chinese people were to exert influence or even power on the bureaucratic polity, they would find themselves ill-equipped to do so. Being an atomistic society, the Chinese society does not have strong and organized political groups to bid for political power. The lack of the institutional appurtenances which enable people in other countries to exercise political power and influence is a further constraint on the political capability of the Hong Kong Chinese. The political passivity of the Chinese, which has not been shaken up by any nationalist or revolutionary movements and the educational or indoctrinating impact they generate, adds an additional hurdle to mobilizing the Hong Kong Chinese into political action.

(3) The low level of interaction between the bureaucratic polity and the Chinese society is a result of the limited functions of the Hong Kong government, the ability of the Chinese to solve many of their problems, the normative inclination of both parties to minimize its contact with each other and the low level of political salience in Hong Kong. The lack of effective linkage devices to integrate both of them is another important contributory factor to the emergence of a minimally-integrated social-political system. Presumably, linking devices of one kind or another can be found in all social-political systems, even though they tend to perform different functions. Kay Lawson, for instance, provided the following checklist of major linkage mechanisms:

Linkage by penetration:
    a. governments locate their agents openly or covertly in citizen organizations;
    b. citizens place some of their members in government (via electoral processes or via acts of revolution, thus establishing a new government altogether).
Linkage by reaction:
    a. governments engage in acts of representative response to citizen views on policy;
    b. governments engage in acts of coercion to which citizens must perforce respond;
    c. governments and citizens exchange rewards for votes. (1980:11)

However, none of these linkage forms can properly be said to exist in Hong Kong. Because the above-quoted devices assume a degree of linkage between polity and society not commensurate with that which exists there. In general, it can be said that, on mundane administrative matters in particular, the Hong Kong government would in many instances "engage in acts of representative

response to citizen views on policy," but this responsiveness is neither automatic nor available in sufficient quantity to effectuate an integration of the
bureaucratic polity and the Chinese society.

The linkage devices in the social-political system of Hong Kong are weak.
They do not enable the Chinese people to affect policy-making in the bureaucracy, and they also fail to provide the necessary leverage to mobilize the
Chinese people to execute self-help or para-administrative functions which
would relieve the administrative burden of the bureaucracy. The extant
linkage devices do serve some purposes: enabling some information flow
between the government and the Chinese society; solving some problems of
the Chinese people which have something to do with the administration of
the colony; playing some "input" role and allowing the bureaucracy some
measure of influence over the Chinese society. However, the crucial point here
is that they do not bring the government and the Chinese society together.
The linkage mechanisms we have discussed in the last chapter, particularly the
traditionalistic organizations, also serve to reinforce the "compartmentalization" between them. This reinforcement function is accomplished in two ways:
first, they take care of some of the problems arising from the unavoidable
interactions between the two and make further integration unnecessary.
Second, they complement the inaequacies of the Chinese familial groups by
acting as an additional channel of resource provision, thus making the Chinese
society even more self-contained and more apolitical.

(4) The British-controlled bureaucratic polity and the Chinese society,
despite their relative isolation from each other and their different forms of
organization (a complex, formal organization versus an informal and particu-
laristically-oriented society), do share some fundamental orientations. They
both adopt political/social stability and economic prosperity as the ultimate
values of Hong Kong, and both parties' avowed purpose is to promote and
maintain them. The consensus also covers the respective roles of the bureaucratic polity (to maintain law and order, and to provide society with the
necessary services which it is unable to deliver for itself) and the Chinese
society (to support the government politically, to engage in diverse economic
pursuits and to maintain order among the Chinese people). Of course, areas of
disagreement can be visualized. Nevertheless, the political significance of the
disagreement pales when compared to the fundamental, though narrow,
consensus. The bureaucratic polity, in executing the functions "assigned" to
it by the consensus, enjoys legitimacy and authority among the Chinese people
in Hong Kong. And, within this agreed-upon realm of activities, the bureaucracy needs not appeal to force or coercion to obtain the conformity of the
Hong Kong Chinese. Of course this does not mean that its coercive capacity
does not count for anything. It in fact does, and it is a prerequisite to the

performance of its "law and order" role. But is is essential to pinpoint the fact that coercion is of little use in enabling the British to impose its rule upon the Chinese society if the narrow consensus is no longer there.

In general, the basic features of the minimally-integrated social-political system have remained stable since the Second World War. Though it is not our concern here, it would not be too off the point to characterize prewar Hong Kong as also a minimally-integrated system, while recognizing some significant differences between prewar and postwar Hong Kong. Among these are the less harmonious relationship between the government and the British merchants (Lethbridge 1969:125), the less favourable attitudes of the Chinese towards the British colonial government (*Ibid.* : 100-101), the more integrated Chinese elite structure, the primarily entrepôt nature of the economy, the more geographically mobile Chinese population, the lesser service-delivery role of the government and the relative insignificance of Chinese participation in the upper echelons of the bureaucratic administration. These differences notwithstanding, the persistence of the minimally-integrated social-political system for such a long time and amidst turbulent changes both in its environment and in the Hong Kong society itself is a magnificent feat. In order to understand the longevity of this system, we shall next deal with the problem of political stability in Hong Kong and the nature of politics in a minimally-integrated social-political system.

POLITICAL STABILITY AND BOUNDARY POLITICS

Admittedly, a minimally-integrated social-political system is not intrinsically conducive to political stability. The distinctive attribute of this system is the "compartmentalization" of the polity and society. This "compartmentalization," however, might be imposed on the society by force by the bureaucracy, which intentionally undertakes to departicipate and depoliticize society. The military regimes in many countries in Africa, as well as the bureaucratic-authoritarian regimes in Latin America are typical examples of "forced compartmentalization." In the same vein, official inauguration and control of all organizations with political relevance in socialist countries is in essence a means to dilute the impact of society on the polity; in this case, it is the calculated and controlled politicization of society by the polity that does the trick. In an era when popular participation in politics is extolled and the state is charged with the burden of nation-building and socioeconomic development, intense interaction between the polity and society is unavoidable. Efforts at imposed "compartmentalization" of polity and society contains within them an inherent element of instability. The incessant incidents of coup d'état, rebellion, assassination, internal war in many developing countries are vivid indicators of the dilemma of participation and departicipation facing the decision-makers in these countries.

In contrast to other developing countries, the minimally-integrated social-political system of Hong Kong is built on a more secure basis. What this means specifically is that the "compartmentalization" of polity and society in Hong Kong is based on consensus, and objective factors have so far not been able to throw this consensus into doubt or demand drastic restructuring of the relationship between the polity and society. We have seen that the limited functions of the bureaucratic polity, the "self-sufficiency" and resourcefulness of the Chinese society, and the tendency of both parties to avoid involvement in the affairs of each other, the absence of effective linkage mechanisms are forces inherent in the system which function to insure political stability by reducing political salience and by facilitating the process of "social accommodation of politics." Under these conditions, activities which might threaten the rule of the bureaucracy are hard even to envisage, not to say, organize. Of course we do not rule out political actions which might be violent, short-lived, poorly organized, with extremely small participant bases or instigated by frustrations of one kind or another. Nevertheless, they are not system-shaking forces.

The co-optation of prominent Chinese into the bureaucratic polity, though not a device whereby the bureaucracy can penetrate into the Chinese society, does enable it to deprive the Chinese society of much of the leadership talent which would be needed if political movements against the system were contemplated. This is not to say that the bureaucracy is able to absorb all leadership talent in the Chinese society into its ranks, but it does mean however that a substantial portion of the individuals deemed as successful in the Chinese society are supportive of the bureaucratic polity and are extremely reluctant to see the status quo altered. While "commending" the Hong Kong government on this achievement, it is also necessary to bear in mind that, upon objective analysis, the co-optive capacity of the bureaucracy is rather limited. Unlike many other governments in the developing world, which can reward their followers and supporters with high political offices, substantial economic benefits and lucrative positions in the bureaucratic administration, the Hong Kong government is prevented from doing so because, aside from the bureaucracy, there are no other powerful political institutions in Hong Kong which can provide attractive positions to its political supporters. Even within the bureaucracy itself, practically speaking no patronized positions are available, thus depriving the government of another kind of leverage for political co-optation. Moreover, the absence of significant state-controlled economic enterprises means that the Hong Kong government cannot employ a spoils system to attract those followers who are intent on pecuniary gains.

To be sure, the government is able to extend symbolic official recognition to the social status of prominent Chinese inhabitants, which is valued in itself in the Chinese society and which has implications for economic success. But still it is these prominent Chinese individuals' support of the existing state of affairs in general and their inability to visualize any viable sociopolitical alternatives which depoliticize (or politically deactivate) them rather than the unqualified co-optive success of the government.

The consensus on the need for political stability and economic prosperity in the Chinese society, which is shared with the bureaucracy, is a powerful stabilizing force. It is indisputably true that Hong Kong as a society has a number of potential lines of division which, if uncontrolled, could tear it apart. They follow race, ethnicity, political inclinations (towards the two Chinese governments) and even possibly class lines. Indeed, to many Hong Kong people. British and Chinese alike, political order in the colony is somewhat precarious, and the dominant presence of the bureaucracy, coupled with political self-restraint on the part of the Chinese, is essential to maintain that order. The consensus on political stability and economic prosperity exerts an overriding constraint on these potential lines of cleavage, and pushes them into secondary importance in the political arena in Hong Kong. This consensus also reins in somewhat the freewheeling self-seeking tendencies derived from utilitarianistic familism, which is prone to hold any conceptions of "common interest" in contempt. Without this consensus, social and political order in Hong Kong is unimaginable.

The services provided by the government is an additional contributory factor to the maintenance of political stability in Hong Kong. The volume of services involved is still fairly small. When however it is measured against the background of a relatively low expectation for services from the public sector on the part of the Chinese inhabitants, these services, delivered to the Chinese apparently upon the initiative of the government, would greatly appeal to the Chinese and put the government in a favourable light. To be sure, the service delivery function of the government is administered in an impersonal manner and in a "political vacuum" which does not involve the recipients or beneficiaries in any organic political relationship with the benefactor. Nonetheless, these services at least serve to complement the capabilities of the familial groups and the voluntary organizations in the Chinese society, and inject a dampening effect on any political heat that might ignite as a result of a shortage of resources.

Perhaps the most important factor underwriting political stability in Hong Kong is the low political mobilizability of the Chinese people. I am talking here primarily in structural terms, though it is important to underscore the stabilizing effects of political passivity and apathy. As a society composed of a huge number of mutually "isolated" familial groups whose members are pooled together to form a society largely by means of a complicated and impersonal system of division of labour engendered by an industrial society and reinforced by a market economy, mobilization of the Chinese people into *sustained*, *large-scale* political action is almost an impossible mission. The shortage of activistic political leadership and organizational networks which can tie the familial groups together and lessen the sentiments of mutual suspicion among them strengthens this political immobilism.

If we look around the world, we see that two types of societies are particularly vulnerable to political activism. One is the so-called mass society in which a mass of alienated and unattached individuals meet face-to-face with the state and the elites, without mediation by effective intermediary organizations (Kornhauser 1959). In such a setting, the mass is amenable to mobilization by counter-elites into extremist political actions against the political system, wreaking incalculable damages upon it. The other type of society is divided into a number of well-organized groups (communal, religious, class, ethnic, regional, etc.) which are readily available for mobilization into political actions against one another when conditions are ripe. Unlike the extremist actions of the mass society, which are inordinately violent and represent short-lived fits of emotional outbursts, political actions in structurally polarized societies are sustained, solidary political movements with explicit and rational goals. In the words of Oberschall:

> The minimum conditions of collective protest are shared targets and objects of hostility held responsible for grievances, hardships, and suffering, augmented in some cases by more deeply rooted sentiments of collective oppression, common interests, and community of fate. These minimum conditions give rise, however, to only short-term, localized, ephemeral outbursts and movements of protest such as riots. For sustained resistance or protest an organizational base and continuity of leadership are also necessary. The organizational base can be rooted in two different types of social structure. The collectivity might be integrated and organized along viable traditional lines based on kinship, village, ethnic or tribal organization, or other forms of community, with recognized leaders and networks of social relations extending to its boundaries. On the other hand, the collectivity might have a dense network of secondary groups based on occupational, religious, civic, economic, and other special interest associations with leaders based on prominent roles in these associations and networks of social relations following occupational ties. Both of these principles of social organization, and they are by no means mutually exclusive, produce horizontal links and sentiments of solidarity within the collectivity that can be activated for the pursuit of collective goals and the formation of conflict groups. (1973:119)

It can easily be seen that the Chinese society in Hong Kong does not fall into either of these categories. Individual Chinese are not uprooted and unattached people, for they are integrated into a multitude of familial groups.

The thin and ineffective layer of extra-familial organizations in the Chinese society is powerless to furnish the leadership for political movements. Moreover, the familial groups in Hong Kong are a potent restraining force on the political behaviour of their members, especially those in the younger generations. By inculcating among their members pervasive attitudes of reticence and respect for authority, the familial groups are significant stabilizing forces. Their sheer number, in addition, will discourage those who would contemplate political mobilization. Even short-lived paroxysms of social and political frustrations, which do occasionally occur, will be swiftly dissipated by the conservative inertia of these familial groups.

Against the large backdrop of political stability in Hong Kong, what then is the nature of politics in the colony? When many large issues which in other countries are breeding grounds of political confrontations are either non-existent or are beyond the control of Hong Kong, when the political monopoly of the bureaucracy is generally recognized and when the Chinese society has neither the will nor the means to challenge the political system, politics in Hong Kong loses all the glamour and "excitement" which characterize politics elsewhere. As a matter of fact, students of politics in Hong Kong are both frustrated and bored by its eventless and colourless nature. The government of Hong Kong is basically a municipal government. I am not denying here that it also has other functions which are normally the jurisdiction of an ordinary municipal government, but they are of secondary importance there. This municipal government administers the city-state in a smooth, pragmatic and no-nonsense manner. In such a setting, politics largely takes the form of disputes set in motion by what the government has done or has not done. To people of other countries, these are mundane and trivial issues, but they constitute the substance of politics in Hong Kong. I would prefer to call the politics in Hong Kong "boundary politics" since it does not involve any serious redefinition of the relationship between the bureaucratic polity and the Chinese society nor restructure the fundamental parameters of the social-political system of Hong Kong. What it involves are minor adjustments between the bureaucracy and the Chinese society, and they might result in some modifications of public policies or some redistribution of resources between the two parties. Resolution of political issues would tend to rest the social-political system at peace, while preserving the "cordial" though "distant" relationship between the bureaucracy and the Chinese society. Besides boundary politics, we can of course talk about politics within the bureaucracy itself and between it and the elites (both Chinese and British). Nevertheless, the submerged nature of politics of these kinds precludes any reliable analysis. Moreover, in the last several decades, politics of these kinds had not been destabilizing to the bureaucratic polity nor detracted it from functioning as an autonomous political institution. Therefore, it will be passed over here.

The nature of boundary politics in Hong Kong can be examined by noting a number of its salient characteristics.

(1) Boundary politics represents the dynamic facet of the minimally-integrated social-political system of Hong Kong, and is triggered by the ineluctable processes of socioeconomic change in the colony and the changing aspirations and expectations of the Chinese society. These changes in the Chinese society also inescapably modify its relationship with the bureaucratic polity. The need for more public housing facilities as a result of population increase and the inability of the private construction sector to cater to the needs of the disadvantaged is a case in point. In a general sense, boundary politics is a reactive adaptation of the bureaucratic polity to the changing Chinese society. Though occasionally it is the bureaucratic polity itself which takes the lead to adjust its relationship with the Chinese society, such as by adopting some sorts of social planning (in the delivery of services) or by making policy moves in anticipation of some popular demands, on the whole political reaction on the part of the bureaucracy forms the core of boundary politics in Hong Kong.

(2) Changes in the social-political system springing from boundary politics are incremental, gradual and minor in nature. Consequently, it is very difficult to identify clearly any particular drift of the social-political system. At most we can talk about a growing tendency of the government to listen to the Chinese people, a greater willingness of the people to bring their cases to the government for resolution, an increasing readiness of the government to assume the responsibility for service delivery, and a creeping process of politicization of the Chinese society. Nevertheless, these processes are still in their incipient stages, and we are not sure whether they would follow a unilinearly upward trajectory.

(3) Boundary politics in Hong Kong is largely informal and non-institutionalized, though given time, the levels of formality and institutionalization would increase simply as a result of repetition and "political learning." In boundary politics, problem-solving is basically undertaken in an *ad hoc*, piecemeal and reactive manner. Normally, issues demanding resolution appear seriatim, and their contents seldom overlap to such an extent that cumulative pressures will be generated on the government. The mode of resolution of one issue might not necessarily serves as a precedent which requires that succeeding issues be dealt with in like manner. This style of problem resolution militates against the establishment of permanent or institutionalized mechanisms to regulate the relationship between the bureaucracy and the Chinese society. If they were to be created, effective linkages would have to be installed which

would enable the public to participate effectively in the decision-making process of the government, and, as we have seen, it is extremely reluctant to share power with others. Consequently, aside from those linking mechanisms which are deliberately set up by the government, which can be easily mani- pulated and changed by it, political institutionalization stimulated by boundary politics is in general meagre. The informal nature of boundary politics serves the same purpose of preventing a fuller integration of the bureaucratic polity and the Chinese society. Through the selection of enforce- ment or non-enforcement of rules, the dampening of issues by means of persuasion, compromise, co-optation, bargaining, cajoling, assuming threatening postures or deliberately setting up informal rules (Chau and Lau 1982), the government is able to avoid formal restructuring of the political institutions in the colony. As informal concessions granted are usually couched in secrecy and are highly diversified and individualistic in nature, they usually fail to aggregate into system-changing forces. "The 'informal' politics is very im- portant and represents the 'real' dimension in the Hong Kong political scene. The meetings of the Legislative Council are obviously the tip of the iceberg where real social issues are observable if not soluble" (Harris 1978:17).

(4) Boundary politics is also non-ideological in nature, and this tightly circumscribes its impact on the system. Both the bureaucratic polity and the Chinese society are guided by material considerations and pragmatic concerns. Non-ideological issues are normally more amenable to peaceful resolution, as they involve low costs and few stakes. More importantly, they do not place the fundamental features of the minimally-integrated social-political system in jeopardy. Hence the bureaucratic polity is more inclined to give in. It is largely in the boundary political situations that the bureaucracy is fairly responsive, and it scores handsomely at this point in terms of support garnered from the Chinese society. While we have no definite idea as to when would the bureaucracy be responsive to demands, entreaties or petitions from the Chinese society, several tentative formulations can be attempted:

(a) Demands which are perceived by the government to be shared by a substantial portion of the public and appear to be "real" grievances would usually receive favourable treatment by it. The campaign to make the ICAC (Independent Commission Against Corruption) take a more "lenient" attitude towards the customary commercial kickback practices in the mid-1970s (Cheng, Lin and Kuan 1979:229; Lee 1977), the Chinese Language Movement in the late 1960s and early 1970s (which demanded that Chinese be listed as an official language in the government), the issues of rent control in residential premises in 1962 and 1980, the Telephone Message Rate System controversy and the demand for drastic measures to block the influx of illegal immigrants from China in 1980 are typical examples.

(b) Demands which can easily be met in terms of resource expenses will be favourably received by the government, as responsiveness in these cases will enhance the popularity of the government. Usually these demands or requests come from small groups of people whose plight is evident to all.

(c) Demands which might not necessarily be small but are self-contained in nature (meaning that conceding to them will not generate additional demands of similar kinds) might be taken care of, though with a little reluctance. The opposition to the Post Office Bill in 1975 is a case in point (Cheng, Lin and Kuan 1979:228).

(d) Demands which come from elite groups will usually receive favourable consideration from the government. The repeal of the Peak District (Residence) Ordinance of 1918, which made it unlawful for a Chinese to reside on the Peak without the consent of the Governor-in-Council, in 1946 can be cited as an example.

(e) Demands which the government perceives as unreasonable (and it might be correct upon objective analysis) will harden its opposition to them. The refusal of the government to give in on the issue of the fare raise by the Star Ferry, which precipitated the 1966 Riot, illustrates this point.

(f) Demands whose gratification by the government is seen by it as a violation of some of its cherished principles of governance or a threat to its fundamental interests will be ignored, even if the pressure from the public is great. The rejection by the government of proposals to regulate the rent of commercial premises in 1962 and 1980 was illustrative, for they ran counter to the principles of a laissez-faire economy which is the cornerstone of the government's economic policy and they would drastically reduce the revenue of the government.

(g) When the risks that the government has to take if the demands are ignored is low, particularly when they come from some disadvantaged groups which have not been able to garner widespread sympathy from the public, it will feel less compelled to gratify them.

(h) Demands the gratification of which will whet appetites and expose government weaknesses will not only be rejected fervently, they may even be arduously dampened. The demands of the Yaumati Typhoon Shelter boat people's demand for resettlement which began in 1977 are a typical example.

Needless to say the above list is far from exhaustive. It should also be remembered that several considerations simultaneously enter into the government's decision-making process with regard to a particular demand coming from society. Moreover, even if a demand is entertained by the government, gratification of it may not necessarily be complete. Judging from available evidence, partial gratification is normally the rule rather than the exception. Besides actual demand gratification, however, the government can manipulate a large number of devices which can weaken the thrust of the demands and eventually blunt their impact on the administration. These devices include: dispensing symbolic satisfaction rather than real satisfaction, dispensing token material satisfaction, organizing and innovating internally (i.e., administrative restructuring) in order to blunt the impetus of demand efforts, appearing to be constrained in its ability to grant concessions, discrediting protest leaders and organizations, and postponing action through the appointment of committees and advisory boards to "study" the matters at hand, so on and so forth.

(5) It should also be borne in mind that boundary politics in an overt form (such as public protests, large-scale publicity campaigns, incidents involving a certain measure of violence) is relatively rare in Hong Kong. The general structural conditions inherent in the minimally-integrated social-political system tend to drastically reduce the volume of issues with political relevance. The resort to informal and "covert" forms of issue resolution by the government is another contributory factor. The fact that the Chinese society is an extremely loosely integrated society with no potent political groups is also a causal factor, for, being unorganized, the Chinese people usually approach the government (when they feel compelled to do so) as demand-making (or more appropriately as request-making) *individuals* rather than as demand-making groups. Individualistic approaches to interest representation are as a rule "covert" in form. The government, on its part, prefers the "covert" forms of interest articulation and representation, for they serve to preserve the image of Hong Kong as a smoothly administered society immune from torrential protest movements from the general public.

When overt interest representations do occur, their mode of action do not fail to reflect the atomistic nature of the Chinese society. These actions are sporadic in nature, and are sparked by specific incidents the termination of which cools things down. Even if this is not done, time will normally be a heat-dissipating factor. No particular organization in the Chinese society is powerful enough to spearhead interest representation in all cases (though of course some are comparatively more active in general than others). In many instances, a number of organizations interested in particular issues have to pool their resources together to create a "public opinion pressure" against the government, or *ad hoc* organizations have to be established to press specific demands. However, true to the spirit of an atomistic society, large-scale mobilization of the Hong Kong Chinese into collective action is rarely attempted, and I suspect that such attempts can hardly be sustained. In many cases, public-opinion pressure oftentimes is simply an aggregation of opinions of organizational officers and newspaper editors. Almost in all of these cases, the government is powerful enough to give a cold shoulder to this pressure, if it is prepared to run the risk of alienating these people. In some occasions, concessions are forthcoming from the government. However, if the government persists in refusing to change its stand, there is comparatively little that the public-opinion pressure can do; and in many instances in the past it quietly vanished from the scene.

As a final note, it should be mentioned that boundary politics is an intrinsic characteristic of a minimally-integrated social-political system. The existence of boundary politics does not indicate that the system is not operating well. On the contrary, a "normal" amount of boundary politics can never be avoided and it might even function to maintain the viability of the minimally-integrated system. The basic constitution of such a system has two crucial structural characteristics: the sluggish and fallacy-prone flow of information across the boundary between the bureaucratic polity and the Chinese society, and the inadequacy and defectiveness of the interest articulation, aggregation and representation mechanisms available to the Chinese society. Since these characteristics make institutionalized absorption of politics difficult, boundary politics "must" break out to bring issues to the fore for attention and resolution. It serves as a barometer signalling that something has changed in the relationship between the polity and the Chinese society, and that boundary adjustments have to be made to redress the situation and to restore the balance. The sporadic and erratic character of boundary politics bespeaks its nonthreatening nature, and the noncumulativeness of boundary political issues underscores its system-maintenance rather than system-changing function.

CONDITIONS FOR THE MINIMALLY-INTEGRATED SYSTEM

The emergence and maintenance of the minimally-integrated social-political system of Hong Kong are a product of a constellation of structural and historical conditions, which together create an environmental setting unique to Hong Kong. In the following paragraphs we shall explicate a number of these conditions which we think have exerted enormous causal impact on the system. The influence of each of these conditions is certainly uneven, and it may be more significant for a particular component of the system. Even taken together we would still doubt that a "complete" explanation can be obtained. Nonetheless, the delineation of these conditions would definitely highlight the processes of formation and maintenance of the minimally-integrated social-political system of Hong Kong.

External Factors

Two crucial external factors underlie the "dependent" position of Hong Kong. One is the China factor, and the other is the open nature of the economy of Hong Kong.

The endorsement of the current political system in Hong Kong by China and her general reluctance to see the status quo altered would render any effort at structural transformation difficult. Even though it is possible to visualize some types of changes in the political constitution of Hong Kong while leaving the hegemony of the British intact, the preclusion of fundamental changes is sufficient to stifle much of the zeal at political reform and create a defeatist attitude among the Chinese (and the reformist British as well) that the status quo is a constant and beyond the power of both the government and the people to meddle with. The closing of the political path naturally leads to whole-hearted devotion of efforts to economic pursuits, opportunities for which are plentiful. The rise of apolitical materialism is a logical response of the Hong Kong Chinese to the unequal availability of political and economic opportunities in the unique setting which they find themselves.

The China factor also relieves the Hong Kong government of a number of functions which a sovereign government is expected to perform. These functions, such as nation-building, ideological inculcation, political mobilization, build-up of a substantial public sector, income redistribution, etc., which would theoretically induce structural transformation in society, are in general absent from the agenda of the bureaucracy in Hong Kong. The dependence of the Hong Kong government on the British government to handle its diplomatic and military affairs also exempts it from being entangled with problems which in other countries constitute major sources of political controversies. In the case of defense, the nonexistence of an autonomous military establishment in Hong Kong, which is both a source of political instability and a source of "imposed" political stability in many developing societies, is a particularly noteworthy fact in relation to the political autonomy of its government. Overall, the political dependent status of Hong Kong makes the government a "limited" government performing limited governmental functions, and eliminates many issues which have the potentiality of seriously politicizing the society of Hong Kong.

The open economy of Hong Kong renders any attempts on the part of the government to guide the economy relatively futile, and serves to immunize the government from pressures directed at making it play a more active economic role, thus releasing it from many political issues which are economic in origin and making it a less attractive target of control by the dominant economic interests in the colony. The open economic system has two other effects which tend to temper social conflicts in the Chinese society and inhibit the rise of conflict groups. The expanding-sum game character of economic competition in Hong Kong tends to dilute class hostility; and the availability of seemingly endless chances for economic mobility makes individualistic efforts at self-improvement more attractive and "economical" than collective efforts.

Society of Immigrants

The fact that immigrants from China constitute a large proportion of the Chinese population of Hong Kong has generated a number of effects on the society of Hong Kong.

(1) That almost half of the immigrants came from cities and towns means that their ultimate social adjustment to the urban setting of Hong Kong is made smoother and reduces the dislocations felt in the Chinese society in the years of large-scale immigrant influx.

(2) As most of the immigrants came to Hong Kong in pursuit of economic opportunities, they largely constituted a self-selected group whose intention is not to question or attack the political system in Hong Kong, which existed prior to their decisions to emigrate. The memories of political disorder in their homeland would make them receptive to a political system whose avowed purpose is to maintain political stability and which has demonstrated a capability of doing so.

(3) Many of the immigrants are well equipped, both psychologically and organizationally, to engage in fierce economic competition befitting a booming commercial and industrial society. Those who came from the urban-industrial centres of China, notably Shanghai, had been accustomed to cut-throat economic competition with one another in order to promote their familial interests. This was also the past experience of many of those who were Cantonese, who comprised the majority of the Chinese population in Hong Kong. Most Cantonese came from that part of Kwangtung Province which is called the Pearl River Delta, where commercialization, invasion of foreign goods, high levels of rural tenancy, poverty, population pressure, banditry and social instability were the order of the day in the last century or so. Competition in the struggle for survival was keen and relentless, and the Cantonese immigrants carried with them habits appropriate to that struggle. Once in Hong Kong, cut off from the moral ties with their home communities, they were exempt from traditional moral sanctions and control. Chinese immigrants in Hong Kong were therefore less bound to the preservation and promotion of family honour and reputation. And, since their home communities were also in the whirlwind of a drastic sociocultural transformation

which cast the criteria of family reputation into doubt, concern for family status in Hong Kong among a people whom they do not care for or respect would seem to be too far-fetched and unnecessary. Chinese immigrants feel a minimum of obligations to one another and to the society of Hong Kong as a whole—a fact which breeds high levels of social and political estrangement. Utilitarian considerations thus creep in to structure interpersonal relationships.

(4) The in-migration of Chinese into Hong Kong in the period 1945-52 took place in an extraordinary form which had long-range effects on intra-familial relationships, and was somewhat different from the pre-1945 im-migrations. Pre-World War II family migrations to Hong Kong were well planned and well coordinated: "first [came] the able-bodied young men, followed by their younger siblings who could learn a trade early, help out in the business. The dependents would come later and make their stay permanent" (Liu 1966:315). This type of mobility would not strain family relationships too severely and would leave the original ideal of kinship ties intact. Family emigration after 1945 "was not well planned and it usually involved drastic interruptions of family relationship because of continuous and morally damaging uprootedness necessitated by events and dictated by risks of personal security" (Ibid.: 315). This disorderly process of family mobility has resulted in an attenuated, fragmentary and dispersed kinship structure, which makes the application of precise and rigorous kinship terminology to regulate interpersonal relationships impossible. The family is also in a weakened position to enforce strict conformity to kinship obligations on its members. The diminution of the patrilineal emphasis, the exercise of selectivity in the choice of kinsmen as interacting partners, and the recruitment of non-relatives into the familial groups through the application of vague kinship labels are thus facilitated.

(5) The Hong Kong into which the postwar immigrants moved was a colonial society with a laissez-faire economic doctrine, its institutional structure geared to the maintenance of law and order and to sustaining an environment appropriate for capitalist endeavours by both foreigners and Chinese. These factors, together with the fact that Hong Kong was—as it still is—dependent on foreign markets for its exports, mean that economic insecurity, both objective and subjective, was an inherent aspect of the colony, alleviated but little by the few institutional structures that promised support and relief in times of need and desperation.

In such an institutional vacuum the Chinese family has to play a prominent role in the accommodation of the new immigrants. The usefulness of the family system can be clearly seen in the absorption of the great influx of refugees pouring into Hong Kong since 1945. Barnett coined the term "social osmosis" to describe the process whereby the refugees, as individuals, families or small groups, are maintained in Hong Kong, largely through the efforts of the family system (1953:1-8). In his words,

> It would be difficult to estimate how many unemployed or partially employed refugee relatives and friends are supported by the well-to-do members of this one web of relationships, but the number is obviously large. The assistance given is in the form both of cash handouts and jobs, and often it is difficult to draw a clear line differentiating the two. The result is that a large number of persons who in other types of societies would probably become public charges are absorbed into the community with a minimum of strain visible to the outsiders. (*Ibid.*: 4)

As a result of the process of "social osmosis," the influx of refugees into Hong Kong has generated a minimum of social disorder. Moreover, the need for mutual help among family members, particularly economic assistance, tends to accentuate the utilitarianistic relationships among them. And, since the available amount of resources is in most cases insufficient to enable all kinsmen to have a share and since it is the natural tendency of each family unit to expand its resource base through enlisting new members, the selective inclusion of kinsmen into the family group and the manipulation of kinship terminology to define relationships with nonkinsmen are natural outcomes.

(6) As a society of immigrants, there are no entrenched power groups in Hong Kong which can make traditionalistic claims on power and privilege, or can muster political challenges to the Hong Kong government by means of mobilizing their subordinate constituents into action. The government is hence relieved of the political necessity of countering the challenge of these groups or coming to terms with them. Either option would entail an expansion of the political arena and the possible sharing of power with groups outside of the bureaucracy, thus threatening the political autonomy of the bureaucratic administration and circumscribing maneuverability. On the part of the Chinese society, the nonexistence of these groups eliminates from the local scene a past history of group oppression, social conflict and irreconcilability of social interests, which is a very important source of social instability plaguing other developing countries. The so-called "Hong Kong families" not only are few in number, but they can trace their origins in Hong Kong for only several generations. They by no means form a "caste-group" which, by articulating a particular set of cultural symbols and an exclusionary theory of status distinctiveness, can deny upward mobility to other Chinese inhabitants. The relative openness of the Chinese society of Hong Kong is highly instrumental in muting social conflict and fostering a certain amount of consensus which endorses the status quo.

The Economy and Sustained Economic Development

Perhaps the most important factor that can be cited to explain the stability of the minimally-integrated social-political system of Hong Kong is the sustained economic development in the postwar period and the economy which underlies it. The enormous economic success which Hong Kong has achieved enables the government not only to justify its acclaimed laissez-faire economic doctrine, it also affords it the luxury of not being required to play an active interventionist role in society, a luxury denied to many developing countries. While governments in many developing countries are compelled to assume the responsibility of promoting economic development, the most extreme forms of which are state capitalism and socialism, it is the private sector in Hong Kong which presents the challenge. Hong Kong is unique in the sense that the essential ingredients of economic development, whose nonavailability or shortage has retarded the progress of development in many countries and made the public sector indispensable, converged at Hong Kong in the late 1940s and early 1950s (except for natural resources), at a time when they were desperately needed to enable her to feed and employ the rising population. Capital and entrepreneurship from China and from abroad, coupled with a disciplined and hardworking (and lowly-paid) labour force, gave Hong Kong the impetus to rapid and sustained economic development and turned it almost overnight from an entrepôt into a vibrant industrial city. While political instability in many developing countries emanates from the failure of their governments to develop their economies and improve the standard of living of the people, the success of economic development in Hong Kong is on the contrary the cornerstone of its political stability.

It is incontestably true that economic development in Hong Kong is accompanied, and even underwritten, by a glaring economic gap between the rich and the poor. With regard to the problem of political stability in Hong Kong, however, it is the gradual impvovement of the absolute standard of living of the masses and the slow but steady narrowing of the economic gap which are critical in maintaining a pro-status quo frame of mind in the Chinese society as a whole. Culling data from various sources and taking into consideration other studies, Chow and Papanek were able to demonstrate the secular trend of diminishing income inequities in Hong Kong:

> There is considerable consistency in the results. Income distribution in Hong Kong was not and is not egalitarian compared to other Asian countries. However, when comparable data sources are used, it seems to have become more egalitarian between the mid-'60's' and the '70's'. At the very least there does not appear to be any evidence that income distribution deteriorated during the period of very rapid growth. The most consistent evidence is that the large majority in the middle increased their share. The poorest 10% may have lost relatively, but not absolutely. The top 10% also have lost relatively. It is the 70% in the third though the ninth deciles who seemed to have gained a greater share of the total income. (1979:13 and 15)

And the absolute increase in real income is particularly impressive:

With income distribution remaining unchanged, or becoming more equitable, a high growth rate with average household income near tripling, meant a dramatic improvement in the absolute income of the poor (as well as elegant profits for the rich). Using the shaky income distribution data one finds that the real income of the poorest 10% increased 150% and of the poorest 20% more than doubled in the roughly two decades between 1957 and 1976. For the next 40%, the poor majority, real income quadrupled over the same period. Over the decade 1966 to 1976, when data from the same source are available, the real income of the poorest 10% more then [sic] doubled, of the poorest 20% increased over 40%, and of the next 40% more than doubled. Whatever years are compared the conclusion is the same: even the poorest of the poor—presumably recent immigrants or handicapped families— saw their real income rise about 4% a year and those slightly less poor by 7% a year. The magnitudes are different for the comparison of 1973/4 with 1963/4, based on different and less reliable data, but the conclusions are the same.

   In current U.S. dollars the change is obviously even more dramatic, but this is a less appropriate index of improvement over time. What it does show, however, is that by 1976 even the poorest 20% had reached a household income of $1,300, way above any poverty index established for any Asian country. (*Ibid.*: 15)

Moreover, the delivery of services by the Hong Kong government also contributes to a slight reduction in the inequality of income distribution in Hong Kong. "Although the reduction in income inequality brought about by fiscal measures is not as far-reaching in Hong Kong as in most developed countries, the improvements are nevertheless significant and apparently greater than those observed in many developing countries. In terms of income, the poor have undoubtedly benefited more than suggested by the 10 per cent overall reduction in the Gini ratio. Benefits from public expenditures net of tax burden exceed 20 per cent of the household income for each of the four lowest income classes" (Ho 1979:177).

The improvement in the standard of living has manifold effects on the minimally-integrated social-political system. First, it directly contributes to a Chinese society which is resourceful enough to allow the familial groups to survive. The capability of the familial groups to draw on their own resources to cater to their needs is instrumental in reducing the salience of political channels of need satisfaction. It hence injects a comfortable buffer between the bureaucratic polity and the Chinese society, and consequently the latter is substantially depoliticized.

Second, continuing increases in the standard of living also foster a spirit of hopefulness among the Hong Kong Chinese, making the existing system all the more appealing, and turning the Chinese into bedrock opponents to social and political instability. Only if their expectations of a better material future for themselves and their offspring are frustrated would political measures be considered. Up to the present moment, such eventualities are unlikely for Hong Kong people.

Third, sustained economic growth in turn furnishes the government with resources large enough to allow it to provide services to the Chinese society and to soothe some of the sores of an industrializing society, which might be politically threatening. These resources undoubtedly also enable the government to dispense benefits to its supporters and to deactivate its opponents, though this point is a minor one when put against the backdrop of the generally secure position enjoyed by the government of Hong Kong.

The proliferation of small, family businesses in the economic structure of Hong Kong is an important, if not determining, factor in the prevalence of utilitarianistic familism in the Chinese society. In the launching of commercial or industrial undertakings, financial resources from family members and relatives oftentimes constitute the most reliable and convenient source of capital and credit. Particularly in Hong Kong, where highly flexible small businesses and dynamic styles of capital investment and retrieval (most times only in small amounts) make possible the miracle of economic prosperity in the colony, family businesses play an extremely significant and indispensable role.

The economic structure of Hong Kong, with its high concentration ratios in both the commercial and industrial sectors, parallels its social structure with a tremendous disparity between the extreme minority of high-income recipients and the vast majority of those earning lower income. In the manufacturing sector, for which statistical figures are available, the share of small manufacturing enterprises (those employing less than fifty persons) in terms of number of establishment steadily increased from 78.7% in 1961 to 86.5% in 1971, and then to 92.1% in 1977. In absolute figures, there were only 1,434 small establishments in 1951. The number increased to 4,365 in 1961; in 1971, it was 23,140. Thus, in twenty years' time, the increase was over sixteenfold. By December 1977, the number increased further to 34,632 establishments. The share of industrial employment by small establishments is equally impressive. In December 1977, they accounted for 40.2% of total manufacturing employment. In more recent years, this share displayed a steady and significant increase, and the trend of increase is expected to continue in the future (Sit et al. 1979:24).

It is not difficult to envision the sociocultural impact of such a large number of family business in Hong Kong. In an export-oriented economy, uncertainty about foreign market demands and about one's employment and advancement opportunities must be relatively great. The proliferation of small family businesses at least injects some hope into many Chinese people that even if things go sour, they may still be able to find comfort psychologically in the possibility of starting a small family business of their own with resources pooled from fellow members of familial groups, even though in the meantime they may have no need for it.

Most of the small businesses are familistic in the sense that ownership is in the hands of one or a few families. On the other hand, since the goals of these businesses are to make profits as soon as possible, and to exploit promptly whatever opportunities present themselves, the management of these businesses cannot be familistic in the traditionalistic sense, with rampant nepotism and particularism. The spirit of utilitarianistic familism is vividly reflected in the operation of these businesses, and the essence of this spirit is to utilize the most capable personnel and the most efficient and effective deployment of resources to further the material interests of the owners. Utilitarianistic familism, when directed to business management, serves as a change-inducing mechanism in that it does not oppose innovation and universalistic orientation whenever they are deemed to be beneficial to the success of the business. And in fact the small businesses in Hong Kong are highly productive and innovative (Mok 1973, 1974). The high rate of failure in the case of small businesses, which cannot survive abrupt changes in market conditions, in turn bolsters the significance of the familial group as the refuge of security in times of financial insolvency for the owners of small businesses and their employees.

The low salience of ascriptive and particularistic orientations in the management of small businesses has been brought out by the study of Ambrose King and his associates (1974, 1975). The hiring of relatives by the owners was cherished by them as an instrumental mechanism to secure somebody whom they can really trust. Consequently, the inclusion of relatives into one's business can be likened to the recruitment of relatives into one's familial group (overlapping of membership in these two groups is of course possible), as rational criteria are employed in both cases. Utilitarianistic familism thus finds its mirror image in the small family businesses.

Urban Society

Hong Kong as a small urban society contributes to the formation of a minimally-integrated social-political system in several ways. First, the insignificance of a rural sector in Hong Kong distinguishes it from other developing countries where the sharp contrast between the urban and rural sectors is a highly destabilizing force. Regionalism and the conflicts derived from it hence do not operate to politicize and polarize society.

Second, geographical mobility and the relaxation of social control in an urban society make the continuation of Chinese families founded on traditional principles impossible, thus allowing utilitarianistic familism to flourish.

Third, while we have already noted before that public demand for urban services on the government is generally low, it should also be noted that as a municipal government, these demands, when they are forthcoming, are of such a nature that confrontation between the government and large organized groups in society can in the main be avoided. This is because of the "divisibility" of urban services, which discourages the formation of broadly-based demand-making groups.

> Citizen demands are deeply fragmented because of the nature or urban public services. Because urban services are personalized and locality specific, they are highly divisible, both in terms of delivery and citizen demands.
>
> Unlike pure public goods like national defense or national parks, urban services tend to be highly divisible, in quantity and quality, between different individuals, blocks, or neighborhoods. . . . Conversely urban administrators can make countless small adjustments and reallocations both in their deployment of street-level bureaucrats and in their definition of what service policies and procedures should be followed in a particular neighborhood. . . .
>
> There is enormous variation in individual needs and demands for city services. Service demands may vary from individual to individual on a block, from block to block, and from neighborhood to neighborhood. . . .
>
> These differences are important because many urban service problems affect a very small public, and the solution of one problem is often entirely independent of the solution of others. . . . In short because the delivery of and the demand for urban services is so locality specific, one resident may be satisfied with service delivery while his neighbor is highly discontented. . . .
>
> Given the number and diversity of cleavages in citizen service demands and given the fact that citizens tend to have a well-crystallized sense of their own service interests (because the services are tangible and visible), the structure of citizen demands for services thus is deeply fragmented. (Yates 1977:21-23)

The non-ideological nature of urban service demands renders them amenable to pragmatic administrative resolution. The fragmentation of demands for urban services makes aggregation of demand over a large geographical area difficult; therefore they can be easily dealt with by the bureaucracy, particularly when the level of demands is as generally low as it is in Hong Kong. The urban nature of Hong Kong thus contributes to pragmatic, *ad hoc* and piecemeal issue resolution, which is in line with the nature of boundary politics as has been explicated before.

It can readily be seen that in attempting to explain the emergence and maintenance of the minimally-integrated social-political system of Hong Kong, we have adopted an eclectic and multifactorial approach. This is done by design, for we cannot envisage a better alternative. In view of the fact that the development of Hong Kong in the last several decades is not the continuation of a process of development of a society inhabited by an indigenous and settled population over an extended time period, a historical approach is not quite appropriate. In our opinion, an eclectic approach has the merit of demonstrating that the minimally-integrated system of Hong Kong is the product of a fortuitious combination of factors which happen to converge at a particular time. While there is nothing unnatural about the social-political system of Hong Kong, this approach does show that because Hong Kong is so unique, its social-political system is highly unlikely to be replicated in other parts of the world.

7. Conclusion

Samuel P. Huntington advocated in his seminal work *Political Order in Changing Societies* (1968) a "gap hypothesis" to explain the endemic political instability in developing countries. This hypothesis in fact consists of three interrelated propositions, each of which suggests a gap between two specific processes of social change. While each of these gaps has destabilizing effects in its own right, together they exert formidable destabilizing impact on the changing societies. Huntington's gap hypothesis provides a helpful starting point for the problem of political stability in Hong Kong which we posed at the beginning of this book.

The first gap, according to Huntington, is the gap between social mobilization and economic development. Specifically, this is a gap between aspiration and expectation, want formation and want satisfaction, or the aspiration function and the level-of-living function. This gap generates social frustration and dissatisfaction. The relationship between social frustration and political instability is mediated in turn by two potential intervening variables: opportunities for social and economic mobility and adaptable political institutions. Conceivably this frustration could be removed through social and economic mobility if the traditional society is sufficiently "open" to offer opportunities for such mobility.

> Apart from urbanization, however, most modernizing countries have low levels of socio-economic mobility. In relatively few societies are the traditional structures likely to encourage economic rather than political activity. Land and any other types of economic wealth in the traditional society are tightly held by a relatively small oligarchy or are controlled by foreign corporations and investors. The values of the traditional society often are hostile to entrepreneurial roles, and such roles consequently may be largely monopolized by an ethnic minority (Greeks and Armenians in the Ottoman Empire; Chinese in southeast Asia; Lebanese in Africa). In addition, the modern values and ideas which are introduced into the system often stress the primacy of government (socialism, the planned economy), and consequently may also lead mobilized individuals to shy away from entrepreneurial roles. (1968:54-55)

The gap between social frustration and mobility opportunities thus channelizes individuals with high aspirations into political activities in order to satisfy their needs.

> In these conditions, political participation becomes the road for advancement of the socially mobilized individual. Social frustration leads to demands on the government and the expansion of political participation to enforce those demands.

The political backwardness of the country in terms of political institutionalization, moreover, makes it difficult if not impossible for the demands upon the government to be expressed through legitimate channels and to be moderated and aggregated within the political system. (*Ibid.*: 55)

Following the lines of Huntington's arguments but turning them upside down, it can be said that the prevalence of political stability in Hong Kong originates from a small gap between social mobilization and economic development. But further elaboration on this point is needed. Economic development in Hong Kong is indeed impressive, but whether, under conditions of glaring inequality of income distribution, it is sufficient to meet the aspirations of the "socially mobilized" Hong Kong Chinese is a moot point. Admittedly the rise in the absolute standard of living produces a soothing effect in the Chinese society; however, judging from the economic expectations and the material motives found in most of the illicit and criminal activities in Hong Kong, social frustration, or more aptly economic frustration, is far from being negligible. Given an open market economy and the values placed on economic achievements, presumably the sentiments of social frustration could be taken care of in Hong Kong. While there is no reason to doubt that opportunities for mobility in Hong Kong are available, they are far from adequate to satisfy the needs of a Chinese society with five million people. As a matter of fact, the labour-intensive nature of the Hong Kong economy is not particularly favourable to rapid upward mobility of an overwhelming majority of the Chinese populace. Objectively speaking, the chances of both intergenerational and intragenerational mobility are not particularly high. Even though in general the Hong Kong Chinese can expect a continuous increase in their standard of living, they do not harbour too much expectation of improvement of the class position of themselves or their offspring. In fact, Mitchell found that 31% of the Hong Kong Chinese felt that they were better off than their parents, which was the lowest community rate compared to other societies in Southeast Asia, whereas 36% said they were worse off, which was the highest rate in the region (1969a, vol. 1:153). Moreover, the adult population of the Chinese society was strikingly pessimistic about its own chances to become successful. Only 18% of the men said there was a great deal of quite a bit of opportunity for themselves to become a success (*Ibid.*: 173). Thus, when it is also recalled that in Chapter 4 we found that many of the Hong Kong Chinese said that there was a lot of opportunity to get rich, these findings seem contradictory.

But upon further analysis they are not, and the "contradictions" can easily be resolved. In the first place, the Hong Kong Chinese are justified in their expectations of an ever-increasing standard of living, in the absolute sense, for themselves and for others, in view of the sustained economic growth of Hong

Kong which has yet showed no signs of abatement. On the other hand, based on the observation that many prominent individuals in Hong Kong have managed to accumulate enormous wealth from scratch and with their bare hands, a grossly exaggerated image of Hong Kong as a land of opportunity has caught the eye of many Chinese people. While they consider that *other* people who are able and fortunate can exploit these opportunities to their own advantage, they do not necessarily consider that they *themselves* can follow suit, either because they think they do not possess the capabilities or they are not unscrupulous enough to engage in illicit activities. Consequently, it is the expectation of increasing standards of living and the psychological gratifications derived from the belief that one is living in a land of opportunities which manage to hold frustrations within bounds. In the long run, even though an individual's objective class position compared to that of his father remains unchanged, the fact that he enjoys a life-style which is materially more comfortable than his father's may instill in him a sense of psychological mobility, and thus lessen the high sense of frustration which might otherwise torment him.

A certain level of social frustration in Hong Kong certainly exists, and can be easily felt by causal observers, even though its magnitude should not be overly exaggerated. In our opinion, however, the normative and structural patterns of Hong Kong's social-political system are capable of maintaining political stability even if the level of social frustration is higher than what it is now. In a minimally-integrated social-political system, it would be difficult for social issues to be converted into political issues, for want of the necessary conversion mechanisms (counter-elites, politicians, electoral machineries, political parties, charismatic leaders, political movements, patron-client networks, etc.). The unorganized nature of an atomistic society naturally immunizes it from large-scale and sustained political mobilization. The lack of a dominant ideology, be it nationalism, communism, ethnicism, regionalism, anarchism, or developmentalism, is another depoliticizing influence, and it in turn reinforces the pragmatic instrumentalism which informs both the government and the Chinese people. The absence of any experience in intense political struggles among the majority of the Hong Kong Chinese further contributes to their apolitical character. As a matter of fact, their decision to flee to Hong Kong rather than to "participate" in the revolutionary changes in their motherland would suggest that they are a group with particularly strong anti-political feelings. Consequently, the conversion of social frustration, even if its level is high, into political participation is difficult to visualize.

Under conditions of low levels of social frustration and political participation, the political institution of Hong Kong (the bureaucratic polity) appears effective enough to maintain political stability in the colony. The cohesiveness

186   Society and Politics in Hong Kong

and solidarity within the bureaucratic polity contrasts sharply with the polities
of many developing countries, which are divided by elite dissensions and
power struggle. Disunities within the polities of these countries leads to
unremitting competitive mobilization of the masses by elites pitting against
one another, resulting in enlargement of the political arena, politicized
societies, and polities which are in themselves sources of political instability.
The dominance of the bureaucratic polity in Hong Kong and the absence of
other viable political institutions are significant stabilizing factors in Hong
Kong. Furthermore, the deliberate decision of the Hong Kong government
not to overextend its capability by confining its limited power and resources
to a narrow range of functions, coupled with a generally low expectation for
the government, and a sense of futility in changing the political system on the
part of the Chinese people, strengthen the basis of political stability in Hong
Kong.

   While Hong Kong's political stability contrasts starkly with the instability
which afflicts many developing countries, it is important to take note of the
fact that Hong Kong's political stability is made possible by a fortuitous set
of circumstances which are not likely to be replicated elsewhere. With the
basic political system "fixed" by external factors, economic development,
urbanization and the influx of immigrants not only do not beget social
disorganization and political turmoil, but they actually capitalize on the still
viable organizational patterns of the Chinese people which are transformed into
the basis of a stable social order. This in turn contributes substantially to
sustained economic development in Hong Kong. Rather than talking about
the disruptive political and social effects of economic development in Hong
Kong, it is more appropriate to talk about the dependency of economic
development on the unique structure of the Chinese society.

   Both the bureaucratic polity and the Chinese society are important in
maintaining political stability in Hong Kong. But, based on our previous
discussion, we can suggest that in view of a polity whose constitutional
makeup and the inherent characteristics of a bureaucratic organization would
limit its adaptability to change, the Chinese society is the more important
factor. Alternatively put, it is social stability which makes political stability
possible and lasting in Hong Kong. And I believe that the last statement can
in fact be universally applied. Huntington's thesis is in essence a theory on the
inability of a polity to contain the disruptive effects ensuing from a rapidly
changing and disorganizing society, in which the mechanisms of social sanction
and control are no longer capable of restraining the conflicting forces released
by an unrelenting process of social mobilization.

   There is no reason to predict that in the foreseeable future the political
stability of Hong Kong will be threatened, as the conditions underlying it are

either unchangeable (the China factor, for example) or gradual in their changes. In any way, some creeping changes can still be detected. Even though these changes are far from revolutionary in character, they still would demand some kind of adjustment in the relationship between the bureaucratic polity and the Chinese society. The general direction of these changing relationship would be, I presume, towards a closer integration between these two components. And this closer relationship is unavoidable in view of the increasing complexity of the economy, the gradually rising aspirations of the Hong Kong Chinese, and the changing nature of social problems which require more and more centralized coordination for their solution.

Among the changing conditions are the following:

(1) There is an emerging middle-income, educated sector which is increasingly inclined to participate in public decision-making and which is beginning to be disillusioned with the responsiveness thus far displayed by the Hong Kong government.[1]

(2) There seems to be a continuous, slow and inexorable process of erosion of utilitarianistic familism, engendered by the modernization of Hong Kong. In the future, we can expect the familial ethos to lose influence, particularly among the younger generation. We will then see the prevalence of utilitarianistic individualism, the weakening of the familial groups, and the proliferation of individuals who are less amenable to social control. The political impact of a less organized Chinese society is difficult to envisage here. But it would certainly mean that the polity has to play a more active role in promoting social "reorganization." Whether it likes it or not, or whether by intention or by default, the policies of the government will be of increasing importance to the structure of the Chinese society. If the part played by the Chinese society in maintaining political stability is reduced in importance, the part played by the government has to be correspondingly increased. The result *has*

---

[1] In 1979(?), the Home Affairs Department of the Hong Kong government conducted a small-scale study of a select group of middle-income employees in a well established commercial organization. The group chosen were successful young Chinese executives in their late twenties to late thirties with an average age of about thirty-three. All had been educated in Hong Kong to at least Form VI level and many had a university degree or a professional qualification. Their salaries averaged around HK$5,000 a month and in most cases they were buying a flat with a loan from their firm. They each had between ten and fifteen years of working experience.

It was found that they were unanimous in believing: (1) that there was a credibility gap between the public and the government; (2) that the system of government by consultation had limitations; (3) that the presence of unofficials from financial, real estate and industrial circles on consultative committees did not safeguard the interests of the wider community; (4) that unofficials on consultative committees did not speak out; (5) that the government needed to make much more effort in community relations. (Walden 1980:4-5) to be a closer relationship between government and Chinese society.

(3) The weakening of social ties in the Chinese society also takes another form. One of the most important social effects of the government's large-scale public housing programme is the rise of new residential communities where community ties and identification are fragile. Admittedly they are also weak in the older neighbourhoods, but the fact that these new communities are more dependent on the government for the provision of facilities injects a new dimension in the relationship between the government and the people. The absence of effective intermediate organizations to mediate between these people and the government is conducive to the emergence of sporadic, *ad hoc* and short-lived protest movements directed against the government (Lau 1981a). Even though we can discount the seriousness of these activities, they still would demand some adjustments, political as well as administrative, by the government.

(4) The trend of decline of intermediaries between the government and the people will continue uninterrupted, and its adverse effects on the flow of information between the two parties will be exacerbated as the structural complexity of Hong Kong continues to increase. The divergence in outlook and political orientations between upper-level and lower-level Chinese elites will be enlarged as modernization continues to exert its differentiating effects. Polarization of the elite structure will further aggravate the linkage problem. Under current constitutional arrangements, it is difficult to foresee the emergence of spontaneously and voluntarily organized groups from within the Chinese society to meet the linkage needs. One of the response to this "communication gap" crisis planned by the government is the setting up of some district boards in the near future, with both appointed and elected (on a universal adult franchise) members, whose functions are to serve as consultative organs for local government officials (*White Paper: District Administration in Hong Kong*, 1981). While these planned measures might have some salutary effects on local administration (which will be becoming more deconcentrated) if the government is determined to make the experiment work, their utility as an effective linkage mechanism is extremely hard to predict. Though any venturing into sociological prediction is always hazardous, we are still inclined not to expect too much from these advisory bodies, at least in the short term, for the simple reason that the necessary structural and psychological conditions which ensure the successful operation of an electoral system are largely unavailable in Hong Kong (Lau, 1982).

(5) The gradual expansion of the service-delivery role of the government will persist both because of objective needs and the rising expectations of the Hong Kong Chinese. And, in view of the stiffer economic competition which Hong Kong will be facing in the international market in the future, this

interventionist role of the government will have to be extended into the economic arena (The Advisory Committee on Diversification 1979), thus revising somewhat the laissez-faire policy so doggedly adhered to in the past. The increasing involvement of the government in the Chinese society would unavoidably bring about more "boundary political issues" which not only would demand adjustments between the polity and society, but would also put the adaptability and capability of the government to severe tests. More importantly, the essence of these tests lies not so much in taxing its capacity to deliver physical resources to society as on demands for political and human-relations skills from the government officials. Increasingly, government officials will be involved in delivering services which contain a significant "human" component (such as social casework, arbitration between competing business interests, administration of housing estates, dealing with labour disputes). Even those services which were considered to be "impersonal" in the past (we have particularly in mind police work) are rapidly gaining their human dimensions, and necessitate remodelling of the behaviour of the service deliverers. Bureaucratic structures are notorious for their "impersonality" and inertial sluggishness in adapting to changes. These changing expectations on the service-delivery roles of government officials, arising from the development of specialist professions and the changing conceptions of the public, have already generated strains among the rank-and-file of the government and friction in their relationships with the people. "Client-oriented" role expectations can only be realized in a more cordial relationship between the government and the people.

The expansion of services delivered by the government spawns another inevitable result. And this is manifested in the growth of professionals and professional orientations in the bureaucratic administration. Among the variegated phenomena generated by the professionalization of the civil service, two are particularly noteworthy because of their possible effects on the relationship between the bureaucracy and the Chinese people. One phenomenon will be the increasing friction between professionals and generalists within the bureaucracy emanating from their different outlooks and identifications. While it is expected that the generalists can maintain their control over the professionals in the foreseeable future, strains stemming from the friction can be readily discerned by outside observers. Another phenomenon is the tendency of professionals to proclaim universalistic values at the same time as their particularistic values are cherished and valued. Professional communities cut across both government and the society, and they emphasize their contributions to "common" interests as against partisan and sectional interests. Consequently the identification of professionals to the government can never be complete and their reference groups usually are located *outside* of the government. A derivative behavioural outcome is hence the proclivity of professionals to involve the general public to arbitrate their differences with the government whenever these occur. The increasing militancy of civil service unions in the last several years (primarily those of professionals and sub-professionals) undoubtedly can be attributed to a number of causes (the discrepancy between the remunerations between the public and private sectors, the gradual loss of social status of civil servants, the impossibility of moving into the private sector on the part of some professional specialties, the high inflation rates, the rigid hierarchical structure within the bureaucracy which fails to adequately incorporate professional evaluations in the promotion system, so on and so forth), the broader identifications of the professionals cannot be discounted as a causal factor. The tendency of a segment of government officials to appeal to the public for support in their quarrels with the government may have the latent effect of drawing the government and the people closer together and undermining the political autonomy of the bureaucracy. While this is only a nascent trend in the meantime, we expect it to continue and become more conspicuous in the future.

In short, the minimally-integrated social-political system of Hong Kong continues to be sustained by a unique constellation of conditions some of which are beyond the control of the people of the colony. Nevertheless, secular changes, though proceeding slowly, in these conditions in a society increasingly populated by a settled population and undergoing dramatic economic development have made many of these conditions lose some of their relevance. While the general configurations of the minimally-integrated social-political system will be maintained, we can expect the closer integration of the bureaucratic polity and the Chinese society to usher in a new era in the history of Hong Kong.

Bibliography

A Group at the Hong Kong Research Project
    1974   *Hong Kong: A Case to Answer*. Nottingham: Spokesman Books.
Adelman, Irma, and Cynthia Taft Morris
    1973   *Economic Growth and Social Equity in Developing Countries*. Stanford:
                Stanford University Press.
Advisory Committee on Diversification, The
    1979   *Report of the Advisory Committee on Diversification 1979*. Hong Kong:
                Government Printer.
Ahern, Emily M.
    1973   *The Cult of the Dead in a Chinese Village*. Stanford: Stanford University
                Press.
Ake, Claude
    1974   "Modernization and political instability: a theoretical exploration."
                World Politics 26, 4 (July): 576-603.
Allen, Charles L.
    1970   *Communication Patterns in Hong Kong*. Hong Kong: The Chinese
                University of Hong Kong.
Almond, Gabriel, and Sidney Verba
    1965   *The Civic Culture*. Boston: Little, Brown and Co.
Annual Departmental Reports of the Commissioner of Registration of Persons. 1963-
                1975. Hong Kong: Registration of Persons Department.
Annual Report of the Secretary for Chinese Affairs. 1958-1959. Hong Kong: Secretariat
                for Chinese Affairs.
Annual Report of the UMELCO Office. 1970-1978. Hong Kong: UMELCO Office.
Annual Report on Hong Kong. 1946. Hong Kong: Government Printer.
Apter, David E.
    1965   *The Politics of Modernization*. Chicago: University of Chicago Press.
Association for Radical East Asian Studies
    1972   *Hong Kong: Britain's Last Colonial Stronghold*. London: Association
                for Radical East Asian Studies.
Babchuk, Nicholas, and Alan Booth
    1969   "Voluntary association membership: a longitudinal analysis." *American
                Sociological Review* 34, 1 (February): 31-45.
Bagehot, Walter
    1955   *The English Constitution*. London: World's Classics Edition.
Baker, Hugh D. R.
    1968   *A Chinese Lineage Village: Sheung Shui*. Stanford: Stanford University
                Press.
Baker, Raymond W.
    1978   *Egypt's Uncertain Revolution Under Nasser and Sadat*. Cambridge:
                Harvard University Press.
Balandier, G.
    1966   "The colonial situation: a theoretical approach." Pp. 34-61 in Immanuel

Wallerstein (ed.), *Social Change: The Colonial Situation*. New York: John Wiley and Sons, Inc.

Barnett, A. Doak
1952   " 'New Force' I—the idea." *American Universities Field Staff Reports, East Asia Series* 1, 2: 1-12.
1953   "Social osmosis—refugees in Hong Kong." *American Universities Field Staff Reports, East Asia Series* 2, 5: 1-8.

Beazer, William F.
1978   *The Commercial Future of Hong Kong*. New York: Praeger Publishers.

Berkowitz, Morris I.; Frederick P. Brandauer; and John H. Reed
1969   *Folk Religion in an Urban Setting*. Hong Kong: Christian Study Centre on Chinese Religion and Culture.

Burton, Robert A.
1958   "Self-help, Chinese style." *American Universities Field Staff Reports, East Asia Series* 6, 9: 1-10.

Campbell, Angus; Gerald Gurin; and Warren E. Miller
1954   *The Voter Decides*. Evanston: Row, Peterson, and Co.

Catron, Gary Wayne
1971   "China and Hong Kong, 1945-1967." Unpublished doctoral dissertation, Harvard University.

Chaney, David C.
1971   "Job satisfaction and unionization," Pp. 261-70 in Keith Hopkins (ed.), *Hong Kong: The Industrial Colony*. Hong Kong: Oxford University Press.
————— and David Podmore
1973   *Young Adults in Hong Kong: Attitudes in a Modernizing Society*. Hong Kong: Centre of Asian Studies, University of Hong Kong.
1974   "Family norms in a rapidly industrializing society: Hong Kong." *Journal of Marriage and the Family* 36, 2 (May): 400-407.

Chau Lam-yan, and Lau Siu-kai
1982   "Development, colonial rule, and intergroup conflict in a Chinese village in Hong Kong." *Human Organization* 41, 2 (Summer): 139-46.

Cheng Tong Yung
1977   *The Economy of Hong Kong*. Hong Kong: Far East Publications.

Cheng Tong-yung; Lin Tzong-biau; and Kuan Hsin-chi
1979   *Economic and Public Affairs for Hong Kong*. Hong Kong: Far East Publications.

Chow, Steven C., and Gustav F. Papanek
1979   "Laissez-faire, growth and equity: Hong Kong." Paper prepared for the Ninth Annual Canadian Council of South East Asian Studies Conference, November 9-11, 1979.

Cohen, Myron L.
1970   "Developmental process in the Chinese domestic group." Pp. 21-36 in Maurice Freedman (ed.), *Family and Kinship in Chinese Society*. Stanford: Stanford University Press.
1976   *House United, House Divided: The Chinese Family in Taiwan*. New York: Columbia University Press.

Collier, David (ed.)
1979   *The New Authoritarianism in Latin America*. Princeton: Princeton University Press.

Connor, Walker
1972   "Nation-building or nation-destroying?" *World Politics* 24, 3 (April): 319-55.
Cornelius, Wayne A., Jr.
1969   "Urbanization as an agent in Latin American political instability: the case of Mexico." *The American Political Science Review* 63, 3 (September): 833-57.
1975   *Politics and the Migrant Poor in Mexico City*. Stanford: Stanford University Press.
Covin, David L.
1970   "Political culture as an analytical instrument: an examination of refugees in Hong Kong." Unpublished doctoral dissertation, Washington State University.
Davies, S.N.G.
1977   "One brand of politics rekindled." *Hong Kong Law Journal* 7, 1: 44-84.
Deutsch, Karl W.
1961   "Social mobilization and political development." *The American Political Science Review* 55, 2 (September): 491-514.
Director of Home Affairs
1973-74   *Annual Report of the Home Affairs Department*. Hong Kong: Department of Home Affairs.
Endacott, G. B.
1964a   *A History of Hong Kong*. Hong Kong: Oxford University Press.
1964b   *Government and People in Hong Kong 1841-1962*. Hong Kong: Hong Kong University Press.
England, Joe, and John Rear
1975   *Chinese Labour Under British Rule*. Hong Kong: Oxford University Press.
Far Eastern Economic Review. Hong Kong. June 25, 1973.
Feierabend, Ivo D. *et al.*
1969   "Social change and political violence: cross-national patterns." In Hugh D. Graham and Ted R. Gurr (eds.), *Violence in America: Historical and Comparative Perspectives*. New York: Signet Books.
Freedman, Maurice
1961-62   "The family in China, past and present." *Pacific Affairs* 34: 223-36.
1966   *Chinese Lineage and Society: Fukien and Kwangtung*. London: Athlone Press.
Furnivall, J. S.
1948   *Colonial Policy and Practice: A Comparative Study of Burma and Netherlands India*. New York: New York University Press.
Geiger, Theodore, and Frances M. Geiger
1975   *The Development Progress of Hong Kong and Singapore*. Hong Kong: Macmillan Publishers, Ltd.
Hambro, Edward I.
1955   *The Problem of Chinese Refugees in Hong Kong*. Leiden: Sijthoff.
Harris, Peter B.
1977   "Government and politics." Pp. 69-85 in *A Quarter-Century of Hong Kong 1951-1976*. Hong Kong: Chung Chi College, The Chinese University of Hong Kong.

1978   *Hong Kong: A Study in Bureaucratic Politics.* Hong Kong: Heineman (Asia).

Hayes, James
1975   "Hong Kong: tale of two cities." Pp. 1-10 in Marjorie Topley (ed.), *Hong Kong: The Interaction of Tradition and Life in the Towns.* Hong Kong: Hong Kong Branch of the Royal Asiatic Society.

Ho, H.C.Y.
1979   *The Fiscal System of Hong Kong.* London: Croom Helm.

Hoadley, John S.
1968   "The government and politics of Hong Kong: a descriptive study with special reference to the analytical framework of Gabriel Almond." Unpublished doctoral dissertation, University of California, Santa Barbara.
1970   "Hong Kong is the lifeboat: notes on political culture and socialization." *Journal of Oriental Studies* 8: 206-18.
1973   "Political participation of Hong Kong Chinese: patterns and trends." *Asian Survey* 13, 6 (June): 604-16.

Hong, Lawrence K.
1970   "The Chinese family in a modern industrial setting: its structure and functions." Unpublished doctoral dissertation, University of Notre Dame.

Hong Kong Annual Report. 1980. Hong Kong: Government Printer.
Hong Kong Hansard. 1947, 1950, 1955 and 1972/73. Hong Kong: Government Printer.
Hong Kong Standard. July 28, 1966; November 13, 1971; and April 5, 1972.

Hong Kong University
1979 (Dec.)   *Convocation Newsletter.* Hong Kong: Hong Kong University.

Hsieh Jiann
1979   "Voluntary associations and cultural continuity: a study of the association of the Waichow Hakka in Hong Kong." Unpublished manuscript in Chinese.
1980   "Persistence and preservation of Hakka culture in urban situations: a preliminary study of voluntary associations of the Waichow Hakak in Hong Kong." Unpublished paper.
1981   *Cultural Persistence and Preservation of the Hweichow Hakka: An Anthropological Study of Voluntary Associations in Urban Situation* (in Chinese). Hong Kong: The Chinese University Press.

Hughes, Richard
1976   *Borrowed Place, Borrowed Time: Hong Kong and Its Many Faces.* London: Andre Deutsch.

Huntington, Samuel P.
1965   "Political development and political decay." *World Politics* 17, 3 (April): 386-430.
1968   *Political Order in Changing Societies.* New Haven: Yale University Press.
————— and Joan M. Nelson
1976   *No Easy Choice: Political Participation in Developing Countries.* Cambridge: Harvard University Press.

Hurwitz, Leon
1973   "Contemporary approaches to political stability." *Comparative Politics* 5, 3 (April): 449-63.

Jackson, Karl D.
1978   "Bureaucratic polity: a theoretical framework for the analysis of power
            and communications in Indonesia." Pp. 3-22 in Karl D. Jackson (ed.),
            Political Power and Communications in Indonesia. Berkeley and Los
            Angeles: University of California Press.

Jarvie, I. C.
1977   *Window on Hong Kong: A Sociological Study of the Hong Kong Film
            Industry and Its Audience*. Hong Kong: Centre of Asian Studies,
            University of Hong Kong.

Johnson, Graham E.
1971   "Migrants and voluntary associations in a colonial Chinese setting."
            Unpublished doctoral dissertation, Cornell University.
1977   "Leaders and leadership in an expanding New Territories town." *The
            China Quarterly* 69 (March): 109-25.

Kan, Angela W. S.
1974   *A Study of Neighborly Interaction in Public Housing: The Case of Hong
            Kong*. Hong Kong: Occasional paper, Social Research Centre, The
            Chinese University of Hong Kong.
1975   *Implications of Concentrated Utilization of Local Facilities and Services
            in Public Housing Estates in Hong Kong*. Hong Kong: Occasional paper,
            Social Research Centre, The Chinese University of Hong Kong.

Key, V. O., Jr.
1961   *Public Opinion and American Democracy*. New York: Alfred A. Knopf.

Khanna, B. S.
1970   "Bureaucracy and development in India." Pp. 219-50 in Edward W.
            Weidner (ed.), *Development Administration in Asia*. Durham: Duke
            University Press.

King, Ambrose Yeo-chi
1972   *The Political Culture of Kwun Tong: A Chinese Community in Hong
            Kong*. Hong Kong: Occasional paper, Social Research Centre, The
            Chinese University of Hong Kong.
1975   "Administrative absorption of politics in Hong Kong: emphasis on the
            grass roots level." *Asian Survey* 15, 5 (May): 422-39.
———— and Peter J. L. Man
1974   *The Role of Small Factory in Economic Development: The Case of
            Hong Kong*. Hong Kong: Occasional paper, Social Research Centre, The
            Chinese University of Hong Kong.
———— and Davy H. K. Leung
1975   *The Chinese Touch in Small Industrial Organizations*. Hong Kong:
            Occasional paper, Social Research Centre, The Chinese University of
            Hong Kong.

Kornhauser, William
1959   *The Politics of Mass Society*. Glencoe: Free Press.

Kulp, Daniel H., II
1925   *Country Life in South China: The Sociology of Familism*. New York:
            Teachers College, Columbia University.

Lang, Olga
1946   *Chinese Family and Society*. New Haven: Yale University Press.

LaPalombara, Joseph
  1967   "An overview of bureaucracy and political development." Pp. 3-33 in
                Joseph LaPalombara (ed.), *Bureaucracy and Political Development*.
                Princeton: Princeton University Press.
Lau Siu-kai
  1977   *Utilitarianistic Familism: An Inquiry into the Basis of Political Stability
                in Hong Kong*. Hong Kong: Social Research Centre, The Chinese
                University of Hong Kong.
  1981a   "The government, intermediate organizations, and grassroots politics in
                Hong Kong." *Asian Survey* 21, 8 (August): 865-84.
  1981b   "Chinese familism in an urban-industrial settings: the case of Hong
                Kong." *Journal of Marriage and the Family* 43, 4 (November): 977-92.
  1982   "Local administrative reform in Hong Kong: promises and limitations."
                Asian Survey 22, 9 (September): 858-873.
————— and Ho Kam-fai
  1982   "Social accommodation of politics: the case of the young Hong Kong
                workers." *Journal of Commonwealth and Comparative Politics* 20, 2
                (July): 172-88.
Lawson, Kay
  1980   "Political parties and linkage." Pp. 3-24 in Kay Lawson (ed.), *Political
                Parties and Linkage: A Comparative Perspective*. New Haven: Yale
                University Press.
Lethbridge, Henry J.
  1969   "Hong Kong under Japanese occupation: changes in social structure."
                Pp. 77-127 in I. C. Jarvie and Joseph Agassi (eds.), *Hong Kong: A
                Society in Transition*. London: Routledge and Kegan Paul.
  1978   *Hong Kong: Stability and Change*. Hong Kong: Oxford University Press.
Lee, Rance P. L.
  1977   "Corruption in Hong Kong: Congruence of Chinese Social Norms with
                Legal Norms." Unpublished paper.
—————; Cheung Tak-sing; and Cheung Yuet-wah
  1979   "Material and non-material conditions and life-satisfaction of urban
                residents in Hong Kong." Pp. 83-94 in Tzong-biau Lin, Rance P. L. Lee,
                and Udo-Ernst Simonis (eds.), *Hong Kong: Economic, Social and
                Political Studies in Development*. White Plains: M. E. Sharpe, Inc.
Lipsky, Michael
  1976   "Toward a theory of street-level bureaucracy." Pp. 196-213 in Willis D.
                Hawley and Michael Lipsky (eds.), *Theoretical Perspectives on Urban
                Politics*. Englewood Cliffs: Prentice-Hall, Inc.
Liu, Hui-chen Wang
  1959   *The Traditional Chinese Clan Rules*. New York: J. J. Augustin Incor-
                porated Publishers.
Liu, William T.
  1966   "Family interaction among local and refugee Chinese families in Hong
                Kong." *Journal of Marriage and the Family* 28, 3 (August): 314-23.
Lockwood, David
  1975   "Sources of variation in working-class images of society." Pp. 16-31 in
                Martin Bulmer (ed.), *Working-Class Images of Society*. London: Rout-
                ledge and Kegan Paul.

Lu, Andrew L. C.
1970   *A Study of Vocational Training for Labour Youth in Hong Kong* (in Chinese). Hong Kong: Centre of Asian Studies, University of Hong Kong.
McKinsey and Co., Inc.
1972   *Strengthening the Machinery of Government.* 2 volumes. Hong Kong: McKinsey and Co., Inc.
Miners, N. J.
1975   "Hong Kong: a case study in political stability." *The Journal of Commonwealth and Comparative Politics* 13, 1 (March): 26-39.
1977   *The Government and Politics of Hong Kong.* Hong Kong: Oxford University Press.
Mitchell, Robert E.
1969a   *Levels of Emotional Strain in Southeast Asian Cities.* 2 volumes. Hong Kong: A Project of the Urban Family Life Survey.
1969b   *Family Life in Urban Hong Kong.* 2 volumes. Hong Kong: Project Report of the Urban Family Life Survey.
1969c   *Pupil, Parent, and School: A Hong Kong Study.* 2 volumes. Hong Kong: A Project of the Urban Family Life Survey.
1971   "Residential patterns and family networks (I)." *International Journal of Sociology of the Family* 2, 1 (March): 23-41.
1972   "Residential patterns and family networks (II)." *International Journal of Sociology of the Family* 3, 2 (September): 212-24.
————— and Irene Lo
1968   "Implications of changes in family authority relations for the development of independence and assertiveness in Hong Kong children." *Asian Survey* 8, 4 (April): 309-22.
Mok, Victor
1973   *The Organization and Management of Factories in Kwun Tong.* Hong Kong: Occasional paper, Social Research Centre, The Chinese University of Hong Kong.
1974   *The Small Factories in Kwun Tong: Problems and Strategies for Development.* Hong Kong: Occasional paper, Social Research Centre, The Chinese University of Hong Kong.
Monthly Reports of the Work of the Urban Council and the Urban Services Department. 1968-1978. Hong Kong: The Urban Council.
Nelson, Joan M.
1970   "The urban poor: disruption or political integration in Third World cities?" *World Politics* 22, 3: 393-414.
1979   *Access to Power: Politics and the Urban Poor in Developing Nations.* Princeton: Princeton University Press.
Nordlinger, Eric A.
1967   *The Working Class Tories.* Berkeley and Los Angeles: University of California Press.
Oberschall, Anthony
1973   *Social Conflict and Social Movements.* Englewood Cliffs: Prentice-Hall, Inc.
O'Donnell, Guillermo A.
1979   *Modernization and Bureaucratic-Authoritarianism: Studies in South*

American Politics. Berkeley: Institute of International Studies, University of California.

Olson, Mancur, Jr.
1963   "Rapid growth as a destabilizing force." *Journal of Economic History* 23, 4 (December): 529-52.

Owen, Nicholas C.
1971   "Economic policy." Pp. 141-206 in Keith Hopkins (ed.), *Hong Kong: The Industrial Colony*. Hong Kong: Oxford University Press.

Pasternak, Burton
1972   *Kinship and Community in Two Chinese Villages*. Stanford: Stanford University Press.

Podmore, David
1971   "Localization in the Hong Kong government services." *Journal of Commonwealth Political Studies* 9: 36-51.

Potter, Jack
1968   *Capitalism and the Chinese Peasant*. Berkeley and Los Angeles: University of California Press.

Price, Robert M.
1975   *Society and Bureaucracy in Contemporary Ghana*. Berkeley and Los Angeles: University of California Press.

Pye, Lucien W.
1962   *Politics, Personality, and Nation Building: Burma's Search for Identity*. New Haven: Yale University Press.
1968   *The Spirit of Chinese Politics: A Psychocultural Study of the Authority Crisis in Political Development*. Cambridge: M.I.T. Press.

Rabushka, Alvin
1976   *Value for Money: The Hong Kong Budgetary Process*. Stanford: Hoover Institute.
1979   *Hong Kong: A Study in Economic Freedom*. Chicago: Graduate School of Business, The University of Chicago.

Rear, John
1971   "One brand of politics." Pp. 55-139 in Keith Hopkins (ed.), *Hong Kong: The Industrial Colony*. Hong Kong: Oxford University Press.

Report of the Director of Social Welfare. 1965-1966. Hong Kong: Department of Social Welfare.

Reports on the Public Service. 1954-1977. Hong Kong: Colonial Secretariat, Establishment Branch.

Report on the Riots in Kowloon and Tsuen Wan, 1956. Hong Kong: Government Printer.

Riches, G.C.P.
1973a   *Community Development in Hong Kong: Sau Mau Ping, A Case Study*. Hong Kong: Centre of Asian Studies, University of Hong Kong.
1973b   *Urban Community Centre and Community Development: Hong Kong and Singapore*. Hong Kong: Centre of Asian Studies, University of Hong Kong.

Rosen, Sherry
1976   *Mei Foo Sun Chuen: Middle-Class Chinese Families in Transition*. Taipei: Orient Cultural Service.

Rothman, Jack
1974   *Planning and Organizing for Social Change: Action Principles from*

Social Science Research. New York and London: Columbia University Press.

Salaff, Janet W.
1976   "Working daughters in the Hong Kong Chinese family: female filial piety or a transformation in the family power structure?" *Journal of Social History* 9, 4 (June): 439-65.

Schermerhorn, R. A.
1970   *Comparative Ethnic Relations*. New York: Random House.

Schmitter, Phillippe C.
1971   *Interest Conflict and Political Change in Brazil*. Stanford: Stanford University Press.

Secretary for Chinese Affairs
1969   *The City District Officer Scheme*. Hong Kong: Secretariat for Chinese Affairs.

Sit, Victor Fung-shuen; Siu-lun Wong; and Tsin-sing Kiang
1979   *Small-Scale Industry in a Laissez-faire Economy: A Hong Kong Study*. Hong Kong: Centre of Asian Studies, University of Hong Kong.

Smith, Carl T.
1971   "The emergence of a Chinese elite in Hong Kong." *Journal of the Hong Kong Branch of the Royal Asiatic Society* 11: 74-115.
1975   "English-educated Chinese elites in nineteenth-century Hong Kong." Pp. 65-96 in Marjorie Topley (ed.), *Hong Kong: The Interaction of Tradition and Life in the Towns*. Hong Kong: Hong Kong Branch of the Royal Asiatic Society.

Smith, M. G.
1965   *The Plural Society in the British West Indies*. Berkeley and Los Angeles: University of California Press.

Social Research Centre
1976   *Housing Policy and Migration: Data Book*. Hong Kong: Social Research Centre, The Chinese University of Hong Kong.

Solomon, Richard H.
1971   *Mao's Revolution and the Chinese Political Culture*. Berkeley and Los Angeles: University of California Press.

South China Morning Post. April 4, 1971; July 25, 1971; October 22, 1972; February 16, 1976; November 1, 1976; November 30, 1977; April 18, 1978; April 19, 1978; October 20, 1978; November 4, 1978; December 6, 1978; March 4, 1979; and September 25, 1979.

Stoodley, Bartlett H.
1967   "Normative family orientations of Chinese college students in Hong Kong." *Journal of Marriage and the Family* 29, 4 (November): 773-82.

Tinker, Hugh
1966   "Structure of the British imperial heritage." Pp. 23-86 in Ralph Braibanti (ed.), *Asian Bureaucratic Systems Emergent from the British Imperial Tradition*. Durham: Duke University Press.

Topley, Marjorie
1969   "The role of savings and wealth among Hong Kong Chinese." Pp. 167-227 in I. C. Jarvie and Joseph Agassi (eds.), *Hong Kong: A Society in Transition*. London: Routledge and Kegan Paul.

Urban Council, The
   1966   *Report of the Ad Hoc Committee on the Future Scope and Operation
               of the Urban Council.* Hong Kong: The Urban Council.
   1969   *Report on the Reform of Local Government.* Hong Kong: The Urban
               Council.
Walden, John
   1979   "The problem of evaluating public opinion." *South China Morning Post*,
               September 25, 1979.
   1980   "A problem of credibility." A talk given to the Hong Kong Observers on
               February 13, 1980. Mimeographed.
White Paper: District Administration in Hong Kong. January 1981. Hong Kong: The
               Government Printer.
White Paper: The Urban Council. 1971. Hong Kong: The Government Printer.
Who's Who in Hong Kong. 1979. Hong Kong: South China Morning Post.
Wolf, Margery
   1968   *The House of Lim.* New York: Appleton Century Crofts.
Wong, Aline K.
   1971   "Chinese voluntary associations in Southeast Asian cities and the Kai-
               fongs in Hong Kong." *Journal of the Hong Kong Branch of the Royal
               Asiatic Society* 11: 62-73.
   1972a   *The Kaifong Associations and the Society of Hong Kong.* Taipei: The
               Orient Cultural Service.
   1972b   "Chinese community leadership in a colonial setting: the Hong Kong
               neighborhood associations." *Asian Survey* 12, 7 (July): 587-601.
   1972c   *The Study of Higher Non-expatriate Civil Servants in Hong Kong.* Hong
               Kong: Occasional paper, Social Research Centre, The Chinese University
               of Hong Kong.
Wong, Andrew W. F.
   1979   "Non-purposive adaptation and administrative change in Hong Kong."
               Paper presented at the Conference on Hong Kong: Dilemmas of Growth.
               December 10-14, 1979, Australian National University, Canberra,
               Australia.
Wong Fai-ming
   1972   "Modern ideology, industrialization, and conjugalism: the Hong Kong
               case." *International Journal of Sociology of the Family* 2, 2 (Septem-
               ber): 139-50.
   1975   "Industrialization and family structure in Hong Kong." *Journal of
               Marriage and the Family* 37, 4 (November): 958-1000.
Working Party on Local Administration, The
   1966   *The Report of the Working Party on Local Administration.* Hong Kong:
               Government Printer.
Yates, Douglas
   1977   *The Ungovernable City: The Politics of Urban Problems and Policy
               Making.* Cambridge: M.I.T. Press.
Young, Crawford
   1976   *The Politics of Cultural Pluralism.* Madison: University of Wisconsin Press.
Young, John A.
   1974   *Business and Sentiment in a Chinese Market Town.* Taipei: The Orient
               Cultural Service.

Zolberg, Aristide
   1966   *Creating Political Order*. Chicago: Rand McNally.
Zysman, John
   1977   *Political Strategies for Industrial Order: State, Market, and Industry in France*. Berkeley and Los Angeles: University of California Press.

Index

Advisory committees, 129-30
Aloofness, political, 102
Aloofness, social, 87-88
Automatic corrective mechanism, 41
Avoidance of involvement with outsiders, 89-92

Balandier, G., 5, 6, 7
Biosocial Survey, The, 22n
Boundary politics, 167; incidence of, 171; and minimally-integrated social-political system, 172; nature of, 168-69; political demands and, 169-71
Bureaucracy: autonomy of, 28-29; and bureaucratic polity, 26; and centralism, 38-39; and common interest, 33-34; and depoliticization, 36-38; and economic laissez-faire, 40-42; and government by consent, 30-31; growth of, 49-51; longevity and continuity of, 27; as an organization, 29; and paternalism, 31-33; and planning, 62; power concentration in, 51-56; and rule by law, 35-36; and social non-interventionism, 42-44; and social services, 44-48, 188-90
Bureaucrats: complacency, 58; defensiveness, 58-59; formalism and legalism, 59-60; inflexibility, 60-62; personalism, 63-64; role orientations, 57-58; technicalism, 62-63
Bureaucratic polity: definition of, 25; and linkage with Chinese society, 122-23; seclusion of, 25-26, 42, 46, 58. See also Bureaucracy

CDOs (City District Offices): performance of, 150-51; tasks of, 150
Chambers of commerce, 132, 138-39
China and Hong Kong, 10-13, 173
Chinese society, 68; atomistic, 121
City District Offices. See CDOs
Civil service, British, 48

Clansmen associations, 132, 136-38, 140
Class consciousness, 98-102
Classes, perception of, 95-98
Colonial society, 5-7; Hong Kong as, 7-9
"Compartmentalization" of polity and society, 144, 162, 163
Conflict, 2, 14; in 1956, 2, 4, 13, 15; in 1966, 2, 13, 15; in 1967, 2, 13, 15-16; potential for, 4
Covin, David L., 12

District associations, 138-40. See also Waichow Hakkas, organization of
District Watchmen, 131

Economy, 173-74, 176-77
Elite, Chinese, 15; composition of, 15, 124-25; co-option of, 126, 164-65; and intermediate organizations, 142; as linkage mechanism, 125-30; political role of, 19; and political stability, 15; and riots, 15-16
Endacott, G. B., 28, 30, 34, 41, 44, 131n
Executive Council, 26, 126n
Expatriates. See Bureaucracy, power concentration in

Familial group, 18-19, 73-74; authority in, 81-82; boundary of, 79-81
Family as status group, 78
Fictive kinship, 80-81
Fiscal policy, 62
Friends, 80-81; 91-92
Frustration, 185
Furnivall, J. S., 5, 6

Generalists. See Bureaucracy, power concentration in
Gentry, Chinese, 123-24
Government, definition of role of, 103-5
Government officials, perception of, 111-13
Governors of Hong Kong, 27-28, 52, 55.